Jim Snyder

# FIVE THOUSAND YEARS
## ON THE
# LOXAHATCHEE

*A Pictorial History of Jupiter / Tequesta, Florida*

*by*
*James D. Snyder*

*Design by*
*Jim Johnston*

Published by Pharos Books, 8657 SE Merritt Way, Jupiter, FL 33458-1007. Phone: 561-575-3430

Cover, interior design, production by Jim Johnston / www.imageblast.com

First printing, first edition. Printed in Hong Kong.

Library of Congress Control Number: 2003095603

## Publisher's Cataloging-in-Publication
  (Provided by Quality Books, Inc.)

Snyder, James D.
      Five thousand years on the Loxahatchee : a pictorial history of Jupiter-Tequesta, Florida / by James D. Snyder ; design by Jim Johnston.
      p. cm.
      Includes index.
      ISBN 0-9675200-4-5

  1. Jupiter (Fla.)—History—Pictorial works.
  2. Tequesta (Fla.)—History—Pictorial works.  I. Title.

F319.J86S69 2003        975.9'32
                        QBI03-200615

## Other books by James D. Snyder

*Life and Death on the Loxahatchee, The Story of Trapper Nelson.* Winner of the 2002 Silver Award for adult non-fiction, Florida Publisher's Association. (Published 2002. 160 pp. ISBN 0-9675200-3-7.)

*The Faith and the Power. The Inspiring Story of the First Christians and How They Survived the Madness of Rome.* A first century history. Finalist (runner-up) for the 2003 Ben Franklin Award for best book on religion, presented by Publishers Marketing Association. (Published 2002: 416 pp. ISBN 0-9675200-2-9.)

*All God's Children. How the First Christians Challenged the Roman World and Shaped the Next 2000 Years.* An historical novel chronicling the tumultuous years AD 31-71. (Published 2000. 680 pp. ISBN 09675200-0-2.)

# CONTENTS

INSIDE COVER PHOTO: Lillian Miller and Ethel Clancy on Celestial Railroad
dock, early 1890s. *(Loxahatchee River Historical Society)*

LEFT: U.S. Life Saving Station (1886-1896) at today's Carlin Park Beach. *(LRHS)*

RIGHT: Jupiter beach scene, turn of the century. *(LRHS)*

# DEDICATED TO

# BESSIE WILSON DUBOIS

She raised four children, ran a restaurant and baked pies for a throng of commercial clients. But the "real" Bessie Wilson DuBois was a born historian. During her seventy-plus years on the Jupiter waterfront she saved hundreds of letters and photos, spoke on local history to countless civic groups and, as her life drew to a close, turned over nearly all of her treasures to the Loxahatchee River Historical Society.

So it was no surprise that as I researched this book in the museum files, "donated by Bessie DuBois" appeared on everything from photos of visiting Seminoles to letters describing the sinking of ships in wartime to the Jupiter centennial celebrations of the 1960s. Her pamphlets and monographs still stand as the best accounts of specific places (the lighthouse, for example). Because so much of this book is based on her life's work, it is gratefully dedicated to Bessie DuBois.

# FROM THE AUTHOR

The first reason I decided to write this book was simply that no one had told the area's long history between two covers. A later and better reason is that the deeper I waded into the subject, the more colorful events and courageous people I encountered.

All towns have their fascinating characters, but in the Indians, fishermen, farmers, fortune seekers and fortune finders who underpin our history, we have far more than our share.

As I learned how their lives revolved around that abundant giver of life—the Loxahatchee River—my growing appreciation and reverence for this great treasure filled me with a desire to instill the same feelings in others. Hopefully, the more you read about its own unique history, the more you'll want to protect the river and its watershed.

My only regret is that the research and writing had to end before the final product began to resemble a telephone book. It is at best a collage of snapshots and stories. I'm painfully aware that out there are many more persons and organizations with memorable stories, valuable photos and major contributions to Jupiter-Tequesta life.

A final note: it may strike some readers as odd that this history, published in 2003, peters out in the mid-1980s (except for chapter 8 on the life of the Loxahatchee). It's simply because my perspective is too myopic to judge the present. Will the history of the past twenty years turn out to have been a laundry list of new golf courses and shopping centers, or of preserving the Loxahatchee and controlling growth? Who are today's memorable characters and shapers of our destiny? These answers I leave to other authors in future generations. — JDS

## ACKNOWLEDGEMENTS

Nearly a hundred persons contributed to this history by sharing their recollections and/or their photographs. Many more, no longer with us, did so by leaving their letters and other records to enlighten us about early life on the Loxahatchee. While many contributors deserve special thanks, I'd like to single out the following here:

The Loxahatchee River Historical Society, from Executive Director Jamie Stuve and Curator Michael Zaidman to the many volunteers who work to preserve and teach about Jupiter-Tequesta history. Thanks for your infectious enthusiasm and your willingness to share your archives and your trust.

The Historical Society of Palm Beach County, and especially Research and Archives Director Debi Murray. Ditto the above.

Lynn Lasseter Drake, Jupiter's unofficial genealogist. Her painstaking collection of maps, photos and facts on area families filled in more gaps in this book than I could possibly count. If you're seeking information on a long-lost aunt or some twig on the family tree, chances are this caring, sharing lady has it in her computer database.

Wilson Horne. Some people are born pack rats and some with a compulsion to record and explain events. Wilson is both. And his writings show a rare talent for touching deep feelings and raw nerves with a prose honed by the precision of a military officer—which he was for many years.

Richard E. Roberts. His official job title with the Florida Park Service reads *Biologist II,* but no one has had a more profound impact on the fate and future of the Loxahatchee River. For over thirty years, Dick has been in the forefront of everything good that's been done to preserve the watershed and in trenches opposing everything bad. He opened his personal files to this writer on the promise that some good would result for the Loxahatchee and its ecology. I hope it has.

My equally heartfelt thanks to so many people and organizations who shared their memories with me:

Richard and Shirley Anschutz, Eric Bailey, Raymond Baird, Richard Bassett, Claudet Benton, Dwight and Margaret Blanchard, Marcus Bressler, Matthew and Lorrie Bressler, Agnes and David Brooker, Marcia Brown, Roger Bursey, Robert S. Carr, Shirley Cato, Philip Celmer III, Ida Simmons Harris Connaway, Robert and Anna Lee Culpepper, Mike Daniel, Richard C. Dent, J. Alden DuBois, John R. DuBois III, Doris Wehage Ebert, Iris Hunter Etheredge, Florida State Archives, Louis and Margie Freeman, Edwin Froelich, Skip Gladwin, Ethel Gravett, Doris (Dodie) DuBois Hawthorne, Patrick Hayes, Marion DuBois Hughart; Jojo Hicks, Jonathan Dickinson State Park, Jim Johnston, Jupiter Inlet District.

Jupiter Medical Center, Jupiter-Tequesta Chamber of Commerce, Marge Ketter, Al and Florence Kuschel, Donny Lainhart, George Lainhart, Peter Leo, Max Little, Loxahatchee River District, Wally McCall, Pat and Bill Magrogan, Charles ("Punch") and Penny Martyn, Beverly Mayo, Brad Mayo, Chuck Milhauser, Judson Minear, Richard Procyk, Kathleen Forst Putnam.

Nathaniel P. Reed, Dimick Reese, A. R. Roebuck, Pam Roebuck, Ella Preston Rollins, Roy and Patricia Rood, Jerry Rupper, Robert Schuh, Lois Shambaugh, Sue S. Snyder, Ramona Horne Pennock Stark, Raymond Swanson, Town of Jupiter Archives, Village of Tequesta, Rose Walton, Gene and Judy Wehage, Nelson and Lilly Wilder, William S. and Judie Wood, and Nancy Davis Young.

Several persons who are knowledgeable about various periods of Jupiter-Tequesta history unselfishly volunteered their time to review parts of the manuscript. I thank the following:

Chuck Milhauser, Richard Procyk and Jamie Stuve for the chapters on Indian history and first settlers. Lynn Drake, Wilson Horne and Raymond Swanson on the period from the turn of the century through World War II.

Ida Simmons Harris Connaway, Lynn Drake, Skip Gladwin, Pat Magrogan, Al and Florence Kuschel, Raymond Swanson, Judy Wehage and Bill Wood on the post war era and beginnings of modern Jupiter.

Rick Dent, Patrick Hayes, Pat Magrogan and Dick Roberts on the final chapter: *The Last Battle of the Loxahatchee.*

Finally, my thanks to the "hard core" team: my wife Sue, who reads every draft first to save the author from embarrassing himself; Milda Enos, who proofreads the final galleys for the same reason; and the remarkably talented Jim Johnston of ImageBlast Inc., who went the last mile in book design, photo preservation and devotion to detail.

# FIVE THOUSAND YEARS
## ON THE
# LOXAHATCHEE

Except for the boat and man's figure, this nineteenth century photo of Jupiter
Inlet's south side appears as it did to the Jeaga/Hobe Indians who lived on it
from at least A.D. 750. Most of the shell-rich mound, or midden, was trucked
away for roadbed in the 1920s. *(Loxahatchee River Historical Society)*

# CHAPTER 1

# EL RÍO
# DE LA CRUZ

John Cabot or Ponce de Leon? It's undecided as to who was the first European to sail into Jupiter Inlet. Because the English explorer Cabot tacked down the North American shoreline in 1496–97 and produced a rough map of Florida's east coast, his proponents insist that he couldn't have resisted the deep, sheltered Jupiter Inlet as a stop for taking on fresh water and firewood.

But the case for the Spanish explorer is better documented. Juan Ponce de Leon had been along on Christopher Columbus' second West Indies expedition in 1493. He had lived for years at the first permanent Spanish colony on Hispanola and later on Puerto Rico. In February 1512 he gained a commission from the King of Spain to discover and govern a legendary island named Bimini (not the one off Miami) and set off with three ships.

After crisscrossing the Bahamas seeking the elusive Bimini, Ponce de Leon sighted the coast of Florida on April 2, 1513, and sailed up as far as the mouth of the St. John's River. There he landed long enough to claim everything he'd seen for the king and to name it *Florida* because he'd discovered it on *Pascua Florida*, the Passover Feast of the Flowers.

A week later Ponce headed south to see just how long his newfound continent stretched. On April 21 he reached Jupiter Inlet and stayed for several days. Before continuing south and around Cape Sable, he named it Río de la Cruz and planted a stone cross that has never been recovered.

Indeed, the Río de la Cruz would have made for a compelling interlude. The inlet at the time faced to the south, a quarter mile down from the present man-made cut. Precisely where the speedy Gulf Stream carried ships closest to the mainland, a captain could quickly veer off towards the shoreline, dodge a few reefs, and glide into the inlet. In a few minutes a bend to the left would bring the ship westward into a small bluewater cove that teemed with fish,

During 1990-92, a group of Florida archeologists and anthropologists burrowed into the shell mounds in DuBois Park and unearthed 241 bone, stone and shell artifacts (plus nearly 3,000 pieces of ceramic shards) that were carbon-dated back to as early as A.D. 750. Large whelks with holes (at top) may have been fastened to sticks for hammering or pulverizing. Smaller ones were strung and worn as necklaces. The two busycon shells below (cousins to the conch) were probably adzes, or cutting tools. Once worn down, they could have served for scooping food. *(Loxahatchee River Historical Society)*

The busycon shell at bottom, the size of a small shovel, was discovered in Jupiter Inlet. *(Florida Bureau of Archeological Research)*

shrimp and oysters. The cove lay at the end of a marshy estuary that extended well into today's Carlin Park. Across the broad blue-green river to the northwest, and perhaps forming the other wing of the rough cross that Ponce may have envisioned, was the mouth of a shallow waterway that wound all the way to today's Titusville.

Just west across that ribbon of water (which would became known as Jupiter Narrows) was a hill nearly fifty feet high that one could climb to survey the table-flat wilderness on all sides. Some 350 years later it would support a lighthouse.

Standing on that sandy dune with a spyglass, one might spot another hill a few miles to the north that was twice as tall. Four hundred fifty or so years later, a ranger tower would be built on its crest and "Hobe Mountain" would become one of the main attractions at Jonathan Dickinson State Park.

Still, the first and most impressive sight that Europeans would notice on their first arrival is not there today except for one hill that supports the Harry and Susan DuBois home in the park that now bears their name. As soon as a ship cleared the original inlet and turned west, it would pass a stretch of lumpy sand hills on the southern shore of the river. They ran for some six hundred feet and stood over twenty feet high. These mounds, or middens, were, in part, deliberately created to provide high ground for dwellings—probably for tribal leaders. In time they would rise as successive generations erected new huts, scattered refuse and buried their dead.

And their descendents were still there to meet the first European explorers when they arrived in the early sixteenth century.

How long had the Indians been there? An archeological team from Florida Atlantic University dated various findings back to A.D. 750, but speculated that the site could have been occupied from as long ago as 5,000 B.C.

Other archeological digs indicate the same age for villages that once dotted the headwaters of the Loxahatchee River. Robert S. Carr, executive director of the Archeological and Historical Conservancy, says the evidence indicates a network of trade and a "well-integrated social life" along well-traveled waterways that wound from the inlet to Lake Okeechobee.

What did these Indians look like? They left no carvings, no imagery. But in 1970, a group of historians and anthropologists discovered a mound containing more than one hundred Indian burials on Hutchinson Island, just 25 miles north of Jupiter Inlet. They concluded that most of the Indians ranged from five feet, eight inches to six feet tall. They had large bones, high cheekbones and heavy-set jaws. The teeth showed an almost total lack of cavities, but many were worn down to the gum-line—due perhaps to the sand that came along with a heavy diet of oysters and clams.

How many Indians were there? Chances are, Jupiter Inlet never contained more than a village of three hundred. But Indian settlements permeated the entire peninsula of Florida. Published estimates of their total numbers by scholars range from 100,000 to 925,000—a further indicator of how little is known.

If only Ponce de Leon had an archeologist aboard, he would have been able to find most of the available information in the middens that lined the south shore of the Río de la Cruz. Unearthed centuries later by both archeologists and curio seekers, they produced a cornucopia of artifacts on daily Indian life, from the residue of meals to jewelry to broken and discarded tools.

By far the biggest portion of the repository consisted of oyster and clam shells. But also included were bones of fish, turtles, birds, raccoons and deer—in short, anything that swam, ran or flew.

Pottery shards were crudely fashioned and poorly fired, with no decorations or marks of ownership. But they were remarkably similar to those found thirty miles southwest in Belle Glade, indicating that these inhabitants were related to or traded with the Indians who lived around the rim of Lake Okeechobee.

Tool remnants abounded. Small animal bones were split lengthwise and sharpened for use as awls to punch holes in animal hides. Large busycon shells were used for breastplates and small ones fashioned into scoops and dippers. Stingray spines were sharpened into fishing spears, and sharks' teeth became carving tools. Flat stones were collected to open shellfish and crack animal bones.

One never knew what the mounds would give up. One day in the 1920s Susan DuBois, whose home still rests atop the last midden, reached down after a storm and picked up a stone ax head. A few hundred feet away and days later, her husband Harry stooped down and picked up a large black stone pendant—jewelry perhaps worn by the wife of a chief, or *cacique*.

Chances are that today's archeologists know much more than Ponce de Leon. He and his men probably had scant opportunity to ask many questions, because the Indians wanted no part of them. Antonio de Herrera, the first official crown historian on the West Indies, used Ponce's logs in 1592 when he wrote,

*Juan Ponce went ashore here, called by the Indians, who promptly tried to steal the launch, the oars, and arms, so as not to provoke the countryside. But because they struck a seaman in the head with a club, from which he was knocked out, they had to do battle with them, who with their arrows and armed shafts, the points of sharpened bones, and fish spines, wounded two Spaniards. The Indians received little injury…Juan Ponce regrouped the Spaniards with great difficulty.*

*He departed from there to a river, where he took on water and firewood [whereupon] Sixty Indians massed to harass him. One of them was taken for a guide and so that he (the Indian) might learn the language. He gave to this river the name of La Cruz and he left at it a cross hewn from quarry stone with an inscription [but] they did not finish taking on water because it was brackish.*

Ponce de Leon had another problem as well. The Spanish ships, in attempting to head down the Florida coast, had found the Gulf Stream such a powerful reverse current that only two of the three had been able to break free of its clutches and veer into Jupiter Inlet. The third vessel actually had slid backward until it disappeared over the northern horizon. A few days later, when the struggling sister ship suddenly hove into sight again, Ponce reasoned that it was best to hightail it out of the inlet and get on with the remainder of the coastal expedition.

This black "celt," found in the DuBois Park Indian mounds, was probably used in ceremonial trades between tribes. The hard ebony rock is the same as that found in Georgia and in Indian archeological sites around Miami.
*(Bureau of Archaeological Research, Division of Historic Resources, Florida Department of State)*

One of 96 sharks' teeth uncovered in the DuBois shell mounds. They made excellent tools for carving in detail, but were just as often strung around the neck as jewelry.
*(Loxahatchee River Historical Society)*

One of the few examples of artistic carving at the DuBois Park site is this fragment of bone with an eel's or turtle's head. Archeologists agree that it was originally long enough to be stuck through a warrior's hair.
*(Department of Anthropology, Florida Atlantic University, Boca Raton, No. A2672)*

## FORT SANTA LUCEA

Ponce de Leon never returned to his river of the cross. Eight years later he was attempting to colonize another group of Indians on Florida's west coast when he was mortally wounded by an arrow, probably made from a splintered fish bone.

Soon it was no longer a novelty for east coast Indians to see Spanish sails billowing along the Gulf Stream. Captains knew the inlet as Barra de Jobe, but whether any stopped there is unknown except for one probable, tragic episode. Pedro Menéndez de Ávilas, the man most responsible for founding St. Augustine in 1565, was also ordered by Philip II of Spain to establish

Large spear point or projectile found in the DuBois Park Indian mounds. Under the nearly-microscopic focus of today's computer technology, one can see each stroke that went into sharpening the tip. *(Loxahatchee River Historical Society)*

settlements along the Florida coast to protect trade routes and convert the local Indians to Catholicism. But after a year or so, the little bands of settlers were sick and starving for lack of sustainable crops. With some of the outposts already in the throes of mutiny, Menéndez decided to consolidate the ones on the southeast coast in a place called Santa Lucea while he sailed to Havana in hopes of bringing back food and supplies.

Some historians have assumed that Santa Lucea referred to today's St. Lucie Inlet because of the similarity in names. However, logs show that the largest garrison, located at Ays Inlet (now Fort Pierce), marched and floated "twenty-three leagues" down the Indian River to found the new settlement of Santa Lucea. Twenty-three leagues is about 66 miles, which would have taken them into the Río de la Cruz. And this, of course, emptied into the inlet called Barra de Jobe, which also offered a more dependable harbor than the shallow and treacherous St. Lucie Inlet.

What was a good geographical choice proved exactly the opposite in terms of hospitality. At first the Jobe (sometimes called Jeaga) Indians seemed at least passive, but soon their harassment and thievery was so incessant that it became impossible to forage for food. The arrival of Menéndez' first supply boat eased the crisis somewhat, but when the second one tried to come ashore, a mutinous faction seized it and headed south, probably in hopes of finding a more cheerful atmosphere at another Menéndez-sponsored settlement on Biscayne Bay.

Bad decision. Most of the mutineers were killed by Tequesta Indians before they reached the fort. Inside, the Spanish soldiers were so hungry and miserable that they decided to head north and try their luck at Santa Lucea.

Another bad decision. As the remaining settlers there chewed on bitter wild berries and cowered behind a flimsy fortification of palmetto stalks, they could not have been thrilled when a ragged band of their countrymen fought their way past angry Jobe Indians and asked "What's for dinner?"

Not much. According to a diarist named Barrientos,

*Provisions…were so low during those almost daily encounters with the Indians that no more than a single pound of maize was issued to ten soldiers. When this supply was gone, a palmetto was sold for one ducat, a snake for four* [and] *a rat cost eight reales—excessive prices because there was very little money. The soldiers began to fall from hunger, and in the end only thirty men were left to bear arms. The bones of animals and fish dead for years were barbecued over the fire and then picked, as were swords, belts and shoes.*

Had they stuck it out, Jupiter might have been the second continuous European settlement in the U.S. But despite the occasional relief ship from Cuba, the withering hostility of the Jobe Indians was too overwhelming. The settlement was abandoned sometime in 1568.

The underlying reason for both the Indian hostility and the abandonment of Fort Santa Lucea was simply that the Jobe had no reserve of food they could share with anyone. They caught fish and shellfish and searched the adjoining scrubland for roots and berries.

## SHIPWRECK AND PLUNDER

No further European arrivals in Jupiter were recorded for more than a hundred years afterward, but the Indians at Barra de Jobe surely felt the ripples of growing activity. By 1574 an estimated 152,000 Spaniards had settled in the Americas and towns like St. Augustine and Pensacola were bustling in Florida. Ships laden with silver and gold rounded the tip of Florida, then used the six-knot Gulf Stream for added thrust before cutting across the Bahama Channel on their way to Spain.

The above suggests more activity for the Jeaga Indians. When hurricanes struck ships or ships struck reefs, the villagers were undoubtedly on the coast to plunder cargo and exploit the survivors for whatever gain they could.

Just what the latter meant is subject to conflicting accounts. In 1987, after Jupiter lifeguard Peter Leo discovered the remains of a Spanish wreck in ten feet of water just off the inlet (see photo, right), the archives of colonial Spain identified the ship as the *San Miguel de Archangel*, sunk in 1659. Logs showed that the 33 survivors lived with local Indians on the "River Jeaga" (amicably, one assumes), until picked up by a rescue vessel from St. Augustine.

And yet, just up the beach, something altogether different happened a year later. In 1570 a ship laden with hides from Spain was seized at sea by an English privateer and its occupants put ashore on Jupiter Island. The Jobe/Jeaga Indians received them by murdering all of the stranded Spaniards except for a mother, her three children and a badly wounded sailor. The five were exchanged for six Indians who had previously been captured by Spaniards to the north.

In 1575 Spain was titillated by the newly published memoirs of one Fontaneda, a Columbian who had been captured by Indians as a teenager and held captive for 17 years. On one page he wrote: "The king of the Ayes [in the Fort Pierce area] and the king of the Jeaga are poor Indians, as respects the land; for there are no mines of silver or of gold where they are; and, in short, they are rich only by the sea, from the many vessels that have been lost well laden with these metals…."

But Indians were already beginning to pay a price for their contact with Europeans and their gold and tools. Some historians speculate that the not all wrecks were caused by hurricanes or pirates. Some ships, they say, probably floundered on the reefs along the Jupiter coast because the entire crew was stricken with plague or other communicable disease. They simply became too weak and short-handed to navigate their ship. If so, each chest the plundering Indians opened on the shore literally would have brought a pox upon them.

## DICKINSON'S INVALUABLE DIARY

When England bested the Spanish Armada in 1588, it weakened Spain's foothold on the New World and opened the door to colonial competition from the British, French and Dutch. Again, there is no record of anything but sporadic contact with the Jobe/Jeaga Indians. But by 1650 the estimated population of the English in North America was 52,000, and it would only be a matter of time before they left their mark on Jupiter.

It came in 1696. Jonathan Dickinson was the 33-year-old son of a well-placed English Quaker family that had been granted a thousand acres near Port Royal, Jamaica, for its service to Oliver Cromwell. On August 23 he set sail from Port Royal for Philadelphia on the barkentine *Reformation* with 25 passengers. Besides Dickinson they included his wife Mary, his six month old son Jonathan, a captain, eight sailors, eleven slaves, an elderly missionary who had been serving in Jamaica and a distant kinsman (perhaps a cousin). Loaded among the farm animals to be slaughtered along the way was £1,500 worth of furniture and tools that were to be the basis of a new family import-export business in flourishing Philadelphia.

The *Reformation* began its voyage as part of a convoy of similar merchants who banded together for self-protection, but rough seas soon scattered the fleet so that one would get only a glimpse of another ship from time to time. Anxiety aboard the *Reformation* turned to angst on the night of September 23 when the wind and waves became violent. Around 1 a.m. the huddled passengers felt the vessel hit something with a thud. It floated free for a few minutes, then rammed another object and stuck fast. Seas rushed over the listing ship, and for another 15 minutes everyone thrashed about helplessly in the cabin as water rose around them. Outside, the skies were black and no land could be seen.

After another petrifying three hours, daylight began to break.

In July 1987, just after a storm, Jupiter lifeguard Peter Leo was taking his usual morning ocean swim just south of the inlet when he noticed a dark object in the water below. A quick dive in the ten feet of water showed it to be an old ship's cannon.

Months later, after forming a treasure hunting company, obtaining a state license and pouring through the archives of colonial Spain in Santo Domingo, Leo and his team brought up some 12,000 coins and artifacts ranging from swords to cannons to the copper bucket (crushed when a cannon toppled on top of it) he's holding in the above photo. The mother load came from the aviso (ore-hauling) ship *San Miguel de Archangel*, sunk in 1659 during a storm just off what the Spaniards called the "River Jeaga." The *San Miguel* was a special find because its coins bore the stamps of five colonial mints: Bogotá, Cartagena, Lima, Mexico City and Potosi (Bolivia).

One "bonus" find from Leo's years of excavations off Jupiter beach is evidence that the ancient Indian midden that ran along the south side of Jupiter Inlet extended for several yards into the ocean. Says Leo: "We found the same black muddy soil, tannic acid and oyster bars underwater that ran along the old shoreline in DuBois Park." *(From* Diving for Treasure, *by John C. Fine, with permission from Richard C. Owen Publishers Inc., Katonah, N.Y.)*

## HOW HO-BAY BECAME JUPITER

For centuries, the Indians who lived at the inlet called their village "Ho-Bay." It seems they were a branch of the Jeaga, a sub-tribe whose domain stretched north perhaps to the end of Jupiter Island. The earliest Spanish visitors wrote the word for the village as *Jobe*. When the English came along in the seventeenth century, they assumed that *Jobe* was Spanish for the Roman god Jove. So they simply made it the English variant, *Jupiter*.

Surprisingly, water receded from the cabin. A clamber up to the quarterdeck quickly revealed that the ship had come to rest on a beach and the tide was going out, leaving it high and dry. The hull's planking was ripped and punctured, and would surely become worse when the tide returned.

Despite near exhaustion, the bone-chilled band began herding the animals that hadn't been washed away and loading boxes of cargo and clothing onto a longboat so they could be brought onto the beach. Despite the continued rain and wind, Dickinson got a fire started and began tending to the many in his party who had broken bones or raging fevers. At the time, he had no idea where he was in Florida. In a few days he was able to place the shipwreck location on today's Jupiter Island—about five miles north of Jobe Inlet.

And it was there history records the first meaningful description of Jupiter's local sons.

*About the eighth or ninth hour came two Indian men (being naked except a small piece of platted work of straws which just hid their private parts, and fastened behind with a horsetail in likeness made of a sort of silk-grass) from the southward, running freely and foaming at the mouth, having no weapons except their knives; and forthwith not making any stop violently seized the two first of our men they met with who were carrying corn from the vessel to the top of the bank, where I stood to receive it and put it in a cask.*

The rest of the passengers also ran or limped to the scene, bringing their wet muskets and asking if they should open fire. This was a pivotal decision for Dickinson. Had he chosen violence, another two hundred Jobe Indians were getting ready to descend on them. Instead, he listened to the aging missionary,

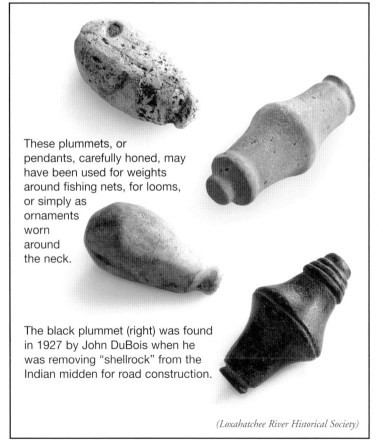

These plummets, or pendants, carefully honed, may have been used for weights around fishing nets, for looms, or simply as ornaments worn around the neck.

The black plummet (right) was found in 1927 by John DuBois when he was removing "shellrock" from the Indian midden for road construction.

*(Loxahatchee River Historical Society)*

Robert Barrow, who urged everyone to remain calm and put their trust in the Lord and their deliverance in the hands of Spaniards— if they could find a Spanish settlement. The two assailants, their hair in a roll with ornamental bones and pins stuck through, kept up their "wild, furious countenance," but Dickinson coolly opened one of the chests that had come ashore and handed them some tobacco and pipes. "Making a snuffing noise like a wild beast, they turned their backs and run away," he reported.

About three hours later, just as a little sun was finally beginning to warm the beach, the busy salvagers began to hear whoops and shouts. Soon "a very great number" of Indians stormed onto the beach, climbing onto the stricken vessel and "taking forth whatever they could lay hold on, except [unexplainably] rum, sugar, molasses, [dried] beef and pork." Next, the "Casseekey" (as Dickinson called the cacique, or chief) and about thirty of his fiercest warriors "came down to us in a furious manner, having a dismal aspect and foaming at the mouth. Their weapons were large Spanish knives, except their Casseekey, who had a bagganet that had belonged to the master of our vessel. They rushed in upon us and cried 'Nickaleer, Nickaleer.'"

Dickinson was to hear the word often. He soon realized it was the Jobe word for Englishman, and the venom accompanying the name left no doubt that these Indians hated anything or anyone English.

"Espania?" the chief asked next. "Si, si!" they all chorused. "Espania!" One of the seamen spoke a little Spanish, and he was enlisted to convince the "Casseekey" that the group wanted to head north immediately in search of a Spanish settlement that would give them shelter. No matter that England had warred off and on with Spain for a century. They'd take their chances.

By now the Indians had formed a menacing circle around the beleaguered survivors. "No Espania!" they shouted over and over. "Nickaleer! Nickaleer!"

At this point only the chief stood between them and the smothering circle of his warriors. Recalled Dickinson: "All had their arms extended with their knives in their hands, ready to execute their bloody design, some taking hold of us by the heads with their knives set against their shoulders. In this posture they seemed to wait for the Casseekey to begin."

But the order to butcher them never came. For a long minute the warriors continued their feverish pitch—"words which we understood not," Dickinson wrote. "But on a sudden it pleased the Lord to work wonderfully for our preservation, and instantly all these savage men were struck dumb," and within fifteen minutes "their countenances fell and they looked like another people."

Obviously, something had compelled the chief to take the forlorn strangers under his wing. Perhaps it was partly because most of the beached chests were locked and the castaways had the keys. In any case, he demanded that all of the chests, trunks and boxes be unlocked and their contents emptied, with the most fetching of prizes going to the chief himself. Next, the Indians clawed and pulled at everyone's clothing, so that all were nearly stripped naked. When the castaways still continued to beg that they be allowed to head north immediately, the chief refused,

## Ⓖⓞⓓⓢ

### PROTECTING PROVIDENCE
*MAN'S*
### SUREST HELP AND DEFENCE
In the times
Of the greateſt difficulty and moſt Imminent danger;
Evidenced in the

## Remarkable Deliberance

Of divers Perſons,
From the devouring Waves of the Sea, amongſt which
they Suffered Shipwrack.
And alſo
From the more cruelly devouring jawes of the inhumane
CANIBALS of FLORIDA.
*Faithfully related by one of the perſons concerned therein;*
*JONATHAN DICKENSON.*

Psal. 93 : 4. *The Lord on high is mightier than the noiſe of many Waters,*
*yea than the mighty Waves of the Sea.*
Psal. 74 : 20. *The dark places of the Earth are full of the habitations*
*of Cruelty.*

Printed in *Philadelphia* by *Reinier Janſen.* 1699.

The hair-raising "Journal" compiled by Jonathan Dickinson after his safe return to Philadelphia was soon printed on a shopworn press from London and distributed to Quakers as proof that God protects the faithful in perilous times. Little did Dickinson know that others would scoop up the dramatic tale and that it would be reprinted 22 times in the eighteenth and nineteenth centuries.

insisting with vivid sign language that "when we came there, we should have our throats and scalps cut and be shot, burnt and eaten."

The cacique's actions in the next several hours would seem to cast further light on his motives. First, it became evident that he knew too much about Europeans for this to have been an initial contact. After all, he and his men were brandishing Spanish-forged swords. Moreover, he must have known the value of cash, having demanded at the outset that all of the survivors' money be collected and given to him personally. Finally, he must have known more of the language than he was letting on. At one point when Dickinson was denying the *Nickaleer* claim for the umpteenth time, the chief sneered at him and spat out, "English son of a bitch!"

Second, even if the chief knew he had ersatz Spaniards on his hands, he still seemed to trust them more than his own men. During that first night on the beach he allowed the party to erect their tents. The chief then hauled all of his personally selected

Looking west from atop the ranger platform on Hobe Mountain, the landscape of Jonathan Dickinson State Park remains much the same as when its namesake first visited in 1696. *(Sue S. Snyder)*

chests inside the Dickinson family tent and slept on top of them. A day later he took two of Dickinson's slaves off into the thicket to help him bury his cash cache, making sure his own men didn't follow.

Reconciled to a five-mile southward journey to the chief's village, the exhausted and threadbare party was grateful for even the smallest of favors. Before trekking in the sand, the chief went down to the wrecked ship and returned with some wet, wooly coats for the Dickinson family. Once they were ferried across the inlet to the Indian village, the cacique took pains to give them sleeping mats and erect a makeshift three-foot fence of palmettos to ward off the incessant wind. A local woman even took Dickinson's infant and nursed him when his mother was too exhausted and dried out from her ordeal.

Dickinson's journal remains the only reliable description of life in the village at Jobe Inlet where DuBois Park and Jupiter Beach stand today. He writes of people living in "little wigwams made of small poles stuck in the ground, which they bended one to another, making an arch, and covered them with a thatch of small palmetto leaves." The Casseekey's wigwam, he adds, "was about man-high to the top."

As the weary and shivering captives lay down to sleep in their first night at the village, the chief "went into his wigwam and seated himself on his cabin cross-legged, having a basket of palmetto berries brought him, which he ate greedily." Later, when Dickinson was offered some, he described their taste as "rotten cheese steeped in tobacco."

In a few days he would crave the berries like manna and miss them even long afterward in Philadelphia.

As the moon rose and the weary guests tried to sleep, Dickinson recalled that the village shaman stood before the moon "making a hideous noise, crying out and acting like a madman for the space of a half hour." This prompted a chorus of males to make "a fearful noise, some like the barking of a dog, wolf and other strange sounds." Then the women chimed in, "making the noise more terrible," and continuing until midnight.

When the fitful party awoke the next morning (their third since the wreck) fires had gone out and they were in "extreme cold." Taking pity, the chief sent his son to the inlet "to strike fish for us" and provided the first glimpse of why thousands of northerners would eventually come surging down to Jupiter:

*… for some of us walked down with him, and though we looked very earnestly when he threw his staff from him, could not see a fish at which time he saw it, and brought it on shore at the end of his staff. Sometimes he would run swiftly pursing a fish, and seldom missed when he darted at them. In two hours' time he got as many fish as would serve twenty men. There were others fishing at the same time, so that fish was plenty.*

That afternoon Dickinson was shocked to see smoke from a great fire billowing over the trees a few miles to the north. He knew that the *Reformation* had been set ablaze and feared that it signaled his party's imminent demise. That night the warriors, as they had on the beach, pressed about them with bows and arrows drawn, and again they thought that their time had surely come. But just when the tension was at its worst, the missionary Robert Barrow rose and read loudly to them from the Bible amidst the din of Indian voices. Soon he had replaced the castaways' dread with an inner calm that "it was His blessed will [that] he would preserve and deliver us from amongst them, that our names might not be buried into oblivion…."

The next morning Dickinson again beseeched the chief to let the party head north, but this time his plea was unexplainably granted. The cacique even produced a longboat from the *Reformation* that the survivors assumed to have burned up with the mother ship. With some in the boat and some wading in the marshes, the still nearly naked party of 24 (a slave girl had died in the storm) set off along the shallow Jupiter Narrows in search of a more friendly civilization.

Along the way they would endure freezing nights, scorching sands by day, searing hunger and more torments at the hands of

other Indian villages. Nearly everyone would become seriously ill and five would simply give up the ghost along the way. The emaciated, blistered survivors finally staggered into hospitable St. Augustine on November 15 after an ordeal of 54 days.

Jonathan Dickinson was convinced that his odyssey was proof of God's divine intervention on behalf of those who prayed and persevered in His name. He published his diary in 1699 as *Jonathan Dickinson's Journal,* and it immediately became popular in the Quaker stronghold of Philadelphia. But it struck a responsive chord elsewhere, too, being reprinted 22 times during the next two centuries. Dickinson, who rose to become mayor of Philadelphia and speaker of the Pennsylvania Assembly, seems to have been undaunted by his harrowing adventure. He passed the Jupiter coast and village of his one-time tormenters many more times on sailing trips between Philadelphia and his Jamaica plantation before his death in 1722 at age 59.

## A TIDAL CHANGE BRINGS THE ENGLISH

More than 60 years would pass without a hint of European activity anywhere around Jupiter Inlet. At the same time, the native Indian population continued to be thinned by disease, internal warfare and raids by slave traders. Of these, diseases brought in by the white population surely took the greatest toll. As just one example of how severely a pox could sweep through a civilization, consider the plight of the Lucayan Indians in the Bahamas. Archeologists estimate the population at about 50,000 when Columbus arrived. In 1513 Spanish explorers couldn't find *anyone.*

It took a far away group of "statesmen" to remove the remaining south Florida Indians altogether. In 1763 the terms ending the French-Indian War ceded all of Canada and America east of the Mississippi to England. Soon afterwards, the Spanish razed their forts in South Florida, snatched up what they believed to be all the remaining Indians—about eighty families—and shipped them to Cuba to work in the sugarcane fields.

Alas, what might have triggered a surge of activity by Florida's

new masters was offset because the British were overwhelmed trying to govern their vast new territory to the north—and later overrun by angry colonists because they tried to impose taxes to help offset their mounting costs.

Curiously, a few eighteenth century English maps show Jupiter Inlet as *Grenville* Inlet. George Grenville was First Lord of the Admiralty in 1762–63 and then served as Prime Minister from 1763–65. Merchants and explorers often named New World discoveries for their patrons or those who granted their charters. The Grenville family was known to have investments in Florida. When the Jupiter Lighthouse was renovated during 1999–2000, project archeologist Jim Pepe found pieces of English clay pipes buried around the base.

However, any "Grenville" settlement in Jupiter would have been brief or sporadic. Some speculate that one of London's many merchant companies might have sponsored an unsuccessful attempt to farm the area, or that the first British Bahamians used it as a camp during periodic visits to hunt for game and salvage. Ironically, the only real population "boomlet" came in late 1782 when nearly 12,000 Loyalists from Charleston and Savannah were evacuated to Florida, the only North American territory not wrested from the British. But again world politics would intervene. In 1783, as part of the Treaty of Paris ending the Revolutionary War, the British handed Florida back to Spain in exchange for the rights to retain their stronghold on Gibraltar. And so the Loyalists were soon packing again and sailing for safer places such as the Bahamas and Jamaica.

Spain, burned once, wasn't about to invest seriously again in Florida. The lands south and east of Lake Okeechobee were as sparsely peopled as they may have been 5,000 years before. In 1786 a survey of all Florida east of the Apalachicola River reported only 1,700 residents. The census of 1800 showed only 21 towns in all of Florida, many of them but a lone trading post in the wilderness. In 1825 the government estimated the population of "south Florida" at 317.

But footsteps from the north would soon break the lull.

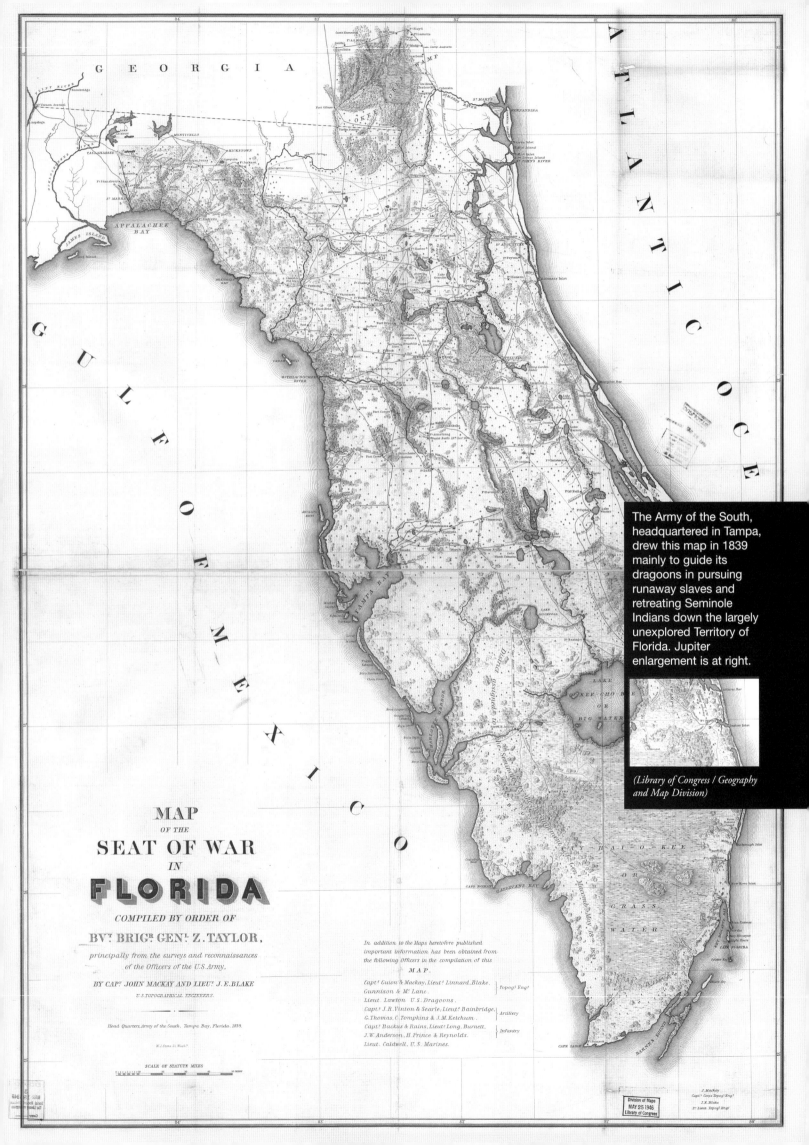

The Army of the South, headquartered in Tampa, drew this map in 1839 mainly to guide its dragoons in pursuing runaway slaves and retreating Seminole Indians down the largely unexplored Territory of Florida. Jupiter enlargement is at right.

MAP
OF THE
SEAT OF WAR
IN
FLORIDA

COMPILED BY ORDER OF

BVᵗ. BRIGᴿ. GENᴸ. Z. TAYLOR,

principally from the surveys and reconnaissances
of the Officers of the U.S. Army.

BY CAPT. JOHN MACKAY AND LIEUT. J. E. BLAKE
U.S.TOPOGRAPHICAL ENGINEERS.

Head Quarters, Army of the South, Tampa Bay, Florida. 1839.

SCALE OF STATUTE MILES

In addition to the Maps heretofore published
important information has been obtained from
the following Officers in the compilation of this
MAP.

Capts Guion & Mackay, Lieuts Linnard, Blake,    | Topogᶫ Engʳ
Gunnison & Mᶜ Lane.
Lieut. Lawton. U.S. Dragoons.
Capts J.R.Vinton & Searle, Lieuts Bainbridge,   | Artillery
G.Thomas, C.Tompkins & J.M.Ketchum.
Capts Backus & Rains, Lieuts Long, Burnett,     | Infantry
J.W.Anderson, H Prince & Reynolds.
Lieut. Caldwell, U.S. Marines.

J.Mackay
Captᵗ Corps Topogᶫ Engʳ
J.E.Blake
1ˢᵗ Lieut. Topogᶫ Engʳ

# CHAPTER 2

# A BEACON IN THE WILDERNESS

Just when the last of the original tribes were fading from south Florida, a much different Indian had begun filtering into the state's northern tier—due to a hard shove from the relentlessly expanding colonists of Alabama, Georgia and the Carolinas.

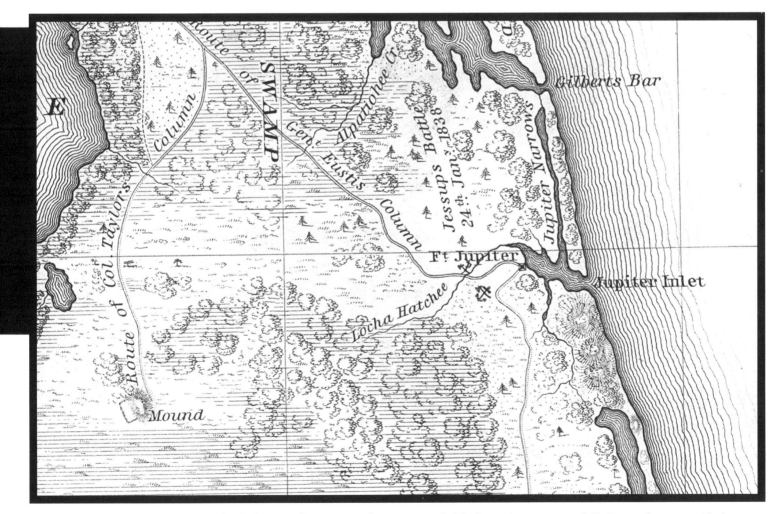

While conflict over land was surely the biggest factor, two others made the political pot boil over. First, Indians of the southern states had often found themselves on the "wrong" side. Many had fought for the English in the Revolutionary War. After 1783, when Spain regained Florida but lacked the resources to rebuild a stronghold there, it encouraged Indian tribes to raid the new Americans.

All that might have been forgiven except for the second factor. When Spain owned Florida, it proved a prosperous haven for an ever-growing stream of escaped slaves. A plantation owner would

Maj. General Thomas S. Jesup (above) reluctantly led the U.S. Army's heavy-handed roundup of the Seminole Indians in Florida. His commander in chief: the pro-slavery Andrew Jackson.
*(U.S. Army Quartermaster Museum)*

Spaniards abandoned Florida in 1783, they turned loose all the cattle and horses they couldn't board on ships for Cuba. Within a generation or two, thousands of range animals were roaming the central grasslands and blacks with their plantation skills were showing Indian chiefs how to round them up into valuable herds.

As Richard Procyk notes in his *Guns Across the Loxahatchee,* "the first American cowboys (vaqueros) were not in the far West but were descendants of the early Spaniards, Indians or blacks, slave or free, in Florida." As for the Indians, Procyk adds that some chiefs "had herds of cattle of well over a thousand head. These Indian ranchers rode fine ponies and…owned many slaves who herded these cattle and grew the crops."

Slaves? Technically, some Indians were indeed slave owners. Occasionally they'd even buy more slaves on the market in exchange for livestock. Yet, the Indian-slave relationship afforded more freedom than in the white South. Blacks usually lived in their own clusters within a tribe's orbit. Since the Indians tended to shun farming, a Negro's only acknowledgment of servitude was supplying a certain percentage of his crops to the tribe. In time, even this distinction would blur, as blacks excelled in special skills, intermarried and became part of tribal councils.

But the Seminoles had scant time in which to enjoy their prosperity. By 1816 white slave owners were livid at the escalated rate of runaways into Florida. At a time when a typical annual wage was $700, a slave could cost $600 to $1,000, and masters were demanding that the federal government help them reclaim their runaway "property" and remove the offending Indians to reservations in Arkansas and Oklahoma. To make a political statement, the U.S. Army crossed into Spanish territory for the first time, sending an armed boat up the Apalachicola River. Its destination was an abandoned earthen fort that had become a center for sheltering black runaways. An estimated three hundred lived there at the time. The ship's gunners scalded cannon balls so that they glowed red and then lobbed them inside the fort. As hoped for, one of them hit a magazine containing seven hundred barrels of powder.

The blast killed 270 people. It also ignited waves of raids by white planters and Seminole ranchers on each other's property so that the combined episodes gradually became known as the First Seminole Indian War. White settlers clamored for more reprisals and, fortunately for them, an ambitious army general was willing to ride the issue all the way to the presidency. He was Maj. Gen. Andrew Jackson and he came from slave-owning Tennessee.

Eventually, he would bring his crusade all the way south to Jupiter until it dissipated ingloriously in the swamps south of Riverbend Park.

Even though Jackson was to write President Monroe in 1817 that "I have long viewed treaties with the Indians as an absurdity…" treaties became the order of the day. When Spain sold Florida to America in 1819 and it became a Territory two years later, the U.S. military found itself with more power to muscle the Indians into one-sided agreements. In the Treaty of Moultrie Creek, for example, the Indians secured some money, livestock and tools in exchange for some central Florida land (along the Peace River south of Ocala) that was scenic but

bristle at learning that runaways had blended beautifully with the Indians in their newfound Florida and that a black man who had cost him perhaps $1,000 now farmed his own spread under the protective wing of an Indian chief. He'd become apoplectic at learning that other runaways had joined the Spanish Black Militia or had formed the first "free" black community at Fort Mose near St. Augustine. The last straw would have been the War of 1812, when hundreds of fugitive slaves signed up to fight for the British.

Just who were these unique, vibrant people? "Seminoles," said the white southerners. The term began with a sloppy pronunciation of *cimarrone*—Spanish for runaway or fugitive— which initially applied only to slaves escaping to Florida. The Indians never accepted the term on grounds that being bullied off one's land at gunpoint isn't the same as running away. But by the early 1800s the two cultures had become so intertwined that *Seminole* became the white's convenient handle for everyone. Indeed, the typical Seminole by then was a mix of African, European, and one of the Creek or Hitchiti tribes. He or she might speak both Indian languages as well as English.

In their first years on the northern tier of Florida, the Indian contingent tried farming—and might have failed without help from runaway slaves who had learned their skills on plantations. In the early 1880s another push southward came as emboldened white settlers forced the Seminoles into the less fertile, open spaces of the interior. But this time luck was with them. Before the

incapable of yielding enough food to live on.

In 1829 Jackson became president and American policy now focused solely on transporting every last Seminole (there were never more than 5,000) to the Wild West. On a gut level, Jackson never forgave the Indians for fighting with the British in 1812. On a more practical level, the U.S. had strained the treasury by paying $5 million to acquire the last lands from Spain and couldn't hope to recoup its investment through land sales until it could assure new settlers their personal safety.

Little did he know that this supposed "housecleaning" of no more than 2,000 Seminole warriors and their black allies would embroil the young nation in its longest war—until Vietnam—and cost more than eight times what it had paid Spain.

By 1835 the lines had been drawn and the leading characters sharpened. On February 16 President Jackson addressed a letter to "My Children" asking them to listen to the "voice of friendship and truth" that they be evacuated. And if not, they would be "removed by force." Jackson's chief Indian agent at the trading post where the letter was read to 150 chiefs and warriors, was Gen. Wiley Thompson, who was already loathed for his overbearing ways. Also present was the handsome 31-year-old son of a Creek woman named Polly and an Englishman named William Powell. He had already risen to be the charismatic symbol of resistance, and his answer to the latest proposed "treaty" was to stab his knife into the parchment. His given name was Billy Powell, but as the Seminoles' fiercest fighter, it would become *Osceola*.

By 1837 around 4,000 of the U.S. Army's 7,130 active troops had already slogged through sand and slough in the battles of the Withlachoochee River and Lake Okeechobee. Nearly always the Seminoles more than held their ground, for example, 7 dead and 11 wounded at Okeechobee vs. 25 and 112 for the army forces. But because the Indians couldn't draft replacements like the army, they decided never again to engage the enemy in direct combat.

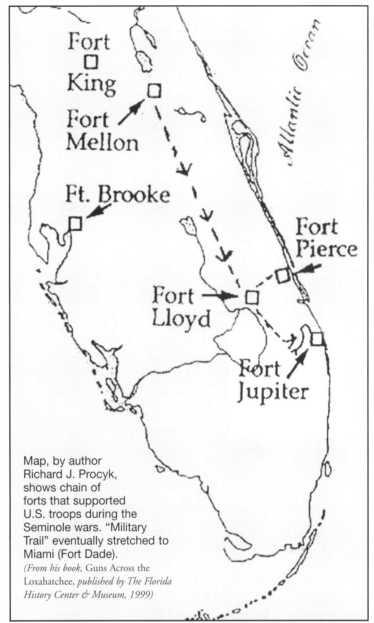

Map, by author Richard J. Procyk, shows chain of forts that supported U.S. troops during the Seminole wars. "Military Trail" eventually stretched to Miami (Fort Dade). *(From his book,* Guns Across the Loxahatchee, *published by The Florida History Center & Museum, 1999)*

Seth Shear, a renowned 19th century photographer, captured the eerie stillness of Jupiter Narrows, which lay at the southern end of the meandering, trip from Titusville to Jupiter. *(Skip Gladwyn Collection, photo by Seth Shear)*

In December 1837 army reconnaissance reported that 150 or so remnants from the Battle of Okeechobee had made their way south to an Indian village along the Loxahatchee. Perhaps 250 to 300 Indian and black warriors were now camped "on a high hammock" a few miles upstream from Fort Jupiter.

By January 1838, 1,535 already footsore soldiers were hacking and wading their way south in one of the most excruciating marches in military history. Horses broke legs and wagons lost wheels. Soldiers howled as the saw palmetto cut their arms, then cursed as the muck of the cypress swamps sucked in their shoes and left over four hundred barefooted. Suddenly on January 24, when they had reached today's Riverbend Park, scouts came upon the Seminole force and officers decided to waste no time in opening fire.

This battle was clearly on the Indians' terms. They had carefully chosen their high ground with an escape route through a dense swamp behind it. They'd chopped the saw palmetto in front of them to have a clearer look at their quarry and they'd even carved notches in tree trunks to steady their muskets. But it was the army who advanced with guns blazing.

After retreating to a second well-rehearsed spot across a narrow finger of the Loxahatchee, the Seminoles unleashed another shower of musket balls before carrying out their new strategy. They vanished into the swamps.

The army, divided and disillusioned, had suffered 7 soldiers killed and 31 wounded. Maj. Gen. Thomas Sidney Jesup, his glasses shot off and cheek torn by an Indian musket, had a bigger wound to heal. Part of his troops were Tennessee Volunteers. Their proud former commander was none other than Andrew Jackson, and the president had bragged that his old unit would whip the Indians quickly and soundly. Truth is, they had buckled under fire. Jesup feared that the fiery commander in chief would simply disbelieve any such report and train his temper on the messenger.

Even more painful was Jesup's conscience. On February 11 he wrote the secretary of war. Why are we down here in this muck? he said in essence. Yes, he could see why conflicts over fertile land in places like Georgia and Alabama required Indians to be removed, but why down here in this miserable buggy, boggy land having no white man and no earthly use? "My decided opinion," he said, "is that unless *immediate* emigration be abandoned, the war will continue for years to come and at constantly accumulating expense."

The Seminoles were tired and hungry, too. Many of them drifted back to Fort Jupiter with their families and received provisions. The thoughtful General Jesup told them frankly about his views and his letter. Soon some five hundred Seminoles were camped nearby in hopes The Great Father would grant them peace in at least this swampland.

On March 17 Jesup opened his reply: a curt and unequivocal rejection. The War Department demanded the prompt capture or

For decades no one seemed to know the site of the Battle of the Loxahatchee, which all but ended the Second Seminole Indian War in 1838. The answer lay in the obvious: the military trail from Okeechobee followed Indiantown Road, and it crossed the Loxahatchee at its shallowest stretch for miles around. The bucolic scene above, where Indians lay on the east side with rifles cocked as army troops prepared to wade across the river, is just a few yards south of where busy commuter traffic now zooms over the Indiantown Road Bridge. *(Sue S. Snyder)*

LEFT, Seminole chief Billy Bowlegs in 1852. *(Florida State Archives)*

BELOW, Billy Powell, son of an Englishman and his Creek wife, soon became known as Osceola, charismatic leader of the Seminole resistance. *(Florida State Archives)*

15

After the Seminole wars the Indians who visited Jupiter didn't exactly disarm, as this 1879 photo shows. Hunting became their chief source of meat and hides a way to trade. *(Loxahatchee River Historical Society)*

destruction of the Indians.

Jesup, though stunned and sickened, managed to rationalize that the Indians would probably perish anyway if left to the dangers of a swampy land that no man could farm. He asked them to assemble at Fort Jupiter under a flag of truce. More than five hundred did so. They were immediately surrounded by troops and taken into custody for the long and demeaning trip westward.

Some, who had never trusted any army offer, fled even deeper into the Everglades. They probably numbered no more than two hundred, and would be the forebears of the Seminoles who live between Miami and Naples today. Some would leave their mark on Jupiter in the years to come.

## IF YOU BUILD IT, THEY WILL COME?

Shortly after the Second Seminole Indian War the army built a crude stockade where today's Pennock Point looks out toward Jupiter Inlet two and a half miles downstream. It was part of a chain of military supply-support facilities that eventually stretched to Fort Dade in what is now Miami. But the first glimmer of a "town" of Jupiter didn't come until May 1855 when the president declared a 9,088-acre military reservation extending four and a half miles west from the ocean. In the middle of it, in today's Pennock Plantation, would be a second "Fort Jupiter" (again a rough wooden stockade) manned by about 85 officers and enlisted men.

What were they guarding out there in the wilderness? They were a symbol of support for new settlers and a new commitment to protect ships at sea.

As the Second Seminole War trailed off, so did the number of active soldiers and pioneers willing to settle in dangerous lands. It was beginning to look like spending $5 million to buy Florida was pure folly until Congress came up with one of the earliest federal handout programs. The Armed Occupation Act of 1842 offered

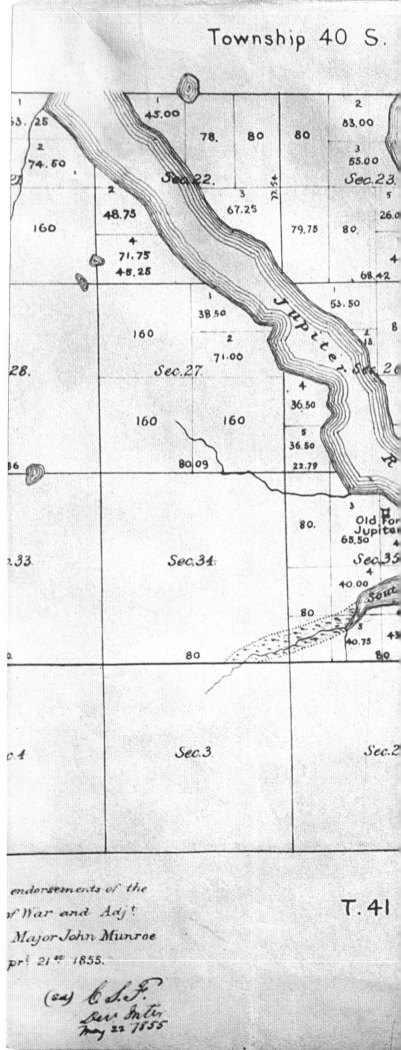

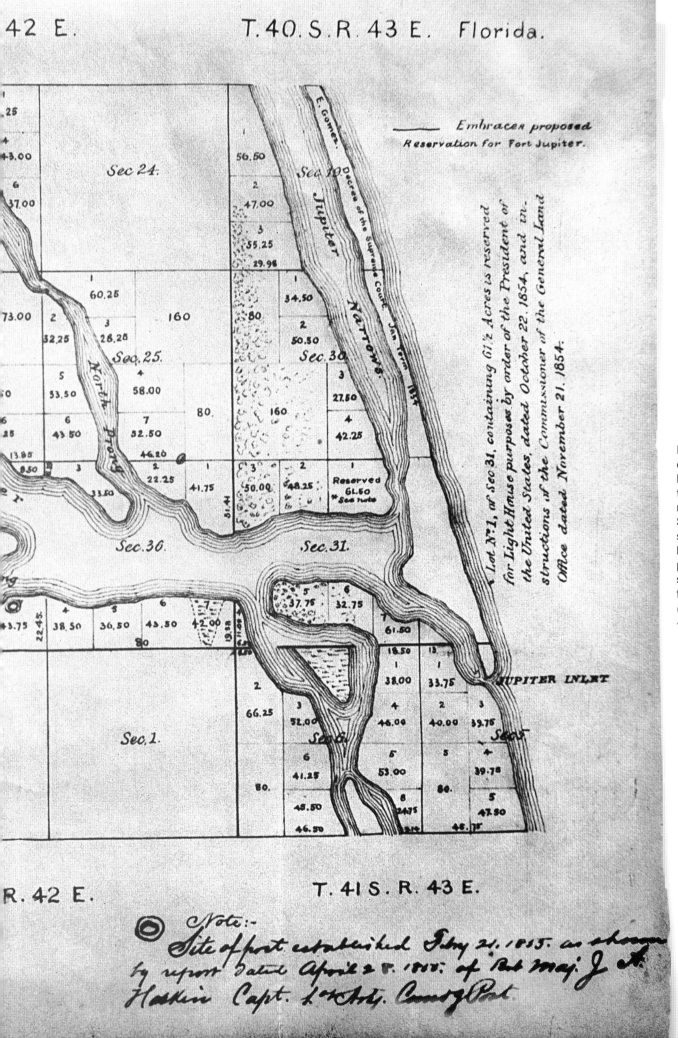

T. 40. S. R. 43 E. Florida.

——— Embraces proposed
Reservation for Fort Jupiter.

Sec 24.

Sec 25.

Sec 30.

Sec 36.

Sec 31.

Sec 1.

JUPITER INLET

Lot Nº 1, of Sec 31, containing 61½ Acres is reserved for Light House purposes by order of the President of the United States, dated October 22. 1854, and in-structions of the Commissioner of the General Land Office dated November 21. 1854.

R. 42 E.

T. 41 S. R. 43 E.

Note:— Site of post established Feby 21. 1855. as shown by report dated April 28. 1855. of Bvt Maj J A Haskin Capt. 1st Arty. Comdg Post.

In 1855 the army drew up the boundaries of the Fort Jupiter reservation. Some of its subdivisions became the first parcels to be sold to settlers a few years later.
*(Loxahatchee River Historical Society)*

17

In 1854, Army Lt. George Meade, an engineer, drew up the plans for the Jupiter Lighthouse. A few years later he would lead the Union forces in the Battle of Gettysburg against Robert E. Lee. In 1849, it was Lee who had surveyed the site. *(Florida State Archives)*

any settler clear title to 160 acres south of a line between Cedar Key and St. Augustine *if* he (1) built a home there and cleared five acres; (2) stayed for five years; (3) lived within two miles of a military post. In the next year the government land office issued some three hundred permits, even including some for as far south as Jupiter.

As urged by the government, settlers banded into self-protection groups, but nothing could shield them from the bugs that preyed on their puny crops. Folks were already starting to pack up when yet another Indian episode hastened their decision. A shopkeeper was murdered and mutilated as he farmed his plot by the Sebastian River. It didn't matter that the nearest Indian chief, Billy Bowlegs, disavowed the act as that of a few renegades, nor that he personally tracked down five of the murderers. Almost all of the frightened settlers headed north, and even a new state law confining all Indians to reservations made no difference.

In 1856 an army report listed only eight families living from Miami to a line 190 miles north.

The federal government was far more generous when it came to protecting the high seas. The most outward evidence of a robust new nation was the rapid expansion of sea trade, but the more that U.S. ships headed down the Florida coast to open new markets, the more they lost men and cargo to storms and reefs. In 1849 Col. Robert E. Lee and a party of surveyors sailed the entire coastline of Florida marking possible sites for a chain of military defenses. His surveys were probably used by another famous name, George Meade, then an Army engineer in charge of building lighthouses. Picking a spot in Jupiter was no doubt easy because Lt. Meade would have been drawn to the natural mound—called a *parabolic dune*—that rose about two miles east of Fort Jupiter (but still within the vast federal reservation).

Jupiter, whose reefs reached so close to the Gulf Stream, got

priority attention, and in 1853 Congress appropriated $35,000 to build a lighthouse of the "first order" (the most powerful of six categories).

George Meade, an engineer who would have laughed at the notion that he'd one day lead Union forces against Robert E. Lee in the Battle of Gettysburg, drew up a blueprint that called for "a 90-foot brick tower with an iron stairway and furnished with a [French-made] Fresnel illuminating apparatus of the first order with flashes." Housing the keeper and his family would be a one-story, 26-by-30-foot brick building.

In 1852 Congress showed its concern for the government's ragtag collection of seventy lighthouses by creating an expert U.S. Lighthouse Board, and Meade's design for Jupiter received swift approval. The devil was in the details. Everyone had assumed that oceangoing cargo ships would haul the estimated five hundred tons of bricks and other materials right through the Jupiter Inlet and tie up to a dock just a few yards from the dune. But Congress didn't reckon with the inlet's unpredictable ways. That year the inlet had amassed an impenetrable sandbar and it became apparent that the only way to get the job done was to "go inside" via the Indian River.

This was nearly the maritime equivalent of the army's slog through the bog to Fort Jupiter a few years back. Parts of the Indian River ran only 18 inches deep at low tide. It meant that ocean vessels had to swerve into Fort Pierce Inlet, then transfer their bulky cargo to three shallow draft barges. The scows would then inch their way south for 35 miles, the last 20 or so snaking through the tricky Jupiter Narrows. Before it was over, the three scows would make fifty trips, each one carrying ten tons.

But that was the easy part. Just when everyone thought the Indian wars had subsided, Congress enacted a Swamps and Overflowed Lands Act, which gave aid to states that drained wetlands for development. Florida couldn't wait to take part, which it took as license to drain the swamps of Indians as well. Soon state surveyors were popping up unannounced on reservations—a violation of an old Indian axiom that land is like air or water and can't be sold or fenced off.

In December 1855 one Lt. George Hartsuff and an armed survey crew ventured into the Big Cypress Swamp and stumbled on the village of Chief Billy Bowlegs. Because someone had earlier burned out two U.S. forts in the area, Hartsuff's men took revenge by destroying the chief's prize banana grove along with his corn and bean crops. Days later the ten-man army crew was ambushed by thirty whooping Indians and the Third Seminole War (or the Billy Bowlegs War, as the press proclaimed it) was again rampaging through Florida. Roving, revengeful Indian bands had even ventured back up to Jupiter, where they hid among the palmetto bushes and took potshots at the twenty-man crew that was beginning to lay a ring of bricks and mortar for the lighthouse tower.

By February 1856 a new army garrison had returned to Jupiter, vowing to resume the Indian roundup and protect the workers. Disdaining the crumbling first fort ("it was bare of timber"), they built a new one on well-wooded and fertile soil a half mile closer to "Jupiter Bar."

Well before the lighthouse reservation got its first dock and boathouse, chickee huts like the one at right may have been used for equipment storage and/or as a place to wash and hang up laundry. *(Florida State Archives)*

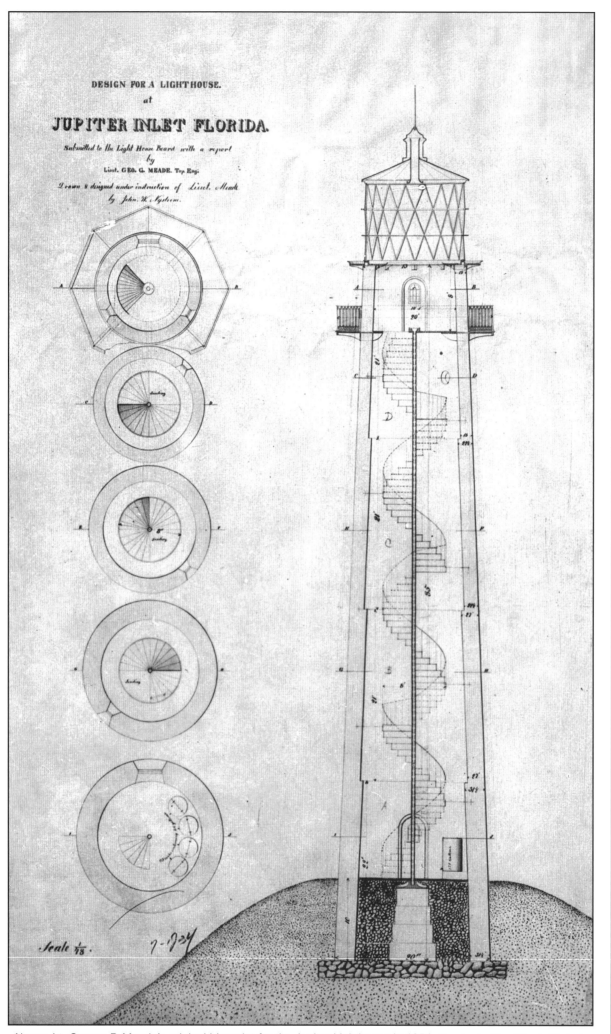

DESIGN FOR A LIGHTHOUSE.
at
JUPITER INLET FLORIDA.

Submitted to the Light House Board with a report
by
Lieut. GEO. G. MEADE. Top. Eng:

Drawn & designed under instruction of Lieut. Meade
by John W. Nystrom.

Scale 1/18.

At right, the lens room keeper's view through the triangle-shaped window panes, called astragals. Just above the ledge were six vents that controlled the amount of air let in to keep the light burning properly and the storm panes from fogging up.

At right, the pedestal, on a cast-iron base, which rotated clockwise on ball bearings. Like a grandfather clock, the pedestal was powered by a 250 lb. weight suspended at the end of a cable that dropped through an opening in the floor. The keeper would have to rewind it every two or three hours.

At right, a look down the 105 cast-iron spiral stairs. A piece of Plexiglas marks the spot where the massive weight snapped free of its steel cable and plunged through the stairs when the keeper wound it too tightly.

At far right, the recessed walls on the first floor were for stacking "butts" (barrels) of lard before their trip to the top of the tower.
*(Photos: Jim Johnston)*

Above, Lt. George P. Meade's original blueprint for the Jupiter Lighthouse in 1854. *(Loxahatchee River Historical Society)*

A sandbar it was indeed at the time, and it was the cause of the greatest single problem for soldier and lighthouse builder alike. The inlet had been closed for a couple of years. The river became clogged with decaying debris and the stagnant water bred the scourge of the tropics in full profusion. The soldiers and workers could only grasp at the cause and call it "Jupiter Fever," but we know it today, of course, as the mosquito's curse, malaria.

The workers became so debilitated that they could scarcely haul another brick. Over at the new Fort Jupiter, 60 of the 68 military personnel on duty were laid up sick. Soon most of the Fort Jupiter contingent was transferred north to Fort Capron, just north of Fort Pierce, to be near the only doctor for miles around.

When the Indians continued to harass the lighthouse workers, Lieutenant Meade in January 1856 urgently wrote the Treasury Department for "small arms ammunition" for his twenty "mechanics and laborers—unarmed & totally defenceless…at points in the immediate vicinity of Indian lines…."

All work ground to a halt. Congress could only shell out another $19,523 and order the construction to go on. It wasn't until September 1856 that work was resumed. In February 1858 a company from Fort Capron marched down to take over Fort Jupiter and supply bodyguards for the last phase of the lighthouse project. A month later Billy Bowlegs signed a pact accepting a cash payment for damage to his cherished crops, but it was a face-saving gesture by the government. Two months later he and his followers were packed off to a reservation out west and the Third Seminole Indian War was pronounced over.

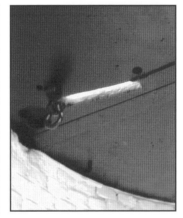

21

## THE LIGHTHOUSE MAKES A BRIEF DEBUT

On July 10, 1860, the Jupiter Lighthouse, by now a $60,860 textbook government cost overrun project, shined its light for the first time. On a clear night it could be seen by ships as far as 24 miles out to sea.

The **tower** stood 108 feet atop the 48-foot dune. It was double walled both for greater strength against a hurricane and for circulating air to keep bricks as dry as possible in the constant humidity. The outer base was 31 inches thick and the top 18 inches. It was 65 feet around at the base and 43 at the top. Inside were 105 cast-iron steps twisting around to the top.

Inside the circular balcony, 79 feet up the tower, was the watchroom containing the pedestal on which rested the lens and turning mechanism. To keep the outer mechanism rotating on its ball bearings, the keeper wound the cable to a 250-pound lead weight around a large cylinder (just like cranking a huge grandfather clock) and watched it descend as it powered the works. He'd repeat the windup process every two to three hours during his routine of oiling the turning mechanism, cleaning the lamp and maintaining his log.

High up on the pedestal was the crown jewel, the **lens.** As a first-order lens, it stood eight feet, six inches in diameter and weighed 12,800 pounds. It was manufactured in Paris using state of the art Fresnel prism technology. Whereas a flame or other common light source dissipates its illumination in all directions, Fresnel prisms were ground in such a way as to capture up to 90 percent of a light source and condense it into a single beam that could travel a great distance. In the case of Jupiter it meant projecting a signal almost halfway across the Bahama Channel so that ships in the Gulf Stream could now steer well clear of the reefs that had claimed victims from Spanish gold ships to American merchantmen.

But not for long. In January 1861 Florida seceded from the Union. On April 12 Confederates fired on Fort Sumter, S.C., igniting the War Between the States.

When President Lincoln ordered a naval blockade of all federal ports, Jupiter Inlet suddenly became a center of activity—not because it was a population center, but because it was *not*.

Confederate blockade runners, sealed off from places like Charleston and St. Augustine, arriving from the Bahamas and Bermuda with salt, flour, gunpowder, liquor and other supplies for a desperate army, found they could sneak into the quiet inlet under cover of darkness and begin winding their way up the Indian River.

Except for one irritant. The Jupiter Lighthouse remained lit— only one of two in Confederate states—and federal gunboats found it helpful in illuminating their quarry as they gave chase. Joseph F. Papy, the head lighthouse keeper, was a Southerner and surely a staunch Confederate. But he felt he had a higher calling in protecting all ships at sea from the dangerous shoreline.

Assistant Keeper Augustus Lang argued with his superior to no avail. On August 7, 1861 he quit his job in anger and soon vented his frustrations to his friend James Paine, who lived several miles up the Indian River. A week later, the two and Paine's neighbor,

In the early years the three lighthouse families could expect one to three supply drops a year from a U.S. Lighthouse Service buoy tender.
*(Loxahatchee River Historical Society)*

If the inlet were open, they'd be brought to the dock. If not, supplies, as shown here, would be dropped on the beach at the high-tide mark. Retrieving them was up to the lighthouse people.
*(Loxahatchee River Historical Society)*

## HISTORICAL HIGHLIGHTS

| | |
|---|---|
| **1821** | U.S. buys Florida back from Spain. |
| **1838** | Battle of the Loxahatchee (Riverbend Park). |
| **1838** | Fort Jupiter established. |
| **1842** | Armed Occupation Act passed to attract south Florida settlers. |
| **1845** | Florida becomes a state. |
| **1849** | Robert E. Lee surveys both coasts of Florida. |
| **1852** | U.S. Lighthouse Board formed. |
| **1853** | Congress appropriates $35,000 to build Jupiter Lighthouse. |
| **1855** | Jupiter Lighthouse construction begins. |
| **1855** | Third Seminole Indian War begins. |
| **1855** | Second Fort Jupiter built at today's Pennock Plantation |
| **1858** | U.S. quits pursuit of remaining Seminoles. |
| **1860** | Jupiter Lighthouse is lit for first time. |
| **1861** | Civil War breaks out. |
| **1861** | Florida secedes from Union. |
| **1861** | Jupiter Lighthouse dark after Confederates seize part of works. |
| **1865** | Andrew Johnson sworn in as 17th president. |
| **1866** | Lighthouse repaired and re-lit. |
| **1867** | U.S. purchases Alaska Territory. |
| **1868** | Florida re-admitted to Union. |
| **1869** | Ulysses Grant becomes 18th president. |

Francis A. Ivy, confronted Papy and demanded he extinguish the light. When he refused and climbed the tower for his nightly routine, the three men soon followed, forcing Papy to go below, and eventually allowing him to take his family by boat to Key West. They then dismantled the works, buried the lamps in Lake Worth Creek and hid the clockworks on Paine's property.

The three felt themselves patriots, even informing the governor of Florida in a letter that added: "At Jupiter we destroyed no property whatever, the light being a revolving one and of a very costly make, we took away only enough of the machinery to make it unserviceable."

They did make off with a sailboat, two muskets, two colt revolvers and three lamps on the conviction that "the arms captured would be much needed in Jupiter in case of attack." Indeed, there were several attacks and counterattacks as one side or the other would capture the tower and use it for makeshift signaling until their rivals forced them off.

By 1864 the Union gunboats had clearly gotten the upper hand. For example, the *Charleston Courier* of February 29 reported "the capture of the British military schooner *Eliza* and the British sloop *Mary,* both of Nassau, while attempting to run out of Jupiter Inlet with cotton."

As the Civil War expired in exhaustion, all southern troops received amnesty from President Lincoln. But it was quite another matter for Confederate President Jefferson Davis and his cabinet. With a price now on their heads and newspapers rumor mongering their whereabouts every day, the only place the desperate cabinet members could head was south into the swampy wilderness.

Confederate Secretary of War John Breckinridge and a few family and friends eventually found themselves in a small boat on the Indian River, hoping to sail out the Jupiter Inlet en route to a sympathetic Cuba. After sweating and swatting mosquitoes down the coast, they were finally nearing their objective when they were warned of a Federal patrol boat lurking just inside the inlet. After finding a relatively narrow stretch on Jupiter Island, they used whatever strength they had left to push their boat through the searing saw palmetto, re-launch it in the ocean and slip past the quiet inlet on their way to Havana.

Had they risked the route through the inlet, they might have been greeted by *The Sagamore,* or one of the many other Union gunboats on which James Arango Armour had served as a volunteer pilot. Born in 1825 in New Amsterdam, N.Y., Armour had moved to the Indian River area in his twenties and knew the shallow, intricate waterway as well as anyone. Oddly, he had enlisted in the Confederate Army, but deserted after just two months in a Florida boot camp. Soon Armour was in Union garb, a rare asset, plying the Indian River in a Federal gunboat.

At the war's end, armed with letters of commendation from two captains, Armour had been rewarded with a government job in Key West as caretaker of "Prize" (or seized) Confederate ships. But before moving, Armour cashed in on a secret he must have learned during his blockading years. He rowed across from the Jupiter Lighthouse to a palmetto hammock and dug up the works that keeper Papy's kidnappers had buried in 1861.

In 1865 a Federal agent arrived in Florida with orders from on high to restore the Jupiter and Cape Florida lights as soon as possible. After meeting the keeper of the missing lighthouse parts in Key West, it's no surprise that the government would find Armour just the man to help restore and run the whole works at Jupiter. He became one of two assistant keepers under Capt. William B. Davis, and would move up to captain himself within two years.

It wasn't until June 28, 1866, that the lighthouse was repaired and officially re-lit. It has remained so every year since—forty of them under the care of James Armour and his family.

Perhaps the earliest photo of the lighthouse extant. Hauling supplies meant donning a yoke, like oxen, and carrying fuel cans or perhaps barrels of flour up wobbly, slippery planking just to reach the base of the tower. Getting to the top with fuel cans meant climbing a 105-foot circular staircase with no handrails.
*(Florida State Archives)*

# THE FICKLE JUPITER INLET

Logistically, the life of Fort Jupiter (on Pennock Point) depended on the army's ability to resupply it by ocean ships coming through Jupiter Inlet. But the inlet didn't always cooperate. Just what the army was up against is evident in this excerpt from a report by Lt. J. C. Ives, a topographical engineer, to the secretary of war in April 1856:

*There is an excellent anchorage* [at Fort Jupiter] *and a good place for loading and unloading boats, making the site of the present Fort preferable to that of the old one, or any other location in the vicinity.*

*Objections exist to it now as a military position, from the fact that the Inlet is closed, and the post rendered inaccessible from the sea to the smallest coasting vessels. The closing of the Inlet causes the locality, at other times salubrious, to be an unhealthy one. The water on the inside of the bar then becoming fresh, and inducing a rapid growth of vegetable matter, which decaying, taints the atmosphere and engenders disease.*

*The alternate opening and closing of this inlet is somewhat remarkable. Between the years 1840 and 1844 it was closed. At the latter period, Capt. Davis, the mail carrier from Fort Capron to Cape Florida, endeavored with a party of four men, to excavate a channel. After digging for several hours, they succeeded by nightfall in starting a stream of water four inches in depth. Upon this they desisted from labor and went to their camp, which was some fifty feet from the*

*(Loxahatchee River Historical Society)*

ditch. *The river inside was unusually high, from a freshet* [rush of water] *in the everglades, and north wind was blowing. At night the sleeping party was awakened by a flood of water, and had to abandon their camp equipage and run for their lives, barely escaping being carried out to sea. The next day there was a channel nearly a quarter of a mile wide, and the rush of water could be traced far out into the ocean.*

*The inlet stayed open till 1847, when it closed till 1853, during which year it opened itself, but remained in that condition only a short time. In 1855, Maj. Haskin, First Artillery, in command of [Fort Jupiter] endeavored again to clear the channel. Sand hills of considerable size, which had accumulated, were cut through, and the*

*attempt would doubtless have been successful but for the low condition of the water during that unusually dry year. A small amount of labor expended under favorable circumstances would, in all probability, effectually open this inlet and render the harbor one of the best upon the eastern coast. At times it has admitted vessels drawing eight feet, and the entrance is protected from north winds by a ledge of rocks.*

Despite these high hopes, the army eventually gave up fighting the fickle inlet and closed Fort Jupiter in 1880. (The above photo, looking southeast around 1916-20, is one of few on record showing the original inlet before it was dredged and straightened in 1922.)

The three lighthouse keepers around 1895. From left, Reinhard Heisser, Capt. James A. Armour and Joseph A. Wells, . *(Loxahatchee River Historical Society)*

# CHAPTER 3

# ALWAYS AT THE CENTER OF THINGS

A lighthouse keeper's life in postwar peacetime was scarcely smoother than it might have been in the days of Ponce de Leon. Nor was the position of keeper especially esteemed. Before 1852 getting a lighthouse job was part of the spoils system and even likely to bring smirks. "A lighthouse," went a common quip, "is a building built on the seashore in which the government maintains a lamp and the friend of a politician."

In 1852, however, Congress took a hard look at the ragtag assortment of seventy lighthouses the federal government had either built or inherited from the states and territories. The result was creation of a Lighthouse Board made up of tough-minded experts. For the first time, keepers had to wear prescribed dress and fatigue uniforms, provided at their own expense. Candidates for

Captain James Armour
*(Loxahatchee River Historical Society)*

The extended Armour family, 1895. Standing, from l. to. r., Charles C. Armour, James A. Armour Jr., William G. Armour, lighthouse Capt. James A. Armour Sr. Seated, Almeda Carlile Armour (the captain's wife), Bertha L. Armour, Lida T. Armour Johnson, Annie Johnson (daughter of Lida), Kate Armour Roberts (who would marry assistant keeper Joseph Wells in 1898) and Lida's son Herbert Johnson.
*(Florida State Archives)*

the job had to show they could read and write, keep accounts and perform the job's many manual labors. The latter included polishing the lens, filling the oil lamps, oiling the clockwork mechanism, whitewashing the tower interior, polishing the copper and brass fixtures, mopping the tower stairs and washing windows. Keepers could be dismissed on the spot for being drunk on the job or allowing the light to go out—especially during a storm.

The relentless force of wind, waves, storms and salt spray made basic maintenance at Jupiter's tower in the wilderness a daily challenge. A smattering of entries from Capt. James Armour's logs shows: "Lantern damaged" (1867), "Damp walls; plaster falling off" (1868); "Windows, casings, inner casings of watchroom and stairway in bad condition" (1874). Here is another perspective, from a government inspector's report in 1879, which the indefatigable Bessie DuBois unearthed from the National Archives:

*One of the lamps has been repaired and returned to the station. This place requires many new panes of lantern glass, a new lightning rod, and a new watch-room lining. The [keeper's] dwelling requires whitewashing and painting and some minor repairs. It was intended to thoroughly overhaul and repair this station, but owing to its isolated position and the absence of the steamer* Geranium, *there was no opportunity to send up a working party. The material for the necessary repairs is already purchased and available.*

The life of a woman intrepid enough to marry a lighthouse keeper was probably even more daunting. In December 1867 Armour went to Le Grange, Fla., and claimed Almeda Catherine Carlile as his bride. Hopefully, as she sailed down the Indian River to his lighthouse preserve, she knew that she would be the only white woman within a hundred-mile radius. When the Armour's daughter Katherine was born the next November, no one could recall another white baby ever having been born in the vicinity.

Although the Armours would raise seven children, life itself was precarious. When their third daughter, Mary Elizabeth, was two years old, she was seized by convulsions. The only doctor was 120 miles upriver in Titusville. Her father's only recourse was to put her in the family sailboat and load it with sand so they could heat water. All during the agonizingly slow journey, Mary's parents alternately bathed her in hot and cold water in a desperate bid to relieve her fever. She died as they watched helplessly.

Raising a family on the lighthouse reservation was as challenging as keeping shipping lanes safe. The first house, 26 by 30 feet, was built in 1859 to house all three keeper families, sharing a single

A construction crew hard at work building the assistant
lighthouse keepers' house in 1883. Until then, three
families shared a house designed for just one.
*(Loxahatchee River Historical Society / Melville Spencer Collection)*

outdoor kitchen. Only 26 years later did they have the luxury of a "remodeling"—the addition of a 14-by-16-foot kitchen building and a new walkway from the house to the tower. It wasn't until 1883 that a new dwelling was built for the head keeper and the original building expanded so as to accommodate one assistant keeper's family on the top floor and the other on the bottom.

All three families had to make do in the most profound sense of the word. Initially, a supply boat arrived only once a year, and even then reports went back to Washington grousing about how difficult the site was to supply. Indeed, the job was left to any of the three tenders that plied the South Atlantic coast lifting and cleaning large buoys. If the inlet were open, the tender crews would load up their skiffs and row right to the lighthouse dock. But during the many periods in which it was closed, the skiffs would beach themselves and unload supplies along the high-tide mark. The keeper and his crew would have to come fetch them.

Either way, a tender was their lifeline. During the first twenty years, the tenders brought large, heavy "butts" (barrels) of lard that were carried up the steps and stored inside the base of the tower before being lugged upstairs to fuel the lighthouse flame. In 1886 fuel arrived in the form of kerosene. Upon unloading the skiffs at the dock, the keeper's crew would break open wooden cases of five-gallon kerosene cans and fix their handles to ropes from wooden yokes across their shoulders. With the pails swinging from their yokes, the men trudged up the steep wooden planks leading up to the oil house. There the keeper would meet them with a cloth to wipe each container carefully with linseed oil so that sand and saltwater residue wouldn't contaminate the fuel and cause the lamp to flicker or die.

After the first priorities—fuel for the light and spare parts for maintenance—came everything else necessary for human health and sanity. Besides flour, sugar, coffee, crockery and the like, they included a portable wooden bookcase containing forty books ranging from novels and histories to adventure stories and religious works. Some served as the mainstay of the children's education and some were intended to entertain the grownups as they read by kerosene lamp in their lonely outpost.

At times the work routine would drone into monotony. But weather and wilderness could also erupt in danger and excitement. On Oct. 20, 1872, for example, the Jupiter light was shining into a roaring northeaster when the assistant keeper on duty spotted a steamer floundering in the surf south of the inlet. After alerting Captain Armour and Charles Carlin, the other assistant, the three jumped into their small sloop and caught up with the ship just as it was breaking up on the reef.

Learning that it was the Mallory steamer *Victor,* the keepers brought all hands ashore safely. As happened often, the crew made fires and camped on the beach while ladies and other passengers were offered all the limited comforts of the keepers' house. Thanks to signaling from the tower, another Mallory ship picked up the survivors on the beach the next day.

Then the real action began. As Bessie DuBois reported in her booklet *The History of Jupiter Lighthouse,* "Almost immediately after the shipwreck, seven canoe loads of Seminoles appeared on one of their rare hunting trips from Fisheating Creek [near Lake Okeechobee]. The *Victor* began to break up, and the cargo of merchandise worth $150,000 began to be strewn up and down the beach."

Indians darted about wild-eyed as crates rolled onto the beach. Cloth and clothing. Barrels of flour and salt bacon. Trunks bursting open with a cornucopia of shoes, shirts, skirts, hats, hankies and undies.

Back at the lighthouse, high tide later brought even more floating largesse. Assistant keeper H. D. Pierce and a lone Seminole were watching the passing parade from the lighthouse dock when both fixed their eyes on a large packing case that was about to surge by. The Indian moved towards it, but Pierce had already read the markings. "That one's mine!" he exclaimed, jumping into a skiff. And so, Mrs. Pierce became the owner of a handsome Wheeler and Wilson sewing machine that she used for the rest of her life.

Added Bessie DuBois, "The Indians camped out on the dunes behind the wreck and had a glorious time. One of the braves found a case of Plantation Bitters and all night long their joyous whoops could be heard all the way up to the lighthouse."

Sometimes Indians were the keepers' only company—if one could use that word to describe their mysterious, unpredictable behavior. One day Almeda Armour opened the door of the keepers' house to find a large Seminole with a knife in his teeth. No use screaming: all the men had gone off on an errand. As Mrs. Armour gulped and stared, the Indian removed the knife from his mouth and handed it to her, handle-first. In the sign language that followed he made it clear that the knife was a sign of friendship and that he was merely seeking permission to camp at the lighthouse for the night.

Sometimes there'd be no knock at all. Mrs. Armour might be pulling weeds in the garden, only to look up and see an Indian staring at her silently. Another time she was inside her kitchen working at the stove. When she turned around a Seminole man was sitting in silence at her kitchen table.

During their 42 years at the lighthouse (1866–1908), episodes like these taught James and Almeda Armour the knack of being gracious and adaptable hosts on an instant's notice. They never knew who might be tossed ashore in a reef wreck or come barging down the Indian River with an entourage of servants and luggage. As Bessie DuBois recorded,

*Capt. Armour was a most important man in this area in those early days. His home was described by early writers and travelers as a haven of hospitality. Prospectors and surveyors relied upon his knowledge. Early settlers came to him for advice and often for assistance in times of shipwreck. When the Pierce family lost their home by fire when they first came to Florida, Capt. Armour sailed upriver and offered Mr. Pierce a job as assistant keeper of the lighthouse until he could find a home. Reserved and self-reliant, kindly to all, his courage in the wilderness was respected and depended upon by all who knew him.*

Life wasn't all somber duty, however. With the rich array of game all about, Armour seems to have been a world-class hunter and fisherman. He fared even better after the *Victor* wreck, when the

Seminoles pose in their unique headdress on the lighthouse grounds not long after the Third Seminole (or "Billy Bowlegs") War ended. Whereas the Indians had often harassed the lighthouse construction crews, they became friendly neighbors and traders after the war.
*(Loxahatchee River Historical Society)*

survivors swimming ashore included three superb hunting dogs. The Armours named them Vic, Storm and Wreck.

Fortunately, many of the captain's trophies were captured in photos by a young assistant keeper who joined him in 1878. Melville E. Spencer was intrigued with the young art of photography and was invariably on hand to produce glass-plate negatives, as, for example, when Armour and friends caught a 360–pound jewfish off the lighthouse dock. Spencer was there when the captain shot a large panther from the lighthouse tower and later a bear near the grounds.

Spencer himself must have had many similar adventures as well. Bessie DuBois reports, for example, that on one summer moonlit night he was walking the beach and stopped by the carcass of a steamer that had been thrown up on the shore years before. There he found a large turtle laying her eggs. When she was done, he rode her back out to sea and then swam back. When he got to the beach a big bear was already digging up the eggs.

Spencer, who later took his photographic talents to Palm Beach, also left us a snapshot of lighthouse economics. When hired in December 1878 his annual pay was $455. A year later he got a $10 raise. At the time, his boss, Captain Armour, was drawing down $820 a year. But with food, housing and other staples all paid by the government, a lighthouse keeper's life seemed princely to any of the few dozen homesteaders struggling to farm the scrub and sand.

# The One That Almost Got Away, Circa 1889

The November, 1889, issue of *The Outing Magazine*, featured an article by one O. A. Mygatt, known to us now only as a die-hard fisherman from New York. He and a chum decided to escape the slush and ice in Manhattan the previous winter and meander down the Indian River in a rented sailboat. After idling up the St. Lucie River, the two, with their hired captain, sailed for Jupiter Inlet.

*While passing through Jupiter Narrows we caught a dozen or so sea trout, trolling with a phantom minnow. The sea trout cooked in brandy and washed down with true old English Bass makes a delicious meal.*

Having been told by the keeper of the Jupiter lighthouse that fishing was "poor" that winter, the party ran into an "old cracker from the upper part of Jupiter Creek" who said he'd seen "hundreds of tarpon up the creek, that they followed his boat like sheep and that they would snap at a piece of rope trolling in the water." The next day they were several miles upstream when author Mygatt saw the old cracker's face break into "the most angelic expression, while his lips parted in a rapturous smile."

*"Great Caesar's ghost, just look at that!" he cried, pointing behind him. A stretch about a hundred yards lay before me, the water smooth as glass, the slanting rays of the setting sun touching the only side of the creek. In this stretch of water some fifty to sixty fish were rolling about like porpoises, but the silver glitter and the large scales visible on the nearer ones made me cry out at once, "Tarpon, by Jove!" They were the first ones we had ever seen, so our excitement may well be imagined. Suddenly one rose within twenty yards of the boat, and, making a beautiful curve, showed almost his whole side and disappeared.*

*I took the rod, and putting on a large bone squib, cast it far out, drawing the squib rapidly back over the surface of the water, winding swiftly on my reel.*

*Two or three times I cast, and suddenly there was a large swirl and a splash. A large tarpon had dashed at the squib and missed it. Time after time this was repeated, sometimes two or three following right up to the boat, but evidently without trying to seize the bait. Here we were, surrounded by these large and beautiful fish, who seemed entirely bent on tantalizing us. After half an hour they ceased doing even that, and we saw the whole band go splashing and cavorting up the stream, where they disappeared around a curve.*

Two days later he finally landed one—a four-footer—but only by accident. Mygatt's hook had hooked the fish in the cartilage above one eye on one of its teasing passes by the boat.

Lighthouse captain Joe Wells caught this jewfish (large grouper) at his supply dock. He estimated its weight at from 300 to 360 pounds.
*(Loxahatchee River Historical Society)*

## MAIL, JUPITER STYLE

It wouldn't be long before the Jupiter Inlet area became a hub of communications even though it was hardly a population or trade center. Indeed, all of Dade County—a vast 7,800-square-mile area that covered all of today's Dade, Broward, Palm Beach and Martin counties—counted only 527 souls in the 1880 census.

But *communications* were another matter. There was something about the inlet, the lighthouse and their close access to that shipping superhighway—the Gulf Stream—that drew communications carriers to Jupiter. Within two decades "progress" would bring a post office, an ocean rescue station, a telegraph cable, a U.S. Weather Bureau outpost, a flotilla of river steamers, wireless radio towers and a short-line railroad. The latter would soon yield to an epochal rail line by Henry Flagler that would stretch from Jacksonville to Key West and change the fate of Florida forever.

It all began with the mail. As early as 1844, couriers from Fort Jupiter doubled as civilian mail carriers when they took army dispatches to Fort Lauderdale and Fort Dallas (Miami) along the Military Trail that still bears that name. In 1856, when the Third Seminole Indian War made regular courier service too risky and "Jupiter Fever" (malaria) decimated the troops, Fort Jupiter stopped carrying civilian mail. Settlers were left to rely on the kindness of traveling friends or hail down ships going in the general direction of their letters. Those with an emergency might appeal to the small navy telegraph outpost on the lighthouse grounds that tapped out official dispatches to its base in Jacksonville.

It wasn't until 1880 that one Valorous Spencer decided to do something about the communications problem confronting ordinary homesteaders. The number of settlers between Jupiter and Miami had been growing, and this Lake Worth farmer decided he'd get as many of them as possible to sign a petition to the Post Office Department seeking a regular mail route. In May 1880 he and his daughter Mattie launched a rowboat on Lake Worth that they'd rigged with a homemade sail. Under a seat was a wooden box containing a fancy looking parchment petition they'd drawn up to impress the neighbors.

The father-daughter team had gathered a goodly number of signatures up the waterway when an early summer squall blew up from nowhere and caught the flimsy sail broadside. In an instant Valorous Spencer and Mattie were thrashing about in the middle of Lake Worth as they saw their boat go under and the box with the prized petition float out of sight. After three hours of treading water, the drained and dejected duo crawled onto a beach and walked until they found a farmer who put them up for the night.

The next morning they were padding along the beach back towards home when they practically tripped over their own wooden box. Inside was a soggy petition, but still intact. It was soon dried out and sent to Washington, where the result was a new post office in Lake Worth—with none other than Valorous T. Spencer as first postmaster.

Soon afterward there were post offices in Jupiter, Miami and Oaklawn (Riviera Beach). The only thing that distinguished them from a thousand other frontier outposts across the expanding continent was the way in which they relayed the mail. Because all of the south Florida post offices were in coastal towns, the straightest line—certainly not through the scrub forests with their sharp saw palmettos—was right down the beach.

And the only way was to walk. Although a mailman could carry or dig out enough fresh water for himself, finding enough for a horse was much too chancy. And so, he walked along the edge of the shoreline where the sand was packed hardest. This meant rolling up his trousers and going barefoot so that the saltwater wouldn't rot his shoes. And so the mailman carried his shoes and gear, along with a locked canvas mail pouch, on his back in a black oilcloth knapsack. He also had authority to charge a "passenger" $5—perhaps a traveling salesman headed for

For a few years, starting around 1870 a "barefoot mailman" departed from the lighthouse and walked the beach each day to Lake Worth.

From a series of Barefoot Mailman murals in the old West Palm Beach Post Office.
*(Historical Society of Palm Beach County)*

Miami—in exchange for his services as guide down the coast.

One of Jupiter's first carriers was assistant keeper Alfred Smith, Mrs. Armour's nephew. He had a large hog named Denny. When Smith would head south with the mail, he'd first row across from the lighthouse. Every time, without fail, Denny would swim behind the boat, then walk the beach with Smith until he realized it was time to head home for dinner.

In 1940 novelist Theodore Pratt wrote a breathless bestseller of danger and daring-do that enshrined *The Barefoot Mailman* in Florida lore forever. A great yarn indeed, but just that. It's very doubtful that any of these sunburned civil servants ever called themselves "barefoot mailmen." Moreover, in keeping with any bureaucracy, the Post Office Department laid out a delivery routine that could be performed by an average employee. In this case, the route from Jupiter to Miami was an uneventful three-day walk with overnight stops at government Houses of Refuge in Orange Grove (Delray Beach) and New River (Fort Lauderdale).

Yes, there was some potential peril in that a mailman encountered three places (Hillsboro Inlet, New River and Biscayne Bay) where he had to untie a government skiff in the bush and row it over deep water. And in one recorded case—the cloth on which author Pratt embroidered his tale—a substitute mailman named James Hamilton did lose his life in October 1887. After staying overnight in the House of Refuge in Delray, he simply disappeared. Days later, at Hillsboro Inlet, searchers found Hamilton's knapsack hanging on a bush with the mail pouch intact. His clothes were scattered on the beach. The boat was tethered on the wrong side of the beach. The only logical conclusion was that someone had illegally used the boat to cross the inlet and that Hamilton had drowned trying to swim across to retrieve it. No trace of his body was ever found—a convenient enigma that allowed Pratt to spin a horrifying account of attack by swarms of sharks and alligators that rivaled *Jaws* of another century.

| | |
|---|---|
| **1870** | Barefoot Mailman begins delivery route on beach. |
| **1879** | Edison invents first commercial incandescent electric lamp. |
| **1880** | U.S. Army abandons Fort Jupiter. |
| **1880** | Census puts population of Dade County (today's Dade, Broward, Palm Beach and Martin counties) at 527. |
| **1884** | Sarah Gleason buys today's DuBois home site from government in first sell-off of Fort Jupiter property. |
| **1885** | Grover Cleveland becomes 22nd U.S. president. |
| **1886** | Jupiter Life Saving Station opens under captaincy of Charles Carlin. |
| **1889** | Juno becomes Dade County seat. |
| **1889** | Opening of Celestial Railroad. |
| **1890** | Census puts 7,800-square-mile Dade County population at 861. |
| **1890** | Carlin House modified to become hotel-resort. |
| **1891** | Edison patents motion picture camera. |
| **1892** | Jupiter-Nassau Western Union telegraph cable completed. |
| **1893** | Economic "panic" ushers in four-year depression. |
| **1894** | Flagler's Florida East Coast Railway opens from Jacksonville to West Palm Beach. |
| **1898** | U.S. declares war on Spain (April). |
| **1898** | Visit to Jupiter by the battleship *U.S.S. Oregon* (May). |
| **1899** | Dade County seat reverts to Miami. |

Like a haunted house, the shell of the abandoned
life station looms over the beach in the early 1900s.
Eventually, it was torn down and the wood carted
off for another generation of Jupiter buildings.
*(Florida State Archives)*

## RESCUE AND REFUGE:
## THE LIFESAVING STATION

In 1885 the lighthouse crew gained a "partner" and mailmen got a new landmark on the beach. The two-story U.S. Life Saving Station was built on a bluff a mile south of the inlet. Charles Carlin, who had been an assistant lighthouse keeper until moving to Titusville in 1875, returned to become captain of the new post. Born in 1842 in Dublin to English parents, Carlin had served in the British Navy before coming to the U.S. as a geodetic surveyor.

The same year that Carlin took over the new lifesaving station he also purchased ten acres on the river from one Sarah Gleason, who had been the first person to buy land (122 acres) in 1884 when the government began offering pieces of the Fort Jupiter reservation to settlers. There, Captain Carlin and his wife Mary began building a three-bedroom house surrounded by roofed porches.

In a sense the home was never completed because it was in a constant state of expansion. The reason was simply that Jupiter was "the end of the line," as the Carlin's grandson Carlin White notes in his *History of the Carlin House.* White, still highly active in his nineties as this was written, noted that "Transportation, such as it was, ended at the Jupiter River and the Carlins were forced to accommodate worn out travelers any way they could long before they were prepared. Over the years Grandmother Carlin said many times that in the beginning she really never knew who or how many would show up for breakfast. Whatever the number, no one was turned away."

And so, the Carlin house soon evolved into The Carlin House— Jupiter's first resort hotel—eventually including a dozen or so guest rooms, several outbuildings and even a tennis court.

Meanwhile, Charles Carlin also had a lifesaving station to run. From September through May he supervised six paid surfmen, then managed alone during the quiet summer months. The building, kept spotless like a fire station, had two stories with a lookout tower on the roof. The ground floor contained a cloakroom, utility room and self-bailing lifeboat mounted on a wagon so that it could be pulled quickly down a wooden ramp to the beach. Upstairs was the immaculate crew's quarters, with iron cots, clothes lockers and a small apartment used by the Carlins until their home was built. Above all this was a tower with windows on four sides. Inside were signal flags and a powerful spyglass atop a tripod.

The crew's regimen was every bit as rigid as that of their counterparts at the lighthouse. On each shift of six hours, one crewman would stand watch on the tower while two others patrolled the beach—each in a different direction. Amidst all this

Carlin drilled his crew constantly on rescue techniques.

Perhaps the trickiest skill was firing the Lyle gun, a small brass canon mounted in the bow of the lifeboat. The canon could project a coiled, lead-tipped rope for up to four hundred yards. The challenge was to fire it from a heaving lifeboat so that it flew over the bow of a distressed ship. Just then it would be snatched by a sailor on board and fastened to the mast. On shore the station crew would have erected a portable mast in the sand to keep the survivors suspended above the churning surf. The wannabe survivors would then grab the taut line and inch their way hand over hand until they dropped into the lifeboat or onto the beach.

Luckily, the lifesaving crew never faced a major disaster at sea during the station's ten-year tenure, but dramatic rescues they had aplenty.

Typical was a dramatic recounting in *The Century Magazine* (June 1893) by a grateful English yachtsman. Lt. William Henn, who had raced in the America's Cup, stopped off in Jupiter in January 1891 in a chartered 29-foot sailboat named *Minnehaha*. It was just one leg on a leisurely fishing trip that would take him, Mrs. Henn, a captain and steward around to Fort Meyers. Having stayed at Carlin House before, the Henns greeted the captain like an old friend and lingered there for a few days of pompano fishing.

Now fast-forward to the night of March 24. After battling tarpon, sharks and mosquitoes on their way through the Florida Straits, the Henn party was headed north along the Gulf Stream on their way back to Jupiter Inlet. They'd sailed all night through a few harmless showers when they began hitting heavy swells at 3 a.m., about ten miles short of their objective. "If Jupiter Bar was impassible, we would be in an awkward predicament," Henn recalled, for alternatives were at least twenty miles away in both directions.

Almost at once they realized that Jupiter was in fact closed. "We could already hear the thunder of the surf on the beach and see the line of white breakers on our lee beam." And the wind was increasing.

Henn then relates the emotions of many a stricken sailor approaching Jupiter: "About four o'clock we caught sight of Jupiter Light, the bright flash of which sent a ray of hope into our hearts,

# JUPITER LIFESAVING STATION FLOOR PLANS

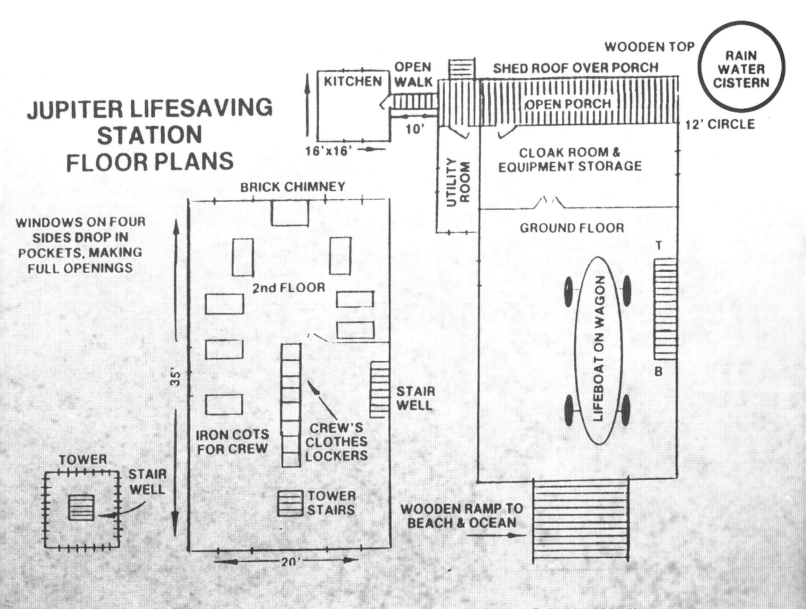

WINDOWS ON FOUR SIDES DROP IN POCKETS, MAKING FULL OPENINGS

KITCHEN

OPEN WALK

16'x16'

10'

WOODEN TOP

RAIN WATER CISTERN

SHED ROOF OVER PORCH

OPEN PORCH

12' CIRCLE

UTILITY ROOM

CLOAK ROOM & EQUIPMENT STORAGE

BRICK CHIMNEY

2nd FLOOR

35'

GROUND FLOOR

T

IRON COTS FOR CREW

CREW'S CLOTHES LOCKERS

STAIR WELL

LIFEBOAT ON WAGON

B

TOWER

STAIR WELL

TOWER STAIRS

WOODEN RAMP TO BEACH & OCEAN

20'

Early photo of the lifesaving station (1889?), on the dune line at today's Carlin Park. The lifeboat was stored in a ground-floor utility room. In an emergency, it could be wheeled down a wooden ramp and launched at sea within a few minutes.
*(Historical Society of Palm Beach County)*

Sometimes on Sundays, the lifesaving crew would take time for a picnic on the beach with friends and families. From top left, Mrs. Fred McGill, Graham King, Fred Cabot, Captain Carlin (in vest), Dan Ross, Harry DuBois, Tom Mitchell and John Grant. Front row: Leah King, Mrs. Ola Grant's mother, Mrs. E.B. King, Tag Kyle, Mrs. Fred Cabot, Lyda McConnell, Ella Aicher, Charles Carlin Jr. and station mascot. *(Florida State Archives)*

for it seemed like an old friend, and told us we should soon be within reach of assistance. Would the night ever pass away?"

The *Minnehaha* was pounding and smashing into the short lop on the long, heavy swell, sending the spray flying everywhere. It was also straining and leaking so badly that the captain kept the pumps on continuously. At dawn "a pale gray light came stealing over the water," revealing a dark, blurred mass, noted Henn. "This quickly took a definite shape and proved to be the buildings of the U.S. life-saving station at Jupiter. But to leeward, as far as the eye could distinguish to the north and south, ran several lines of furious breakers, the spray from which rose in sheets of vapor enveloping the sand hills in clouds of mist."

Two months beforehand the captain-owner had let the intrepid yachtsman talk him into taking the aging sloop "outside" after he'd argued that it was fit only for Indian River trips. Now, as the swells grew, Henn rated their chances "small" and the already-seasick captain was downright morose.

So it was time for Henn to show some English pluck. Now about a half mile from the beach and in about 18 feet of water, he

ordered the skipper to hoist the ensign "union down" and prepare to "lay the boat to." They waited for a breaker to slam into the beam and turn the boat's stern to the beach. Then Henn ordered the pale skipper to heave out his mud hook.

"It'll never hold on; she'll go clean under," wailed the captain. When they felt the anchor catch, he moaned that the line was "old and untrustworthy."

But the "thread," as Henn called it, held as the sloop lurched up and down, sometimes dipping its mast into the foam. Captain Carlin and his crew could be seen lined up on the beach with their lifeboat, but the surf had swatted them back on shore every time they had tried to launch it. Henn continues:

*We had no lifebuoys or anything on board that would float, except the oars of the skiff and the setting-poles, which wouldn't have been of much account; and to add to my anxiety…my wife and the steward were unable to swim. The danger in beaching the sloop was very great, as there was an outer line of breakers, with deep water between them and the shore. If we were swamped in crossing it, we could sink before we reached the beach, and there was an additional risk of encountering sharks, several of which were actually visible. We emptied the water-casks and improvised a couple of lifebuoys by slinging and attaching to them beckets [loops of rope] for lifelines. Then we could do no more but await developments.*

Toward noon the waves seemed to slack a bit and Henn could see Carlin's crew cluster about the lifeboat. The *Minnehaha's* line of vision disappeared for an agonizing minute as it dipped into a swell. As it rose again the lifeboat was coming straight at them, having "cleared the breakers like a sea-gull."

*They approached cautiously, and the bowmen, laying in their oars, flung a grapnel to us, which was quickly made fast. Then, hauling up alongside, Carlin and two of his crew sprang on board. A warm grasp of the hand, then to business. We had no need to explain the situation; a few hurried words settled everything.*

*"Carlin, you must take my wife and the steward ashore, for they can't swim. Lend us an anchor and cable and a couple of cork lifejackets and I think we can hold on. We want to save the boat and gear if possible."*

Henn and the captain watched the lifeboat shooting the crests of the rollers, losing sight of her in the hollows. "At last, to my great joy," he wrote, "I saw her run again on the beach, and all hands land in safety."

Henn was so relieved he realized he hadn't eaten in 24 hours. He rummaged in the small galley, finding a box of crackers, some sardines and "the ribs and trucks" of a ham. As he downed his concoction eagerly, the captain took one glance and retched over the railing.

By midnight the wind was ebbing to the point where both men slept soundly despite the fact that a twelve-foot shark circled incessantly. When they awoke the next morning the seas had fallen off even more and both men felt chipper enough to make a breakfast. By 8:30 a.m. Captain Carlin and crew were mustered on the beach hoisting a flag and pointing it in the direction of the inlet. Even the optimistic Henn had his doubts. "Four formidable lines of breakers were roaring and flinging their snowy crests in the air as they curled and broke," he wrote. Several sharks were visible. Henn and the captain stripped down to cork jackets and trousers, cut the tether to their dinghy (which was filled with water and dragging), and began sailing along the outer edge of the rollers.

The only good news was that it was high tide.

*The men on shore were still in line, as if on parade. Suddenly it struck me that this was not merely accidental; they had been placed in range to show us the best course through the breakers. By keeping them*

After a picnic, the crew would show off their boat and rowing ability in a little ride around Jupiter Inlet. *(Florida State Archives)*

Capt. Carlin at the helm of his self-bailing lifeboat, with his spit-and-polish crew of six surfmen. Besides keeping a 24-hour watch for stricken ships and stranded sailors, they practiced intricate rescue techniques almost daily. *(Historical Society of Palm Beach County)*

Resourceful Mary Carlin, bred in South Carolina, cooked and baked for her husband's lifesaving crew of seven, then for many more as The Carlin House grew from a home to a busy hotel. In 1886 she also became Jupiter's postmistress.
*(Town of Jupiter Archives / Carlin White Collection)*

*"end on" we should strike the deepest water on the bar. We instantly altered course, and, jumping forward on the deckhouse, I held onto the mast, directing Skipper how to steer. We rapidly approached the broken water and seemed to fly. As the first roller lifted and literally hurled us forward, the water seethed and boiled in over our decks, but comparatively little of it found its way into the cockpit, as it broke ahead, expending itself in an acre of foam…*

*I held my breath; the critical moment was at hand. For if the roller did not break before it overtook us, to a certainty we should be swamped. Skipper's teeth were hard set, and his whole weight was thrown against the tiller to keep the sloop straight. Suddenly I felt her dragging; she was touching the ground and the roller was almost overshadowing us, when in an instant the green was changed to a flood of milk-white foam, which, surging down on us, lifted the sloop, tossing and bearing her onward at a tremendous pace. A flood of water swept in over the stern and weather-quarter, and half-filled the cockpit, nearly washing Skipper overboard, as we almost broached to; but we were safe. We had crossed the shallowest spot. When the next breaker thundered astern of us, we shot into smooth water, and all our troubles were over.*

*A loud cheer went up from our friends as we ran the* Minnehaha *alongside the beach at our old camping ground, and there securely moored her.*

And just as soon as he could, Lt. Henn wrote the secretary of the treasury urging a letter of commendation for Captain Carlin and his crew. Indeed, a lavish letter of praise arrived a few months later.

The Carlin House in 1890, just after it was first modified to accommodate paying guests. Note the extension of upstairs bedrooms. *(Town of Jupiter Archives / Carlin White Collection)*

English-born Charles R. Carlin began in Jupiter as an assistant lighthouse keeper. Later he became captain of the U.S. Life Saving Station while his family expanded their home on the Jupiter River to a busy resort hotel.
*(Town of Jupiter Archives / Carlin White Collection)*

One of the merchant sloops that plied the Indian River from Titusville to Jupiter, stopping to sell staples and sundries of all kinds. If it happened to be Walter Kitching, he'd blow a conch shell before he got to a town landing, and before he tied up people would be waiting in line. *(Loxahatchee River Historical Society)*

## RIVERBOATS: BRINGING COMMERCE TO THE CUSTOMER

With no paved roads to speak of and three rivers converging just outside their back doors, it's not surprising that settlers would go by water to buy, sell or visit. At first they'd jump in a skiff or sloop and ply the river until they reached a far-flung general store, which might be no more than an ill-supplied, dirt-floored palmetto shack.

Then in the early 1880s, as more settlers lined the waterways, a few entrepreneurial souls got the idea of going to the customer with dock-to-dock service. It began with sloops full of general merchandise, but in time it would include people like Dr. Moses Holbrook, who made house calls for seventy miles along the Indian River. An optician named Hawks went downriver every two months selling eyeglasses, and a Dr. Houghton ran a dental boat. Sometimes he'd set up his equipment on shore and stay for as long as people lined up to see him.

But the model, or most successful trade-boat operator, was probably Walter Kitching. Born in Leeds, England, in 1846, he left a successful family brokerage business in 1867 when he read of fortunes to be made in the untamed and expanding U.S. Eventually lured to south Florida by ads touting cheap homesteads, he put down roots in the Stuart area where he bought 15 acres and opened a general merchandise store.

In 1887 Kitching and another entrepreneur, S. F. Travis, outfitted a sloop named *Wave* and went calling on customers from Cocoa to Jupiter on a two-hundred-mile round trip that would take between thirty and forty days. The arrival of *Wave* was something akin to the Good Humor truck in modern America. Walter would blow on a conch shell to announce the event, and by the time it tied up—most often at a public landing—shoppers would be lining up on the waterfront. One reason was his ample inventory, which included clothing, fabrics, shoes, groceries, medicines, kerosene, building materials and other staples that settlers badly needed. Another reason was that Kitching had become a notary public and was able to validate various deeds and licenses that would have taken people days of travel to execute.

Kitching's most endearing appeal seems to have been his reasonable prices. *The History of Martin County* quotes one local woman's reaction:

*Most of us were buying our groceries from John Clark & Son of Jacksonville, for we had no department stores… So when Walter Kitching started his first trade boat and gave us smoked bacon, full sides, at nine cents a pound, we took to him like bees to a sugar tree. Later he got a larger boat and carried a splendid stock of goods, which he sold at fair prices for small profit and sure-enough come-again trade.*

The profits weren't too miniscule, because the "larger boat" referred to above was a splendid sixty-foot schooner named *Merchant.* Besides drawing only five feet, it had a twenty-foot beam with rows of built-in shelves and a much wider selection of merchandise said to be worth over $5,000. The former *Wave* was a converted fisherman; to carry as many goods as possible, Kitching had to pile all sorts of items inside its covered bow. It required hiring a very small cabin boy, so that when Kitching needed something that wasn't stored in the open center section, the boy would burrow into the bow and holler "all right" when he'd located what was wanted. With that, Kitching would pull him out by his feet.

Coming and going. The popular *St. Augustine* riverboat steamer departs Titusville for the 120-mile trip to Jupiter's Celestial Railroad dock in 1895. While providing commodious accommodations for passengers, steamers like the *St. Augustine* also brought furniture and building materials to the southern frontier and returned with pineapples, coconuts, lumber and other produce.
*(Loxahatchee River Historical Society)*

This riverboat has no smokestacks, probably because they were no longer needed. In the 1890s two paddlewheel steamers were moored in the Jupiter River as floating hotels. While getting stuck on a sandbar may have been the initial reason for "permanently parking," the hotel steamers provided a romantic setting and elegant service. And the fishing couldn't be beat.
*(Loxahatchee River Historical Society)*

*St. Lucie* was a popular passenger boat in its heyday. But after the demise of Jupiter's little railroad, it hauled lumber to build Flagler's new hotels and railroad. In 1906 the tired old ship sank in a hurricane and when raised months later, all that remained was the skeleton below.
*(Florida State Archives)*

This panoramic view from the lighthouse shows four steamers in the Jupiter River in the 1880s.

Inset shows closer view of boxed area. Note the Lifesaving station looming on the distant ocean dune line.

*(Loxahatchee River Historical Society)*

Walter Kitching assigned his trade-boat business to a nephew in 1896 and concentrated on his bustling general merchandise store in Stuart. But sometime before that he must have sailed upriver on the Loxahatchee and spied a cypress-lined creek that he found especially beautiful. In 1886 a family member, Susan Kitching of Berndly, England, showed up on the Tallahassee property rolls as owning 37 acres along the narrow waterway in today's Jonathan Dickinson State Park. Although later sold to the DuBois family, it is still aptly named "Kitching Creek."

Still, sloops like *Merchant* were dwarfed by a new leviathan plying the Indian and Jupiter rivers in the late 1880s. Paddlewheel steamboats had become the rage on Midwestern waterways, and shipping entrepreneurs soon found the flat-bottomed, shallow-draft floating platforms quite serviceable in south Florida's inland waters.

The first paddlewheel steamers arrived in Jupiter because it was the turnaround point on a 240-mile round trip from the northern terminus, Titusville. Since there was no more navigable water from Jupiter to Lake Worth, many steamers featured day excursions, hiring local horse-drawn carriages to take passengers sightseeing along the rough roads overlooking the Jupiter River.

Probably the first steamer was the *Santa Lucia,* which came down in 1887 after a 3,000-mile trip from the Mississippi and Ohio rivers. It was 200 feet long and 30 feet wide, so big that it practically straddled the Jupiter Narrows and was constantly being pulled off sandbars. More nimble was the *St. Lucie,* a 122-foot sister ship that brought passengers and staples down from Titusville and took back pineapples and coconuts. On the way through Jupiter Narrows, its colorful captain, Steve Bravo, would impress passengers by opening the lid of a fish box on the stern deck and hanging a lantern over it. Then they'd watch pompano jump into the box until it overflowed. In 1890 the *Titusville East Coast Advocate* reported,

*Last Wednesday, as the St. Lucie was plowing through the Narrows, the officers and crew were startled by hearing cries of distress issuing from the shore. As quickly as possible, Captain Bravo stopped the steamer and hastened to the assistance of the imperiled person. Arriving opposite the spot, a Mr. Ballard was found snuggly ensconced in the top of a tree, while at its foot sat a huge black bear gazing wistfully upward. Mr. Bruin, evidently tiring of his plentiful palmetto buries, coco plums and sea grapes, and evidently desiring a little meat, attacked Mr. Ballard, who defended himself as well as he could with a brush hook, inflicting several wounds on his lordship with little effect except to render him still more furious. With the assistance of a few revolvers, Mr. Bruin was induced to be quiet while he was pulled aboard and divested of his winter overcoat.*

By the mid-1890s, with the arrival of the Celestial Railroad from Jupiter to Juno (see story below), literally dozens of paddlewheel steamers were showing up in Jupiter, the most conspicuous among them the *St. Augustine* and *St. Sebastian.* Another regular visitor, *The Swan,* was described by the Titusville newspaper as "a big 185-foot three-decker, with such a shallow draft that she could float on a heavy dew." With a crew of twenty, she could accommodate eighty passengers and carry forty carriages.

Some steamer owners found it easier to moor their lumbering leviathans in the Jupiter River and use them as hotels. One, perhaps the *St. Augustine,* ran aground near the lighthouse dock and simply stayed on as a sort of elegant fish camp. "Among the first guests were President and Mrs. Grover Cleveland," Bessie DuBois recorded. "The former first lady, to her great joy, landed a huge and gleaming tarpon."

Across the river was another moored steamer, probably the *St. Sebastian.* St. George Rathbone, a fishing enthusiast who extolled Jupiter in an 1891 article for *The Outing Magazine,* wrote that "she looked like a Mississippi River Boat…and we were served royal meals all the time we stayed."

The steamer served as Rathbone's base for excursions up the Loxahatchee.

*We amused ourselves between times by catching mullet from the side of the steamer. This is a fish that was once said never to touch bait, and that one had never been caught on a hook. We took dozens of them. A fine leader, a trout hook, a piece of dough from the cook's galley and no sinker—the tide carries the dough along—a tiny morsel on the dainty hook. It sinks a foot or so; there is a jerk and up comes a mullet nearly a foot long, his white sides glittering like silver in the light.*

*Small [catfish] could be taken at the rate of one a minute. It was nothing to say "I'll fish until I have twenty five," for they never stopped biting that I knew of, day or night. Probably the refuse thrown out from the cook's galley brought these schools of small fish around.*

A view from the Jupiter River's southern shoreline at The Carlin House in mid-1890s. Steamer passing the lighthouse may be the *St. Augustine*.

*(Loxahatchee River Historical Society)*

## JUPITER'S MINI-RAILROAD

Jupiter got its first railroad, essentially, because northern Dade County people were sick of making the three-day trip to the county seat of Miami to transact official business.

They were also tired of being bounced about on ox carts that hauled people and freight between Jupiter and Lake Worth.

Which exasperation came first probably doesn't matter. In 1885 some small investors named Dimick and Brelsford began operating a line of freight wagons, or "bull trains," over the seven and a half miles of lumpy, sandy scrubland that separated Jupiter and Lake Worth. Most of the traffic involved steamer cargo on its way to West Palm Beach and Miami. The rest consisted of people going to and from Jupiter.

Jupitarians probably would have continued to gripe at being jarred and jostled in ox carts had it not been for some ambitious railroad developers. The state government's Internal Improvement Fund was awarding generous land grants to anyone who would build rail lines, and a New York investment group saw Jupiter–Lake Worth as a chance to make a fast buck. They bought out the freight-wagon investors, formed the Jupiter and Lake Worth Railway, quickly secured a federal mail delivery contract and then "flipped" their tiny franchise to the more established Jacksonville, Tampa and Key West Railroad Company.

Well, even the *prospect* of a railroad was all the citizens of Juno (located on the northern edge of Lake Worth) needed to launch a power grab. There were no roads to Miami, the county seat, which meant that people from the Jupiter area had to emulate the barefoot mailman's hundred-mile trek to conduct official county business. What made their smoldering resentment boil over was J.W. Ewan, who was county treasurer and known as the "Duke of Dade." Ewan had been charging the county $5 a month to store its records in a building he owned. When he summarily announced that the new rent would be $15, tempers flared. Residents of the Lake Worth area circulated a petition calling for a special election to determine the location of the county seat for the next ten years. A.M. Fields, the northern commissioner, promised to rent the county a room in *his* home at the old $5 a month.

On Feb. 19, 1889, the Miami contingent went down to defeat by a vote of 107 to 80. After a tense, intrigue-filled night in which northern commissioners actually had to smuggle county records into the hold of a boat, Juno became the official seat of Dade County. Mr. Fields, now the new county boss, soon announced that the rent for storing the official records would be $15 a month —the same rate that had sparked the revolution.

Older Jupiter, on the ocean, was now wedded to Juno, his bride on Lake Worth. Having tapped Mount Olympus for the first names, railroad planners quickly followed with Venus and Mars for the two stops en route. That Mars never survived its

Little Dora Doster poses on the cowcatcher of Celestial Railroad engine No. 1, with her aunt, Lucy Doster Miller, and cousin, Lillian Miller in the cab. One wonders how ladies kept their long light dresses clean with all that soot flying at them! *(Loxahatchee River Historical Society)*

The Celestial Railroad comes to life in 1889 as construction nears completion on a wharf and warehouse where steamers would transfer their cargo and passengers to rail cars. Site is just east of the present Suni Sands dock.
*(Loxahatchee River Historical Society)*

christening and that Venus was to remain but a vision of its sole resident, was something few cared to mention. Two years later, when a reporter from *Harper's Magazine* wrote a lighthearted feature on the little line, his headline stuck: the "Celestial Railroad."

Emboldened and wishing to entrench their victory, the new county commissioners ponied up $1,495 to build a courthouse, a two-story building 30 by 35 feet with offices on the first floor and the courtroom on the second. It also served as lodge hall, church and ballroom, renting for $5 a night.

By this time, Juno also had a newspaper, and on July 4, 1889, the *Tropical Sun* reported that locals celebrated with a free ride over "their" new railroad. "Just think of riding on a steamboat and in the [rail] cars in this country—both in one day!" enthused editor Guy Metcalf, who also ran the post office and a real estate office. "For the first time in history in this part of the country we could do it."

Indeed, about 75 local luminaries boarded the steamer *Lake Worth* at 8:30 a.m., met the train—"consisting of one coach and one flatcar"—at 10:15 a.m., where "away we went to Jupiter…"

At 11 a.m. they were met by James Armour of the lighthouse, all of Jupiter's finest, and the captain of the elegant steamer *Chattahoochee*, "who threw open the steamer for our use and did everything in his power to make our visit both enjoyable and memorable."

*The table was set in the cabin, and there were nearly a hundred in all to eat, and the table not being large enough, the old people and children were served first, after which came the middle aged and young, but no one went away hungry, for there was enough to spare and all kinds of good things…*

*Visiting the Lighthouse and Signal Station, strolling on the beach and sailing around the harbor were some of the diversions indulged in by the picnickers to pass away the time. We left for home on the train at 4:15 p.m., being accompanied to the head of the lake by all our Jupiter friends. A little time was spent in getting the steamer off the mud, where the falling tide had left her, but we finally bid our Jupiter friends adieu and started down the lake. The trip down was a delightful one and enlivened by our singing patriotic songs.*

Then the residents and railroad settled down to getting to know one another. In the off-season the railroad ran one trip a day, two in season. Usually with the engine pulling two passenger cars and three freight cars, the line made the most of its monopoly by charging 75 cents one way and 20 cents per hundred pounds for freight.

A large wharf was built on the Jupiter River (just east of today's Suni Sands dock) and rail schedules were set to match the arrival of steamers. But passenger boats, with all their weather woes and sandbar groundings, often made the train late as well. And so did finicky locomotives. "Old No. 3," (it went only forward to Juno and then backward to Jupiter) broke down frequently, meaning that all transport ceased until it could be fixed, which sometimes meant awaiting spare parts from Titusville. When the train jumped the track in November 1894, it took everyone who could be mustered eight hours to set it right.

Meanwhile, the *Tropical Sun* editorialized incessantly that the rail station at Juno, which "has to answer for the purpose of a waiting room for passengers, a storehouse for freight, a distributing room for mails, tickets and telephone offices, is one of the most unsightly buildings to be found in this entire country." At a time when other houses in the area "are neatly painted and the surroundings fairly well kept," editor Metcalf fumed, "the freight house of the big J.T. & K.W. Line is too small, unpainted, undeniably shabby and unquestionably uncomfortable…."

But the colorful conductors, engineers and wharf workers did their best to joke their way through adversity—and even to entertain passengers. Local kids used the wharf for diving and swimming. It also served as Jupiter's official polling place. Blus Rice, the popular engineer, would play his rendition of "Dixie" on his one-note train whistle and pretty soon people would be singing the tune and forgetting their long wait before climbing aboard. Many passengers brought guns aboard to shoot deer and wild turkeys along the way. And if they were lucky enough to score a hit from their lurching perch, Rice would stop while they jumped off and brought back their quarry. On Oct. 18, 1894, the train stopped and passengers leaned out their windows to watch Blus Rice shoot a nine-foot, eight-inch alligator that had been sunning itself on the track.

Another benefit—albeit short-lived—was that people who owned land along the right-of-way saw prices escalate to $75 an acre. But then, poof! After just six years of operation, the little railway was sucked up in the whirlwind of railroad consolidations, bankruptcies and confusion that Henry M. Flagler touched off when he decided to forge a major line from St. Augustine to as far south as he could blast his way.

Flagler, who had been John D. Rockefeller's partner in founding Standard Oil, achieved an immense fortune by age 53 and spent the rest of his years spending it on bold ventures for which he, at best, broke even. But the sheer size of his projects changed lives and fortunes wherever they impacted. For example, Flagler had been dismayed during an 1887–88 trip to Jacksonville to find transportation so primitive. So he brought a rail line to St. Augustine—a dilapidated town of 2,500—built the outlandish Ponce de Leon Hotel and soon filled it with vacationing northerners.

In 1893 Flagler confirmed long-time rumors that he wanted to do the same in West Palm Beach by bringing down a major rail line and connecting it by a bridge over Lake Worth to Palm Beach. There, near the beach, he would build one of the world's largest wooden buildings (soon to be named the Royal Poinciana Hotel).

By now Flagler had hit on a workable formula for achieving his goals. He had already received a million acres of right-of-way from the state as a building incentive. Now he asked the city fathers of Palm Beach to raise $30,000 in earnest money. Then he spent just about that much lavishly entertaining the same "first families" during the 1893 social season. All this had a predictable leavening effect.

A week after Flagler and party departed, *The Tropical Sun* gushed that $400,000 in real estate had changed hands between Lake

Fireman Milton Messer polishes the headlight of locomotive No. 2. At far left is conductor, Captain Matheson with engineer Blus Rice in the center holding his oil can. In the cab: Rice's hound dog, who proved handy retrieving wild turkeys and other game that passengers might shoot out the windows during their 7.5 mile trip to Juno. *(Lynn Drake Collection)*

Worth and Jupiter. Anxious steamboat owners were pacified by contracts to haul railroad construction materials from Titusville to Jupiter. The Celestial Railroad and steamers from Lake Worth to Palm Beach got contracts to deliver building materials for the new resort hotel. The little rail line, for example, took in an estimated $84,000 from Flagler to build a hotel (the Royal Poinciana) that would consume 5 million feet of lumber, 1,400 kegs of nails and 20 acres of plaster. The sudden income spurt was more than the estimated value of the railroad's entire rolling stock.

But it was already clear that the whistles of the steamboats and "Old No. 3" would soon be drowned out by the roar of Flagler's high-speed, wide-gauge railcars. One foot was put in the grave when Flagler tried to buy the Jupiter and Lake Worth line. Its parent, the Jacksonville, Tampa and Key West Railroad, was in financial distress at the time. Its owners reckoned that the land just to the west was too boggy for a rail bed and they gambled that

Flagler would pay an outlandish price. Instead he was repulsed by their gall and vowed to bypass Juno with his new railroad. His engineers built a bridge across the Loxahatchee and laid the tracks on the flatlands into West Palm Beach (costing Flagler more than had he bought the Celestial). Then just for good measure, he got state permission to widen the marshy waterway from Jupiter to Lake Worth into a canal. Soon even boats could go from Titusville to Lake Worth and the little railway was obsolete.

Juno, the once-proud county seat, was now the terminus of a bypassed, narrow-gauge railroad that had to back up to go one way.

Meanwhile, its troubled parent, the JT & KW, sank into receivership and then into oblivion. Like so many dominos, the steamship owners began to topple as well. When the largest holdout, the Indian River Line, laid up its steamer fleet in April 1895, service on the Celestial Railroad was suspended.

The demise of the Celestial Railroad left Jupiter saddened. Dora

Once the new Celestial Railroad wharf was in business, it became a gathering place for everyone in town. People tied up rowboats, kids swam, men fished and just about every visitor (including these Seminoles) had to have his photo taken with the lighthouse looming in the background. From left to right: Cypress Tiger, Jimmy Gopher and Billy Stuart in 1891.
*(Loxahatchee River Historical Society)*

As soon as Henry Flagler's Florida East Coast Railroad bypassed Juno by building his Jacksonville–Palm Beach line to the west, he also commissioned the dredge *Montanzas* to cut a straight canal through the meandering Jupiter River to Lake Worth. Photo at right, taken several years later, shows the dredge's handiwork.
*(ABOVE, Loxahatchee River Historical Society. RIGHT, Jupiter–Tequesta Chamber of Commerce)*

Doster Utz, who had posed on the locomotive as a young girl, years later summed up the town's sagging spirits in a letter:

*So, the Celestial fell into disuse, and Papa was commissioned to dismantle it. Some of the river steamers, such as the* St. Sebastian *and* St. Lucie, *were beached along the river and rotted away there. The big railroad carried the mail now, supplanting the primitive years of boat, stagecoach, and even the barefooted mailmen* [who] *walked the route along the beach.*

*The hotel was abandoned, and the nearby saloon vacated, becoming the meeting place of more respectable pursuits, like dances, for instance.*

*There was something sad about how quickly the little stops along the Celestial right-of-way were abandoned, but it was natural that they should because transportation for their produce was no longer available. So shacks were left with their doors ajar, and the odoriferous pineapple patches ripened and perfumed the air with their golden fruit unpicked.*

*The jungles and the underbrush were fast claiming the right-of-way,* *and the sorrowful call of the Mourning Dove seemed to be sounding a requiem to its passing.*

As for the beached steamers, Bessie DuBois adds: "Early settlers of the Fort Jupiter reservation used the stateroom windows and doors in their shacks. The steamers gradually rusted away…relics of a priceless era…."

In 1899 the seat of Dade County was moved back to Miami. In fact, the jail cells, with prisoners still inside, were put on a barge and towed to Miami by the steamer *Lake Worth*.

The next year the Juno courthouse was consumed by fire. So little was left of the town that in the 1930s a group of pioneers erected a monument with a bronze medallion marking the spot where today's Route 1 crossed the rail line right-of-way. Ten years later the state was widening the road when a bulldozer knocked the monument over and smashed it to pieces. Evidence of Juno and the Celestial Railroad were merely memories for many years to come.

One of two steamers that were towed upriver in 1896 after Henry Flagler's Florida East Coast Railroad completed its leg to Palm Beach and put Jupiter's steamers and Celestial Railroad out of business. Settlers tore off doors, planking and furnishings for their own homes. In just a few years, the humidity and jungle had reclaimed all but the rusted husks. *(Loxahatchee River Historical Society)*

The British cable ship *Westmeath* laid a Western Union line from Nassau, Bahamas, to Jupiter. When completed in 1892, its captain paused while awaiting permission from Washington to bring the cable onto the U.S. shore at today's Carlin Park. *(Loxahatchee River Historical Society)*

## HUB OF THE HEMISPHERE?
## JUPITER MEETS MORSE AND MARCONI

Although a farmer or fisherman would scarcely notice it, Jupiter suddenly became a vital center of hemispheric communications in the early 1890s when a Western Union telegraph office and U.S. Weather Bureau station arrived at almost the same time.

For several months the British schooner *Westmeath* had been laying a cable from Nassau in the Bahamas to Jupiter. When completed in 1892, the cable surfaced on the beach at today's Carlin Park. From there lines ran overhead on poles to a new Western Union building (*shed* would be more accurate) that had gone up right next to the equally new Carlin House hotel. From there the telegraph line became a cable again as it snaked along the bottom of the Jupiter River. It surfaced again at the Lighthouse complex campus near the three-story building operated by the U.S. Weather Bureau in the southeast corner.

The result of all this linkage was that Jupiter had become the southernmost electronic communications point in the U.S.—a critical link in a chain that ran from South America to Central America to the Bahamas to Jacksonville and points north.

Both facilities worked together in a way that made the sum greater than the parts. For example, the Weather Bureau's main role was to relay storm alerts; but its observers also scanned the ocean for ships from their third-floor balcony and learned to read signal flags through high-powered field glasses so they could pass vital messages to the telegraph office.

The improvement in weather information was dramatic. Carlin White noted in his *History of the Carlin House* that until then "the only tools that the folks had were the usual weather almanac, the barometers and a few seafaring truisms" such as watching the behavior of frigate birds. Now they could get daily reports from places like Cuba and Puerto Rico.

It seems that Turks Island (just off the southeastern tip of the Bahamas) was an especially valuable source. As White's chronicle notes:

*The telegraph operator on Turks Island was an old friend of Percy King, the local telegrapher. In those days… because of their limited numbers, most cable telegraphers knew each other. The Turks Island telegrapher received bad weather information promptly. When this data was passed on to Carlin House, Grandmother would make sure that the cows and the livestock, which normally were allowed to roam freely, were kept close to the barn. The family did many other things, also. They would collect and stow all loose items, outdoor furniture, boats, etc. The similarity of the weather in Turks Island and that of Jupiter was uncanny; except for the timing it was almost identical."*

The telegraph link to Jacksonville was a big attraction to Carlin House guests as well. Most were affluent, and, notes White, "They would have all the quiet romance of a frontier and [still] keep daily track of their investments."

The U.S. military was probably the biggest beneficiary. Naval vessels still lacked wireless ship-to-shore communications, so it was common when passing a telegraph station to lower a skiff and row in. There, they'd report on their whereabouts or wait for new orders.

For Jupiter, the most memorable of many such visits was on May 24, 1898. As Carlin White reports, the tourist season was ending and the few guests remaining at Carlin House were taking their usual morning beach walk when they noticed a giant vessel looming on the distant horizon. It looked as big as a battleship—but whose? At the time the U.S. and Spain were trading threats over who held sway over Cuba and war seemed imminent. Could this be a Spanish man-of-war bent on invading Florida or bombarding the coast?

A second account by Bessie DuBois adds that some of the Carlin ladies were rocking on the front porch when "[they] saw a fiery rocket curving toward the lighthouse."

*Their screams brought the men on the run. Arms were hastily assembled and joined by the lighthouse keepers, and [with] the rest of the Life Saving crew they set sail for the inlet determined to repel the invaders at any cost. All the men, that is except one timorous soul who gathered all his valuables and hid out with them in the woods.*

As the mysterious gray giant loomed nearer it was headed dead on for the inlet, its rows of long guns pointed right at the lighthouse reservation. Then it went dead in the water. Soon a longboat approached, full of men. Hearts were in throats for a long moment until the men at the inlet suddenly let up a cheer! They recognized the uniforms of the U.S. Navy. Added Bessie: "It was a gala night at the lighthouse for all except the fellow who hid out in the woods. He was ragged unmercifully."

Why the landing? The *U.S.S. Oregon,* the nation's first battleship, had left San Francisco 67 days beforehand on a good will voyage. Despite all the might embodied in this floating fortress, it still lacked wireless communications. Its captain had no idea of the military tension in Cuba or whether he might be ordered to join the U.S. blockade of Havana harbor. And on the other end, Washington knew not whether its flagship was still intact or lost at sea.

After a homemade meal by Mrs. Carlin and her daughters while the emissaries transmitted orders back and forth at the navy telegraph office (the ship went on to play a major role in the Battle of Santiago), the officer in charge presented Captain Carlin with his Springfield rifle. The gesture may have been a bit chauvinistic, because it was Mary Carlin who had done most of the work—and then some. Mrs. Carlin had just been made postmistress of Jupiter and, after all her cooking, she was faced with sorting what seemed like a ton of letters brought to her by sailors who hadn't been able to write home for over two months.

The *Oregon's* plight demonstrated why Jupiter would soon have another type of communications office on the lighthouse grounds. Developing a wireless ship-to-shore radio capability was a top priority for both naval and merchant shipping leaders and all sorts of rewards were offered to anyone with a way to make it work. When Italy's Guglielmo Marconi did it by sending electric impulses from Newfoundland to Scotland, newspapers proclaimed

This mid–1890s close-up shows (from left) the assistant keepers' quarters just in front of the lighthouse, the oil house, the captain's quarters, boat dock and U.S. Weather Bureau building. Gone by then was the lush foliage pictured in photos of a decade earlier. *(Florida State Archives)*

it the achievement of the century.

The U.S. Navy quickly established an experimental wireless telegraphy facility in Arlington, Va. Top brass decided that a fair test of the technology should involve two stations 1,000 miles apart. When they looked on the map for some existing federal real estate to fill the bill, it came up Jupiter. One reason, no doubt, was that Jupiter already had a telegraph office that could transmit back-up data if the wireless version sputtered. And if it

worked, one could then test ship-to-shore communications in the Gulf and Caribbean.

Before long the old navy outpost at the lighthouse had been expanded into a two-story wireless telegraphy building, storage house, boathouse, dock, upstairs personnel quarters and a 120-foot rotating wooden antenna that resembled a ship's mast. Just outside was a separate concrete power building housing a 50 horsepower diesel engine that was used mostly to charge the large

Panoramic view from the lighthouse shows the Weather Bureau building and both sides of the inlet. Note the wrap-around observation decks and wind gauges. *(Florida State Archives)*

storage batteries.

Once the hubbub of construction was over, three wireless telegraphers traded monotonous watches spent hunkered down at desks listening to weak raspy signals through primitive headphones. Although they could communicate with Arlington, they didn't do much to advance ship-to-shore communications because the majority of vessels didn't have wireless equipment for another dozen years or so.

When a ship did have the latest wireless gear, its wave signal would be picked up by the rotating antenna in Jupiter and indicate the signal's compass direction. However, it was only a *line of position*. While useful to a navigator, it did nothing to position a ship in relation to Earth's longitude and latitude. Ships would need to rely on many more wireless stations in strategic locations before they would be able to triangulate a fixed position.

Adam Bryant, called "Old Daddy" by everyone at Carlin House, was once a
slave on the South Carolina plantation where Mary Carlin grew up. He joined
the Carlins in 1886 just in time to help build Carlin House. He remained at
the center of its life until his death in 1944. *(Loxahatchee River Historical Society)*

# CHAPTER 4
# TURN-OF-THE-CENTURY LIFE IN JUPITER

"When my mother was married [at 17] she didn't know how to do a thing. She couldn't sew and knew nothing about cooking. Having been raised on a South Carolina plantation with slaves doing all the work, she was lost. She had a New Home sewing machine that my father taught her how to use. He had to show her how to cut a pattern, too."

So wrote Emily Carlin Turner about her mother Mary. By 1888, when the Carlins outgrew their small apartment in the Jupiter Life Saving Station, she had six children, had learned to cook for a crew of six men, was using her home as the town's first school, was baking fifty loaves of bread a day for Bowers Grocery and would soon supervise a round-the-clock hotel operation in elegant fashion.

She was the town postmistress as well.

When first built, Carlin House was simply a family residence, with two bedrooms upstairs and two more downstairs, all surrounded by covered porches. At first, running a commercial hotel was probably the furthest thing from the Carlins' minds, but circumstances almost compelled it. Jupiter was at the end of the Indian River and travelers just seemed to gravitate towards the hospitable house on the inlet. "Mary Carlin never knew what was around the corner," her grandson Carlin White would later write. "People would sail in during the night and the first time she'd meet them would be at breakfast.

"The decision to create a commercial hotel caused a beehive of activity," wrote White in his self-published *History of the Carlin House.* "First they built a two story attached addition south,

Guests on the Sperry House front porch in 1907, perhaps taking in the morning air after a sumptuous breakfast at the neighboring Carlin House. Seated at left is William Sperry. His wife, Emily ("Nana") leans against column. Other guests are not identified. *(Loxahatchee River Historical Society)*

between the house and kitchen. This added two bedrooms, a west porch with stairs to the upper level, two porches and a large dining area below. This modification closed in the upper and lower halls, thus providing space for a library and three bathing areas.

"When the calendar turned to the new century," he added, "The Carlin House consisted of almost all the necessary entities plus a few amenities. In addition to the main house, which by then was an eleven–room structure, there were five permanent cottages—two for guests, three for the family and hired help. There was also a windmill and two large water-storage tanks. One was located south of the dining room, at ground level, and used as a water cistern. The other was perched on a twenty–foot tower and in conjunction with the windmill, comprised the hotel's sanitary water system. Included were a pigpen [and] a barn for four cows, one mule and feed storage. Drinking water came from a special pitcher–pumped well, at the west edge of the property and this water was carried to the hotel in white porcelain–lined buckets, as needed. The collected rainwater was used for washing clothes. The sanitary water, containing some salt, was too hard for this purpose. Also near the supply buildings stood the washing/ironing shed with its wash lines and the proverbial outdoor wood-fired iron wash kettle nearby."

The center of outdoor life, however, was the 200-foot-long pine board dock that ran at a right angle to a 20-by-25 foot pier. All that bulk was needed because everything came by boat—guests and supplies alike. At the end of the dock was a thirty-foot flagpole with a crossbar just below the top. At one end of the crossbar

guests would display their respective yacht club flags. At the other end the Carlins would fly signal flags with all sorts of messages for passing boats.

The Carlins' guests were an eclectic lot, but usually came from the northeast with impressive financial or scholarly credentials. A season might be flavored by visits from Dr. L.S. Stanford, a renowned ornithologist, and Maj. Allan Brooks, a wildlife painter for *National Geographic.* One year three taxidermists who had accompanied Theodore Roosevelt in his wildlife collecting expeditions stayed at Carlin House while they studied the elusive Carolina Parakeet (which seems to have settled in Jupiter). William Henry Jackson, known worldwide for his photography of the American West, came to Carlin House for his winter respites and stored his large glass negatives in its attic for many years.

One visitor arrived by boat with an entire entourage of horses, bound for an equestrian show in Miami. When Captain Carlin obliged by giving the horses water and walking them on the beach, the grateful owner saw to it that he was supplied with free pipe tobacco for the rest of his life. His name was P. Lorillard.

Interspersed would be the steady visits to Mrs. Carlin's popular table by Palm Beach locals. They included society guests from the Breakers and Royal Poinciana hotels with names like Woolworth and Flagler. One regular was "Colonel" Edward R. Bradley, who owned the most flourishing bistro in Palm Beach. After his first meal at the hotel he took Mary Carlin aside and told her that she was being too generous to charge $1 for such sumptuous fare. "Make it $5!" Bradley urged. She did, and noticed no drop in

John Cleminson in 1900. This native Englander began as a guest at Carlin House and stayed on long enough to become a mail carrier, schoolmaster, violin player at dances and eager porch chair debater on almost any scholarly subject.
*(Florida State Archives)*

Still the busy owner-manager of Carlin House, Mary Carlin feeds her turkeys outside the kitchen door sometime just after World War I. She was now widowed and known to most as "Grandmother Carlin." But to "Old Daddy," Adam Bryant, she was always "Ole Miss." *(Town of Jupiter Archives / Carlin White Collection)*

business whatever.

For the most part, the hotel's guests consisted of a few "regulars." In fact, the Carlins kept no guest registry and rarely had room for "walk–in" trade. Mary's eldest daughter, Nauman, who ran the business side, found reservations the least of her worries. Explains Carlin White:

*Almost without exception* [guests] *were members of the same or closely related social clubs and were good friends. Because of the limited available space and the slowness of the mail, they found it more effective if they made their annual schedules among themselves. This they would send to Aunt Nauman in mid-summer. This procedure eliminated much of Aunt Nauman's accommodation problems and in a sense made the hotel operate as a private club; so much so that if Nauman received a lodging request from someone she didn't know, she would, before replying, send it north for the regular attendants' comments. If the comment were negative, they would not be accommodated.*

One of most colorful guests was John Cleminson, an Englishman known as a scholar and musician. He taught school. He delivered mail, fiddled at local dances and held forth on almost any subject from his rocker on the Carlin front porch. He was also known for his predictions. "Charlie," he'd tell Captain Carlin, "the day will come when we'll be able to sit here and see pictures that are being taken in New York." He didn't use the term "television," but he had the right idea.

Another mainstay was Robert Dixon. An outdoor enthusiast and officer of the New York Athletic Club, he owned a commercial farm produce business in New York. Dixon had camped along the Jupiter River for several winters and befriended the Carlins even before they left the Lighthouse Service. When they opened the hotel, he became its first permanent guest, occupying a large upstairs bedroom that was built just for him. Each summer he'd pay for the season in advance, and his early arrival would be accompanied by trunks full of pennants, photos, boat models and other paraphernalia for decorating the "Dixon Room."

After Dixon, the biggest influence in the hotel's early years was probably William Sperry, co–founder of the Sperry & Hutchinson green stamp company. Always attired in wool knickers, wool socks, wool coat, celluloid collar and tie, he was, as Carlin White wrote, "fastidious to a fault." His obsession with what he called "the finer things in life" had its pluses and minuses for the Carlins. In the hotel's early years he assumed the task of tutoring the Carlin girls on proper service, even to the point of taking daughter Nauman to Long Island to show her how a "proper" hotel was run. Because he had traveled the world and expected the finest, he saw to it that the Carlin dining room used only white linen tablecloths, cut–glass water tumblers, sterling silver utensils and English Haviland china. He also insisted that when the Carlin girls waited tables, they wear white, full-length, starched linen dresses with frilly white aprons—regardless of the temperature.

Sperry also enjoyed the role of self–appointed guardian of the

Young Carlin White, son of Emily Carlin, in 1913 at age six. He would become an engineer, mayor of Jupiter and author of *The History of The Carlin House.*
*(Town of Jupiter Archives / Carlin White Collection)*

Looking southeast on the shore opposite the lighthouse stood an early home built by the William S. Tancre family around 1889. Susan DuBois boarded there when she taught at the Octagon Schoolhouse. After being used later as a boardinghouse (perhaps for Celestial Railroad builders), it was rolled on logs to the river's edge around 1896 and barged down to West Palm Beach. *(Loxahatchee River Historical Society)*

The DuBois home, perched atop the ridge of Indian mounds, 1899 or 1900. *(Loxahatchee River Historical Society)*

local "social register." Afternoon dinner parties were held in the dining room every day at 3 p.m.—and by "appointment only." Invitations might go out to tourists staying in yachts or to the increasing numbers who had begun to build winter homes on the river. Special dinner parties were held later in the evening, always with the same menu of broiled and baked fish, oyster cocktail, scalloped potatoes, macaroni and cheese, baked ham, string beans, fresh garden salad and Mary Carlin's unique strawberry shortcake.

Neither the afternoon dinners nor evening dinner parties involved alcohol. As Carlin White wrote, "although the patrons were not against the use of spirits, few used any and those that did confined its use to their rooms."

The Sperry family continued to dine regularly at Carlin House, even after they bought up the Celestial Railroad property next door, built their own winter home and brought in their personal Chinese chef. White's *History* offers a glimpse of what the Carlins had to endure from Sperry day after day. Late one afternoon Captain Carlin heard shrieks of "Help!" coming from down by the dock. Mustering two of his sons, he rushed toward the noise. It came from the boathouse. Inside, Sperry's enraged "personal chef" had him pinned to the ground

*…and was threatening to take him apart with a meat cleaver. It seems that Mr. Sperry had committed a Chinese cook's unpardonable sin by going into the kitchen while food was being prepared, or some other ridiculous far east custom. While wielding the cleaver over his head the chinaman kept loudly repeating, "Stay the hellliee out mee keechon."*

At Carlin House, the kitchen was certainly the busiest place on the property. Wrote White,

*It was large enough to accommodate a big wood stove a sink and two good-sized tables. Attached to the east side of the kitchen was a pantry-pastry making area. In this small room Grandma kept the things that she needed in a hurry: spices, seasonings, etc. In addition to the baking that was done daily for the hotel, Mrs. Carlin baked fifty loaves of bread for the local store. Until around 1918…the bread was delivered by the family in boats, seven days a week.*

*During the season all of the cooking and some of the baking was done on the wood stove; the heavy baking was reserved for the brick oven. The stove also heated hot water for all of the sinks—the big ones in the kitchen and the small ones that were eventually installed in all of the bedrooms.*

The library, between the dining area and parlor, contained several hundred books along with an atlas, a globe and a large Webster's dictionary on an ornate stand. Most of the books were given to Mrs. Carlin by guests or friends. "My grandmother only attended school through the third grade," said White. "However, she loved to read, especially during the long summers. In this way she continued improving her knowledge throughout her years by reading anything and everything she could find. She read *Gone With the Wind* five times."

Christmas at Carlin House was a season's highlight, with perhaps forty dinner guests around a large tree in the dining room. Emily Carlin Turner recalled that her mother was known for her holiday plum pudding, which was well-laced with rum and brandy. She still remembers some woozy teetotalers praising their hostess for its delicious "vanilla flavor."

If Mary Carlin was the inner hub of Carlin House, Adam Bryant was Mr. Outside. "Old Daddy," as everyone called him, wasn't sure of his age, only that he was around 15 when the Civil War ended and could recall as a boy seeing slaves bought on an auction block in his native South Carolina. He'd drifted to Jupiter in the 1890s and wound up laying the crossties that supported Flagler's tracks. In 1894, as the railroad neared completion, Bryant was among hundreds of workers laid off. But it was also the time when Carlin House was looking for a handyman—and with his husky six-foot-plus build, he was a natural for the job.

Officially, Bryant's primary task was finding and hauling enough driftwood, pine and castoff rail timbers to supply the hotel's never-ending need for its kitchen stove and laundry tubs. But he soon became the glue that held Carlin House together. No one could cast a net like Old Daddy, and no one could handle a hand line as well when it came to fishing for snook, blues or jack. He'd get up every day at 5 a.m. and make coffee with a whole egg—shell and all. It was so strong, guests said, "the spoon would stand up in the cup." Often at night he'd build a campfire where everyone from New York tycoons to children of the Carlins' maids would sit with chin in hands as he spun tales from his plantation days.

Each summer Old Daddy would pack up a trunk of various fabrics donated by guests and set off for his family home in Georgia. There the ladies would sew the scraps together into colorful quilts. When he returned each fall, Old Daddy's trunk would be filled with paper shell pecans, which he'd dole out to the local kids who followed him about.

But mostly he was remembered as a thoughtful, gentle man whose wisdom belied the fact that he couldn't read or write. When "Ole Miss," as he called Mary Carlin, died at 93 in 1944, Adam Bryant, her contemporary, was still alive.

## HARRY AND SUSAN DUBOIS START A FAMILY

Bessie DuBois tells the story of a man known only as "Captain Stone." Seems that sometime after the Civil War he ambled along a spot opposite the lighthouse called "Banana Point" by locals and decided he'd make the most of it. For a couple of years he raised bananas and sent them off to northern markets. One day he was walking the beach and discovered a Spanish chest containing some gold coins.

Suddenly bananas weren't quite as glamorous. He took the coins to New York, chartered a schooner and brought it back down through Jupiter Inlet to his old haunts. Captain Stone's new vision was to build a big business cutting down palmetto logs on the

On the DuBois front porch in 1908 or 1909: Susan Dubois with children Anna to her right. Next are friends of the family: George Rowley, his mother Rose, Anne Farquard, Henry DuBois, and two other children. *(Loxahatchee River Historical Society)*

Harry DuBois in his banana grove. *(Loxahatchee River Historical Society)*

In 1905 the major buildings of the lighthouse reservation stand out clearly where once they'd been almost hidden by foliage. From left to right, the tower and oil house, assistant keepers' house (with kitchen outbuilding at left), the head keeper's house and the U.S. Weather Bureau station. *(Town of Jupiter Archives/Carlin White Collection)*

Jupiter River and shipping them to lumber–starved Key West for docks and homes.

Alas, while he was sawing and loading, the inlet silted up so that he couldn't get the (now much heavier) schooner back out. Leaving the vessel with its cargo of logs to rot away, the hapless Stone walked up the beach to Cape Canaveral, subsisting on turtle eggs and a washed-up bottle of rum.

Although he wasn't heard from again, "Banana Point" had by then become known as "Stone's Point" when Harry and Susan DuBois bought the property and built a home atop the Indian mounds that stretched from there to the inlet.

Harry DuBois, raised on a Monmouth County, N.J., farm, came to Florida at age 16 to spend the winter working in an orange grove on Merritt Island. He'd always return to the family farm during summers, but when he became of age he lived mostly in Florida. When Flagler decided to bring his railroad and a hotel to Palm Beach, DuBois bought himself a forty–foot sharpie sailboat and began contracting to haul building supplies. Along the way he'd sail into various inlets. He was especially impressed with the shell mounds at Jupiter and thought they'd make a nice high and dry perch for a home one day.

That day came sooner than DuBois had imagined when he found a steady job with Captain Carlin's newly formed lifesaving crew. Soon afterward he saved up enough money to buy twenty acres of land along what's now the Intracoastal Waterway and put up a one-story 14-by-28 foot cabin. When he wasn't working and a-building, DuBois farmed pineapples on ten of his acres.

What he needed now was a wife. As his eldest son John recalled in *The Loxahatchee Lament* series,

*Dad met my mother, Susan Sanders, on a blind date. She was a teacher at the old Octagon School. It was located in the area of today's Pa-Ja Villas… Their date was arranged by Charles Carlin and his girl friend. It was a dark night and they rowed across the river to the lighthouse. They really didn't see one another until they reached the other side of the river. They took to one another and started dating. When Dad proposed to her they became engaged in the lighthouse.*

*Dad didn't want to take his bride to the pineapple patch, so he bought the land that is now DuBois Park. Then he started building a home on the shell mound to avoid high water. He planned a seashore type of house…like those on Cape Cod or the New Jersey coast.*

By 1896, with the lifesaving station now closed and Harry's regular government paycheck just a memory, the young couple encountered some anxious moments. They tried raising oranges, but weren't successful. As four children came along, the DuBoises got along by fishing, raising their own vegetables, and finally finding a cash crop in bananas. Harry would use the sharpie to haul his bananas to West Palm Beach, where he was paid "a penny a finger."

Susan's main farm job was caring for the chicken coop, which was a constant battle against hawks, snakes and possums. In the summer, swarms of mosquitoes were so bad that the chickens all but stopped laying in protest. The coop had a little swinging door for the chickens to go in and out, and whenever Harry or Susan would forget to lock it shut at night, a coachwhip snake would be ready to crawl in. As John DuBois recalled,

*They'd get so fat they couldn't crawl back out the door again.*

*Mother raised biddies, too. She had a problem with chicken hawks, though. They were always trying to carry off her biddies. So Dad got her a double-barreled shotgun. She didn't hesitate to use it on those hawks, either. The chickens were her department.*

When the DuBoises needed something they couldn't produce themselves, they got in their motorboat and went to Bowers Grocery, which was built on pilings on the shore just east of the railroad tracks. There they'd buy flour by the barrel along with dried prunes, apricots, rice and oatmeal. Meat came from Pennington Kitching, who had a butcher shop next to the railroad depot. Some supplies—cases of canned milk, beans, tomatoes and ten pound buckets of margarine—came by train all the way from Tyler Grocery in Jacksonville.

All this might indicate a subsistence-level life until one reads the memoirs of Bessie Wilson, who was taken under the wing of Susan DuBois shortly after arriving from New Jersey in 1914.

*Her daughter, Anna, was only eight days older than I. We became fast friends. I was often a guest and loved nothing better than to stand by the well-polished old wood range and watch Mrs. DuBois cook, She prepared better food, I am sure, than the plush patrons of the Royal Poinciana Hotel were pushing around on their plates 17 miles away.*

After describing Mrs. DuBois' "famous" chicken perleau, "huge platters of fried rabbit," the elaborate "ambrosia of oranges" dessert and a table with "a gleaming white linen cloth and fairly groaning with food," Bessie continues,

*How one woman could have prepared so much I do not know! When she took off her apron and seated herself, the family and guests quieted down for the blessing, the father, Harry DuBois, looked at the vast array with a twinkle in his eye. Then he remarked in a plaintive voice, "Susie, is this all we have to eat?"*

*I always hesitated to unfold the big white linen napkin. I knew the effort it took to iron them with the old fashioned flat irons heated on the back of the wood stove.*

## A NEW 'WATCH' AT THE LIGHTHOUSE

Over on the lighthouse side, the reservation kept "upgrading." The oil house was rebuilt in 1905 and two years later came a new windmill and boathouse. In 1917, for the first time, galvanized

Surfing was just as much the rage in 1917 as it is today. The latest "technology" for these Jupiter kids was their homemade, square wooden boards, each with names and slogans (like "Fast Flyer" carved in). Standing, from left, Graham King, Henry DuBois, John DuBois, Authur E. Sims, Bland Futch and Neil DuBois. Sitting are John R. Wilson, Bessie Wilson DuBois, Anna DuBois Nelms and Edgar Sims.
*(Loxahatchee River Historical Society)*

Kate and Joe Wells relaxing on the steps of the chief lighthouse keeper's residence. In the background is the four-story Weather Bureau building. *(Loxahatchee River Historical Society)*

pipe handrails were installed along the stairs. Until then, crewmen had no way to brace themselves while going up the steep incline with heavy fuel cans.

But the most memorable, practical "improvement" probably came in 1910 when the keepers were able to pry some money from Washington to erect a wire screen around the windows that projected the light. The reason was that panes of glass were constantly being replaced because flocks of migrating ducks flew smack into them at night.

The new screen had both good and bad results from the standpoints of lighthouse families. On one hand, they could pick up a tub full of dead ducks on a lucky morning. On the other hand, the screen would become so encrusted with bugs that the men would have to scour it clean before the light could shine properly.

In 1908, when James Armour inherited a tidy sum and retired as head lighthouse keeper, the post was taken by his assistant and son-in-law, Joseph Wells. When World War I came, Wells and his assistants saw their workload increase steeply because passing Allied ships were required to keep a radio silence. A platform was built on the Weather Bureau building and signalmen were stationed round the clock with flags. Each vessel passing the lighthouse was required to stop and signal its name and destination. Often it created a nautical traffic jam as several ships circled the buoy marking Jupiter Inlet, each awaiting its turn to identify itself.

### 'INDIAN RIVER' COUNTRY

Beyond the little cluster of buildings on both sides of the inlet area, the arrival of Flagler's railroad in 1894 and the widening of the Jupiter Narrows into today's Intracoastal Waterway a year later encouraged people to settle in several surrounding areas.

Just to the north was the now-easier-to-navigate Indian River, and typical of the first to move in was John H. Grant, who began in the Carlin orbit and eventually settled his family on Jupiter Island. A native Londoner, he explored Florida from inlet to inlet with two friends in a sailboat. In 1887 they found themselves tied up across from Carlin House where Jupiter Inlet Colony stands today. At night the three would play musical instruments, and the sound so pleased Mary Carlin that she sent them a loaf of homemade bread and a crock of baked beans. As Grant's daughter, Ola May, would recount, her dad had planned on going to California, but said he was so captivated by Mrs. Carlin's cooking that he stayed and became a member of the Jupiter lifesaving crew.

Grant met his future wife Ola in 1895 when he spied a comely redhead shopping in Doster's grocery on the Celestial Railroad dock. After the lifesaving crew disbanded in 1896, John and Ola Grant wound up raising pineapples in an area along the Indian River known then as the "English Colony." It was all part of a tract owned by the London-based Indian River Associates Company that included the Gomez Grant and Jupiter Island. To make ends meet John was Hobe Sound's postmaster-mailman and Ola ran a rough–hewn hotel called "The Wigwam" where the Hobe Sound Water Co. later stood.

Just west of Hobe Sound was the North Fork of the Loxahatchee and a trail that ran alongside it that would one day become Riverside Drive. In 1893 the Young family began homesteading 66 acres of beans, peppers, potatoes and onions in what is now Bermuda Terrace. And as far as one could go up the North Fork, by County Line Road, Dr. Charles Jackson had ten acres planted in pineapples—all in addition to his regular jobs as town doctor, schoolmaster and Sunday school leader.

## 'WEST' JUPITER

Back on the river's southern shore, the arrival of Flagler's rail depot gave rise to a cluster of wooden shops—most of them built on pilings—that meant people could now think about living further west than they ever did before. Center Street, an east-west dirt road, soon sprouted a few cabins and stores where it intersected Old Dixie.

Further out Center Street was a creek where only the most intrepid would live. When the Sims family became the first to do so in 1895, they got to name the creek. Their closest neighbors were the Hepburns, a mile and a half away.

Arthur E. Sims, one of five children, remembered a two and a half mile walk to the one-room schoolhouse on Dixie Highway. Sims, interviewed in *The Loxahatchee Lament,* talked of "lots of alligators up Sims Creek. We could hear them holler at night. We went up the creek one time and got about 25 alligator eggs that we brought back to the house and put in a nest inside a fenced area. There were so many alligators we couldn't swim in the creek. Instead, we used to fill a boat with water, and when the sun heated the water we'd use it to take our bath."

Still further, where the river meets today's C–18 Canal, the Pennock Plantation would begin putting down roots in 1895 with dairy barns, fern sheds and worker cabins. In those days the canal was but a shallow creek, and the dairymen would sometimes walk their herd across it to graze on the pasture on the other side. It would become known as Pennock Point.

But even before that much of the Pennock site was occupied by the Tindall family, noted today chiefly by the fact that its home is preserved on the grounds of the Loxahatchee River Historical Society as the best available example of a Florida "cracker" home (circa 1894).

The Tindall family story is worth preserving as well. The family of nine actually arrived by mule wagon from Kissimmee around 1890 and subsisted in various makeshift dwellings as George Tindall tried his luck at pineapple farming and worked part-time in a lumber mill. Great grandson Leo Albert (Al) Kuschel Jr. remembers his grandmother, Stella, Tindall's eldest daughter, describing a Seminole cattle drive through Jupiter's outskirts that took three days. She recalled how she had bright red hair, how the Indian men flocked around her to admire it, and how she froze with fear because she'd read that they liked to hang human scalps from their belts.

Kuschel also has a priceless letter that his grandmother Stella wrote sometime in her seventies after her offspring pressed her for a memoir. After the family went as far south as they could and wound up in Jupiter, Stella recalled,

*When we got to Jupiter we could get neither food for us nor our horses, so they ate salt grass until they died with Salt Grass Sickness. And we were only left to fight mosquitoes and fleas. As soon as you put your foot on the ground you were covered with fleas.*

*But we could not leave so we stayed.*

*We found out that it was homestead land, and we settled down where the Henry Pennock house is. We cleared up and built a palmetto shack on it so we had a place to live. We lived there a year and a man came and told us we were on his place and we had to move about three hundred yards to get on the land we filed for. And then we built another palmetto shack.*

*We cooked our meals out in the open on a brick stove. Our table was made from some old boards from the beach, and we sat on boxes to eat. You had to hold on tight to your bread or the jaybirds would have it.*

*We were there two years and my mother fell ill with a stroke. The only doctor was in West Palm Beach, so we sent down and brought Dr. Potter up to Jupiter in a rowboat to tell us what was wrong with her.*

The doctor said Mary Tindall's only hope was to go back up north to the care of her parents. The only way to get her there was to wait for one of the sporadic paddle–wheel steamers that came to Jupiter Inlet. George Tindall carried Mary in his arms to the dock, the seven children following behind. A steamer eventually took them to Titusville, where the family lived for two years trying to nurse Mrs. Tindall back to health.

Strangely enough, they were again drawn to Jupiter, even though Mary Tindall was described as still "crippled" by her stroke. At some point during the record freeze that jarred south Florida in 1894 the family rode Henry Flagler's new railroad south and found themselves deposited at the Jupiter depot on a bitterly cold night. George Tindall was unexplainably absent during another family ordeal, as described by Stella:

*My father was gone from home and we had no way to get from the train and it was over a mile to go. We asked the station agent if he knew of a place she could go in until morning. He took them up to [a livery stable] and the woman there said she had no place for them. But there was a horse [barn] and up above the horses was a hayloft.*

*He took my mother in his arms and climbed the ladder and put her on the hay, and the children climbed up themselves. Then he went down to where the horses were and got the horse blankets and covered them up and kept them from freezing. The next morning he came and helped them down, and they walked home.*

Lest the reader remember early arrivals in Jupiter only as frosty and forbidding, here is another first impression from no less than Bessie Wilson DuBois. Her father, John Wilson, was a New Jersey greenhouse operator who had fought frustrating battles when frigid winters disabled his boilers and froze his water pipes. In the winter of 1914, after an ice storm had destroyed all his greenhouses in a single night, Wilson picked a spot on the Florida map where the Gulf Stream ran nearest ("It should be the place least likely to freeze," he said) and headed for Jupiter. In September his wife and four children followed, and Bessie picks it up from there.

*We traveled by the Florida East Coast Railway from Jacksonville to Jupiter. The view from the windows of the yellow coach was not encouraging to say the least. The only living things we saw, around some of the tiny stations at which we stopped, were razor back hogs. They were lean, vicious looking and rooting around. It was nightfall* when the conductor finally called, "Jupiter." We stepped off the train at the end of a long bridge.

Papa was there to meet us. He looked very brown. It was quite evident that he had missed Mama's cooking. He was thin. He must have sensed our weary disillusionment. He had us wait until the train disappeared down the track.

Then he said, "Listen."

We became conscious of a vast rustling sound in the river below us. It sounded as though it were filled with a great school of fish. Indeed it was!

This was our first intimation that our steak and chop days were over. Our seafood days were about to begin. If only we had known it!

Then the beam of the Jupiter Lighthouse…swept over us. It gave us a welcome that was warm and reassuring. All our doubts dissolved, then and there. Jupiter became the place Papa had described to us. So it has been to this day.

## BLACK PIONEERS MAKE THEIR MARK

At the turn of the century, Jupiter's African-Americans didn't gather in any one particular area—they lived just about anywhere. Just as it was for whites, Carlin House was one reason several black families got a foothold on Jupiter. For Will Bostick, it was a circuitous beginning. As his daughter Josephine told the *Jupiter Courier* in 1975,

In 1879 he ran away from home and got a job on a riverboat heading south. He was only ten years old. When the boat to Jupiter landed, he decided to get off and stay there. He knew he had to find work. While looking around he met a white man who said he could work for him at his cowboy camp. His place was west of here in the area now known as Indiantown. He told him how to get there and Dad said he'd think about it.

When he decided to take the job he started walking west. When he came to a fork in the road he didn't know which way to go. He finally thought he was on the right road when he saw some campfires ahead.

It wasn't the cowboy camp, though. It was a Seminole Indian village. He said he was sure scared. Even when they gave him food to eat he thought they planned on feeding him before they killed him. When he finished eating they asked him to go hunting with them. Then he knew they were friendly and meant no harm.

Dad lived with the Seminoles until he was 25 years old. He learned to speak their language and spoke it fluently. They liked him so much they even offered him a squaw as a wife, but he said he wasn't interested. When the Indians left this area and moved to the big cypress country, Dad decided to go home.

Out for a stroll. Two Seminole Indian ladies and their children stop to greet Emily ("Nana") Sperry and her daughter Dorothy—perhaps the most 'proper' New Yorkers they would ever meet. *(Loxahatchee River Historical Society)*

Leading ladies of Jupiter, Mrs. Sam Barfield, Mrs. Armour and Lulu Barfield.
*(Loxahatchee River Historical Society)*

But after marrying there was something about Jupiter that lured Bostick back. He and his new wife lived in one of the railroad workers' cabins near the Celestial Railroad dock and soon the couple was working for Carlin House. "My mother did the washing and ironing," daughter Josephine later recalled. "My father did all sorts of chores around the place. He worked on the grounds. He chopped wood for the stoves. He knew the Loxahatchee River, too, for he had worked on the steamers *St. Augustine* and *St. Sebastian.*"

When her mother was doing Carlin House laundry, Josephine would fish off the hotel dock. Sometimes on summer evenings Josephine and the Carlin kids would go down to the beach to watch turtles laying their eggs. "We never went near their eggs," she said, "but when the turtles finished laying we would ride them back into the ocean."

Another black pioneer, Lewis Davis, may have had a unique distinction: he walked all the way from Georgia to Jupiter, where he first worked on the railroad. After getting married in 1905, Lewis and his wife Mary worked and lived at Pennock Plantation where he did everything from horseshoeing to bricklaying. He became one of the first settlers further west along Limestone Creek Road when he began homesteading.

His daughter, Georgia Mae Davis Walker, remembered her one-room schoolhouse on Limestone Creek Road. She also recalled when

*Riverside Drive was just a wagon road. The Simmons family lived over there and Dad used to visit them. He had a mule named Jane. That mule took him all over the area. I've always said my father and Mr. Simmons built Riverside Drive. Their visiting back and forth started the route that is pretty much the same today.*

From Grace Simmons Carter: her mom and dad moved to Neptune, which became known as West Jupiter. "There weren't many colored people here then—just a few from Georgia and South Carolina. Everyone was so kind, though—both blacks and whites. They were so friendly it wasn't long before they began to feel right at home.

"Dad raised pineapples for Dr. Jackson, and for a long time we were the only black family on Riverside Drive."

Another indicator that African–Americans lived in all quarters of Jupiter comes from the diary of Elsie Dolby Jackson in 1916. She noted that "the southwestern portion of the [lighthouse] reservation has since been taken up mainly by colored people. Many of them have become quite successful farmers."

More leading ladies. From left, Mrs. Kitching, for whom the creek in the state park is named; Kate Armour Wells, the first child born to lighthouse parents, and then the wife of a keeper; Mrs. Robert (Elsie) Jackson with her two oldest children, Margaret and Howard; Mrs. Ann D. DuBois, in back wearing black hat; Mrs. Henry Pennock, holding daughter Shirley's hand; and Susan DuBois, wife of Harry. *(Loxahatchee River Historical Society)*

## JUPITER GETS A 'DOWNTOWN'

Dora Doster Utz, the little girl photographed standing on the Celestial Railroad engine (see p. 52) later described the row of buildings that led to her father's general store. Flagler's newly built railroad ran a short spur to the east on the south side of the Jupiter River so that paddle-wheelers and barges could pull up to the wharf and transfer cargo to freight cars. Dora, in a letter much later, recalls her girlhood living in an entire street of structures built to avoid floodwaters.

*Adjacent to the tracks on our left, built on pilings out over the swamp, was the little two-story hotel [called Jupiter Hotel and Wayside Inn at different times] and another one story frame building —a saloon. The stairway of the hotel was on the outside of the building. Its kitchen was around a boardwalk in the back and its outhouses further out on pilings over the swamp. One had to practically "walk the plank" to get to them. Once, when a tiny girl, I fell into the swamp from the outside stairway of the hotel and had to be fished from the morass of underbrush, logs, snakes and perhaps an alligator or two from a precarious footing of rolling logs. Perhaps the only thing that kept me from drowning was the fact that there was not enough open water in which to sink.*

*The hotel dining room was large and ran down one side of the structure, commanding a lovely view of the rivers. Dances and entertainments of various kinds were held in this large room. For instance, one Christmas a community celebration was held in this room. A large pine tree which touched the ceiling was erected and beautifully decorated with candles, strings of popcorn…and Chinese firecrackers. Quite a combination!*

Two more fixtures were the post office and Bowers Grocery. Ruby Bowers McGehee wrote in *The Loxahatchee Lament* that the store (and family home) was located on the south side of the river, east of the tracks. "The railroad had a switch-line that came in front of the store," she said. "When the engineer saw me he would blow his whistle and let me ride in the engine's cab. Most of the merchandise came in by boat. We had a dock in the rear of the store where I fished lying flat on my stomach."

By 1913, Jupiter had another commercial center—of sorts— when Aicher's Store opened on Dixie Highway just north of Center Street. Facing the railroad tracks, Aicher's offered sugar, flour, coffee, beans and pickles from a barrel.

One of Jupiter's "school boats." Tradition has it that the first one was a converted captain's yawl from the ill-fated battleship *Maine*—acquired perhaps through a military surplus sale. Charles Jackson manned the school boat for a few years beginning in 1904. After 1910 the job was handled by "Doc" Blanchard, who worked his way up and down the river from his home at the site of today's Boy Scout camp. *(Florida State Archives)*

## JUPITER'S FLOATING 'SCHOOL BUS'

Emily Carlin Turner, the youngest of the five Carlin children, recalled in a *Jupiter Courier* interview that the first "school" in Jupiter was for the children of the lighthouse crew, the Carlin House, the Western Union operator and the Broadwells, who ran a pharmacy where Shuey's would later build a motor court and cottages. Carlin House served as the school. "The teacher lived in our house and wasn't charged for room and board," she said.

In the mid–nineties the school switched to the front room of the Ziegler home just south of today's Alternate AIA Bridge. Then came the first "official" school, a one-room, yellow, octagon-shaped building scarcely large enough for a dozen children. Its primary teacher from Ziegler days (1895–96) to around 1910 was the multi-talented Dr. Charles P. Jackson, already the town physician and community Sunday school teacher.

What made going to school in Jupiter different is that most kids went by water. Somehow—it isn't clear—the community had obtained a thirty-foot "double-ender" that—it can't be confirmed—was supposed to have served as the captain's yawl on the legendary battleship *Maine*. Outfitted with benches and a wooden sunroof, the *Maine* made a splendid school "bus."

Around 1908 the school boat job went to "Doc" Blanchard, a widower with two school–age boys who lived way up the Loxahatchee where the Boy Scout camp is today. Each school day he'd wend his way down with one of his sons, picking up kids on both sides of the river. Boys would troll along the way and if they brought in a snook or jack, it usually found its way into a fish stew that Doc kept in his fireless cooker for lunch.

Once the last of the children had been collected from the lighthouse dock, the old yawl would cross the river and tie up at the railroad wharf near the post office. From there the kids would walk to the schoolhouse.

White and black children went to different schools, but they used the same school boat. Josephine Bostick remembered when her parents were resident caretakers of a home she referred to only as the "Hooley place" on today's Anchorage Point (actually the home owned by Edwin S. Hooley after he sold his prime land adjoining The Carlin House to William Sperry).

*Susan* [her sister] *and I attended the colored school not far from the old Hepburn place. Everyone traveled by boat in those days. Dr. Jackson ran the school boat that took the white children down to the school at the Ziegler house. We would wait on the dock for him and on the way back he would pick us up and take us to school. When school was over for the day he would pick us up again before he went back to Ziegler's for the rest of the children.*

The school boat often figured in several special community events as well. Bessie DuBois, writing in *The Jupiter Courier*, recalls the time when,

*…a local bachelor brought home a bride from Miami, the entire Jupiter population met them at the depot, The bride and groom were placed in the school boat, which was lighted with Japanese lanterns, and led a procession of motorboats to the home of the happy couple. In the bridegroom's absence, the ladies of the village had entirely refurnished the house.*

Another milestone in the school boat's life came in 1911 when William Sperry, the Carlins' winter neighbor, paid to send the entire student body on a two and a half hour ride to West Palm Beach to witness something they could scarcely believe. Arriving at a public park and lake on the Intracoastal, Bessie reports,

*They gazed in amazement at the contraption of wires, wings, ropes and pedals that was supposed to be able to fly. Finally, a man climbed into the open seat, the motor behind him began to roar, and he was off down the field. The children, carefully herded at a distance, watched open-mouthed as he circled the field at an altitude of from 500 to 1,000 feet. He was plainly visible to them at all times, staring down through his goggles.*

*After he landed lunch was served, and they embarked for the journey home. They little dreamed that this new airplane would become a common method of transportation while the old familiar school boat would become a relic of the past.*

## DOWN BY THE RIVERSIDE

Jupiter's first church was simply a "Community Sunday School." It had no building and no official minister. Sunday lessons for all ages were conducted by many townspeople, usually coordinated by the versatile Dr. Charles Jackson. Another example of this "grassroots Christianity" was the town's annual Christmas Eve celebration. Families would begin arriving in the early evening —many by boat. The center of their attention was a community tree, decorated with chains of popcorn and colored paper. At its foot were paper bags, each with the name of a Jupiter child. After conducting the Christmas Eve service, kids delved into their bags, which typically included hard candy, an orange or apple and a small toy.

Later when the schoolhouse was built, near the site of the (first) Town Hall, the second–floor auditorium was used for Sunday services and the annual community Christmas party. In 1913, as was already the tradition, Santa Claus climbed up a ladder and made his appearance through a second-story window while ringing bells and shouting encouragement to his reindeer. Henry Pennock played the role perfectly until he was handing out presents. Then his beard caught fire from a wall candle and all the children saw Santa go into a dance they would never forget.

Jupiter got its first "official" church in 1899 when St. Martin's Episcopal was built on the former Celestial Railroad terminus where the Suni Sands recreation hall now stands. Most of Jupiter's few families had Episcopalian backgrounds, and once they decided they wanted a church, they launched a fund-raising flurry of suppers, bake sales and plays. Once they had raised $400, a committee paid a call on Henry Flagler, who quickly agreed to match it.

As Harry Jackson, Charles Jackson's son, wrote in *The Loxahatchee Lament*,

*They bought lumber from the nearest sawmill and had it brought down by boat. A contractor from Palm Beach sent a man to supervise the building and everybody in town, whether Episcopalian or not, helped with the work. The inside was not plastered or even ceiled, and there was no need for a basement, so the building was completed in about a month. It was strong and well built with great beams of hard and durable yellow pine and a good roof over all.*

When the church's 25 members were conducting the dedication service, Henry Flagler arrived unnoticed and stood quietly in the back of the church. When he saw someone he knew—the Carlins' married daughter Susan Albertson—sitting just in front of him, he dropped a handful of coins in her lap and told her to give them to her mother for the church. Susan thanked him and put them in her purse, thinking they were nickels or quarters. After the service she looked inside and realized they were gold pieces.

The new church was inspiration enough for Charles Jackson to "graduate" from being a lay Sunday school leader to taking his holy

Jupiter's first "real" church building was St. Martin's Episcopal, built in 1899 near the river's edge where Suni Sands mobile home park is today. People put on plays to raise the money for materials. Sitting on steps is Mildred Carlin.
*(Town of Jupiter Archives / Carlin White Collection)*

Charles Jackson became the community's spiritual leader, in addition to farming a sizeable pineapple plantation.
*(Loxahatchee River Historical Society)*

# A Popular Pastime in Old Jupiter

Despite improvements in ship-to-shore communications, Jupiter saw many ships wreck on her reefs and many tortured hulks of other stricken ships bob along the Gulf Stream on their way to a final resting place on the ocean bottom. For years men fished off the rigging of the three-masted schooner *Martha Thomas* near the beach on Hobe Sound. Kids played in the wreckage of the *Melrose*, which finally stuck fast on a Jupiter Island beach after first becoming disabled off North Carolina. In 1917 Harry DuBois and his son John were rowing their skiff just south of the inlet and saw "the bottom of a ship" adrift in the waves. As Bessie DuBois would later write in her *Shipwrecks in the Vicinity of Jupiter Inlet,*

*All that remained of the upper part of the craft was the captain's cabin on the after part. They circled the wreck but could see no life aboard. They came up on the lee side, and Harry stayed in the skiff after bringing it up close enough to the wreck for John to scramble aboard. John carried a rope that was payed off and his father fended the skiff off the wreck with an oar.*

*The captain's cabin had evidently been hastily abandoned, for all his personal effects remained, including his razor. John, who had just reached the age to find this instrument useful, took it for his own use. He also salvaged the ship's bell from the roof of the cabin. The compass could be seen, set in gimbals, by the ship's wheel. He went down into the cabin. The wreck was moving and water came to his waist. He managed to find the sextant, taffrail log and sounding lead, also the ship's log, the captain's raincoat, a big straw hat, and a pair of very antiquated handcuffs. The ship's log gave the name of the vessel as the* Evadne; *she was of British registry and the master's name was Walters.* [Records showed it to be an old, barely seaworthy boat that the British navy had hired to haul lumber during World War I.]

*A day or so later the wreck washed up on the beach, and Harry and his son were able to salvage rope and plumbing fixtures. A hatch under the wheel disclosed a lazarette* [storage compartment] *holding a heavy storm sail bound with rope. It was the wettest, heaviest canvas they had ever seen. By this time other people had come to the wreck, among them an old sailor who with no ado chopped the sail out of the lazarette, cut off the rope, and spread the canvas out on the beach. When it was dry, he folded it up and took it home.*

Like yesterday's Thanksgiving turkey, the ship's carcass was picked apart for many inventive purposes. One man pried out several yellow metal spikes and forged them into andirons for his fireplace. Another retrieved a long hawser (tow line) and sold it for enough to go out on a "grand spree," as Bessie described it.

In 1963 some scuba divers raised the wheel of the *Evadne* among the rocks near Carlin Park. It marks the entrance today.

orders as an Episcopal priest. This was a huge decision, because Jackson was already town physician, pharmacist, schoolteacher, pineapple grower and sometime carpenter. And on Sundays he was counted on to pick up members of the congregation in the school boat. But from 1908 on, Reverend Jackson focused his energies on the church. In 1911 the Episcopal bishop reassigned him to open another new church in Coconut Grove.

In 1914 or so William Sperry, the S & H Green Stamp founder, bought all the land around the church area and St. Martin's was moved. It was taken through the woods and barged across the Loxahatchee to "West Jupiter," and relocated on the southeast corner of Town Hall and Florida avenues. But by then membership was declining, and those remaining decided to join the Union (community) Sunday School that was being held in the upstairs of the new school building.

With no permanent church, it's understandable that early Jupiter lacked a permanent graveyard as well. Before 1900 people who died were buried at home or out in the scrub pine. In 1901 volunteer citizens formed a Jupiter Cemetery Association and sold "shares" for $5 each to local families. Each share was entitled to one burial plot.

However, it wasn't until six years later that the association got around to buying a burial ground. On Nov. 11, 1907, the board voted to pay Dr. Charles Jackson (its secretary) $10 for a two and a half acre property on the North Fork of the Loxahatchee. It also authorized Dr. Jackson to buy enough material to build a forty-foot dock leading to the property. Herbert Young got the job of transporting coffins because he owned a scow for shipping vegetables to the railroad loading dock.

In 1912, when Capt. Charles Carlin died at age seventy, his family was the first to conduct a funeral with a horse-drawn hearse. The elegant black and brass cart was brought down by train, then pulled over sandy roads to the cemetery on Riverside Drive.

Perhaps one reason the cemetery wound up on the out-of-the-way North Fork was that just up from Anchorage Point lived a Captain Herring, a cabinetmaker who often got the job of building caskets.

## THE 'WILD WEST'

As the twentieth century began, anything more than a mile or so beyond the rough circle encompassing the lighthouse, inlet area, railroad and lower North Fork was seen as something akin to Outer Mongolia. That is, by those living in Jupiter. To those in the somewhat more urbane Palm Beach area, the area out around today's Riverbend Park and the cypress–canopied upper Loxahatchee was seen increasingly as a scenic spot for a vacation cabin and/or a chance to make extra money from fruit groves. In 1899 a sufficient number of well-connected Palm Beachers had interests there that the Dade County commissioners were prevailed upon to spend $425 to cut a road (actually a trail) from Jupiter to Indiantown on the edge of Lake Okeechobee. In 1909, when Palm Beach County was carved away from Dade, one the new government's first actions was to rename Orange Grove Road Indiantown Road and "pave" it with shellrock. A better wooden bridge was built over the Loxahatchee so that owners of groves could take their produce wagons back and forth.

Even farther out—a grueling dozen or so miles west of the inlet—was an area called Philo Farms where a few brave homesteaders were trying to force their often-swampy plots to yield up enough tomatoes, beans, onions and oranges to sustain a family. Today it's part of Jupiter Farms.

Edgar W. Philo had been vice president of the Jupiter Fruit Farms Company. In 1913 he acquired a chunk of his former employer's tract, platted it into neat rectangles, and began running ads in rural newspapers up north. New Jersey seems to have been his favorite target—and usually in winter—so that freezing farmers would read about the chance to reap rich, multi-crop harvests in a balmy clime with plenty of water.

Ah, yes, *plenty* of water. During a bitter cold winter in New Jersey, William Wilkerson was hunkered near his wood stove reading a newspaper when he saw an ad that read: *Buy a Chicken Farm in Florida!* He felt warmer already and immediately sent a money order for ten acres unseen. That spring he packed up 4,000 chickens in cages and took a steamer to Jacksonville with his wife and seven kids. After transferring the whole gaggle to a train, Wilkinson arrived in Jupiter and set out on horseback on the arduous ten-mile trek to Philo Farms.

And found all his land under water.

After sloshing over his new property, Wilkinson threw up his hands in disgust, clopped back to Jupiter on the same horse and bought some land near what is now Old Dixie and Toney Penna Drive. But feeding the chickens was soon costing more than the chickens sold for at market. Wilkinson let the chickens run wild and went to work for the Pennock Plantation fernery.

But he didn't forget that first purchase. One day Wilkinson hitched his horse to a wagon and rode out to Philo Farms to seek out Mr. Philo himself. On the bench beside him was a shotgun, which he intended to use if he didn't get a full refund for the flooded acres.

He got the refund.

One family that did try farming the boggy Philo Farms was the Roods. On Christmas day, 1914, Homer, Sophia and their seven children took a train from their native Ripon, Wis., down to Jupiter and stayed in the Wayside Inn. The next day they headed out to Philo Farms, where they'd bought a plot sight unseen, and started raising vegetables and sugar cane. Harlow Rood would recall how in 1917 he and his sister Bernice came

Sometime in 1898 the Carlin and DuBois families got together for a picnic at Will Joyner's beach cottage just inside the inlet. Above steps in black hat is Charles Carlin, with Harry DuBois to his left. Facing Harry below is his wife Susan. Others are unidentified. *(Loxahatchee River Historical Society)*

87

At one point in the early 1900s pineapple groves like this one this lined the Indian River and parts of today's Juno Beach. But after two severe freezes in a single year, growers threw up their arms en masse. *(Florida State Archives)*

down with malaria. "But Mother pulled us through it with good care, quinine and rye whiskey," he later wrote.

The Roods had a mill for squeezing cane into syrup, but cash was hard to come by in a family that would grow to eleven children. So Sophia Rood, in addition to all her other chores, became postmistress of the new Rood Post Office in Philo Farms. When the mail came in by rail to the main post office by Bowers Grocery, it was driven out to Rood's. Then Harlow Rood, in his Model T Ford, would drive it out to Indiantown. That lasted until 1919 when Mr. Rood accepted an offer to work at the fernery down at Pennock Plantation.

## THAT ELUSIVE 'STABLE' ECONOMY

The trouble with Jupiter was that aside from the yachtsmen and hotel guests who enjoyed it in winter, it was difficult, erratic, tenuous going for those who had to make a living year around. Jupiter, in short, had no economic base.

The inlet itself symbolized why settlers were always on edge and off balance. When the town's artery to the sea was blocked by sand and silt, the river would swell and stagnation would take its toll in terms of smell and mosquitoes. But when the inlet was open, spirits were brighter. In 1894 Juno's *Tropical Sun* newspaper noted,

*Jupiter Inlet is in the best shape it has been in years. Soundings by the Life Saving Crew show a depth of 9 feet on the outer bar and 7-1/2 feet on the inner bar. On up the river to the railroad wharf there is twenty feet for a long distance. The people of Jupiter feel proud of their inlet and well they should.*

Just what could happen when the inlet closed is this snapshot of

autumn, 1910, by Bessie DuBois.

*The fall rains were torrential and Jupiter experienced its worst flood. Storekeepers waited upon customers in bathing suits wading in water. Cows had to be led up to high ground to be milked. Boats, the only means of travel in those days, could not pass under the railroad bridge since the water came up to the bridge ties. The residents went down to the inlet with shovels and a mule and scoop. The water went out so fast they had to run for high ground to escape being washed out to sea. One resident said that every leaf bore a cargo of insects. If one so much as touched a worker the insects were upon him biting lustily. Five years later the inlet was closed again.*

John DuBois, who wouldn't marry Bessie until 14 years later, adds his own boyhood memories to the same event:

*About twenty of us with shovels dug a six-foot trench providing a five to six foot fall. Within two days the inlet was a half-mile wide. The water line dropped one foot an hour for the first couple of hours.*

*At that time the Loxahatchee drained from Delray to way back of Hobe Sound* [there was no Palm Beach inlet at the time]. *In normal times, before people started drainage projects, the river would frequently run high and with such force that it would hold back the incoming tide—maybe for two or three weeks at a time. All that water kept the river cleaned out real good.*

Things were still so primitive that "good times" could mean a week or two following a wreck. In 1909, for example, a fruit boat hit the reef near the abandoned lifesaving station and the waves tossed up so many oranges, mangoes and bananas that the local ladies tossed everything into a boiling iron pot and made enough preserves to last a year. On another occasion Bessie DuBois wrote of barrels of Pillsbury flour rolling along the shoreline. "The water formed a paste on the outside of the flour, but the flour inside was dry. The flour was used for many a loaf of homemade bread by the pioneer families who salvaged it."

"Industry" was tentative and usually exploitive. As the Celestial Railroad was being built, two steamboats, The *Rockledge* and the *Steadfast,* were anchored nearby to serve as rooming houses for the workers who streamed in from the north to lay the tracks. Once the railroad was running and the steamboats drew up to its wharf, they needed men to keep their furnaces stoked with cordwood. As John DuBois noted, "Fellows around here would cut and haul by oxen to the river bank, then the lighter wood to the railroad dock."

Later, many of the same men helped load and offload lumber headed for Henry Flagler's 1,200–room Royal Poinciana Hotel in Palm Beach. As Harry Jackson would recall many years later, "A small army of men" was kept at each of four points on the way to Palm Beach "where they worked night and day, seven days a week." But when the hotel was built, the task was over along with the Celestial Railroad.

When the Celestial died, Jupiter's most ambitious entrepreneur, Fred M. Cabot, won a contract to supply ties for Flagler's new wide-gauge line. Cabot's camp was two miles below the Jupiter River out in the flat pinewoods. The land around the planned Jupiter train depot was a large shell mound. Around 1893 he bought the land it was on, brought in crews and put up palmetto shacks as temporary homes. The gangs dug out the shell mounds and sent the shellrock in flatcars to Palm Beach and St. Augustine

for roadbed. Because he had construction crews and because the railroad passengers would one day need a way station while they waited for the next train, Cabot built himself a hotel along the tracks and called it Wayside Inn.

The energetic Cabot was into everything. In 1895 he got an Army Corps of Engineers contract to straighten Jupiter Narrows and in 1896 used the same equipment to unclog Jupiter Inlet. The same year Flagler paid him to deepen the Jupiter River south to Lake Worth. He had just built Jupiter's first concrete school building in 1906 when he was killed by a freight train speeding along the tracks he had worked so hard to make possible. His hotel had already burned down in 1902 and virtually none of his other creations remained in terms of providing his successors steady employment.

In 1910 the men of Jupiter found work for awhile when the Champion Bridge Co. of Wilmington, Ohio, got a county contract to build Jupiter's first bridge over the Loxahatchee. The 1,224–foot pedestrian and carriage causeway consisted of a concrete deck and draw-span costing $20,891.95. A newspaper story heralding its completion proclaimed, "The bridge is not only artistically beautiful but the permanency of its structure indicates it will be a joy forever."

The hurricane of 1926 blew it down like a Tinker Toy set.

When there weren't cutting-hauling-building projects to produce a flurry of cash, unemployed men would find other short-term ways to sustain themselves. Plumage plunder, for example. So that style-setting ladies could display the most colorful, exotic feathers in their bonnets at Easter parades, numbers of scruffy "hunters" plied their way through south Florida preying on egrets

The "Big House," west side view, taken from roof of A.L. Pennock's home (circa 1905).
*(Ramona Horne Pennock Stark Collection)*

Just a few yards away from the depot stood the Jupiter Hotel, post office and Bowers' store. Photo taken 1910–12. *(Loxahatchee River Historical Society)*

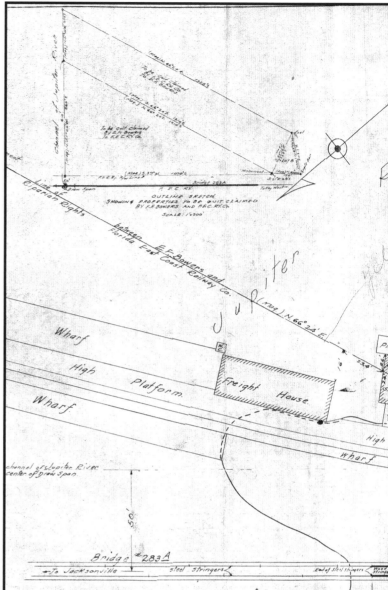

RIGHT: Identifying sites in turn-of-the-century Jupiter is difficult because many of them no longer exist. This 1913 architectural drawing was intended to show how the Florida East Coast Railway crossed the river paralleling Dixie Highway and how a spur (a half-mile down on the river's south side) was designed so that freight cars could be backed up to a wharf on the river and take cargo from barges at the dock. It was along this spur that the first semblance of a "town" formed. Straddling the tracks to the east—most of them built on pilings to escape flood damage—were a fish house, machine shop, hotel-saloon, two general stores and a boarding house. Along the main tracks stood a passenger station and a platform where mail could be placed on a large hook and snatched up if the train decided not to stop. *(Matthew Bressler Collection)*

Jupiter's first rail depot was located on a spur of Flagler's railroad that jutted into the river. Later it was moved to a spot east of Dixie Highway and Jupiter Beach road. *(Historical Society of Palm Beach County)*

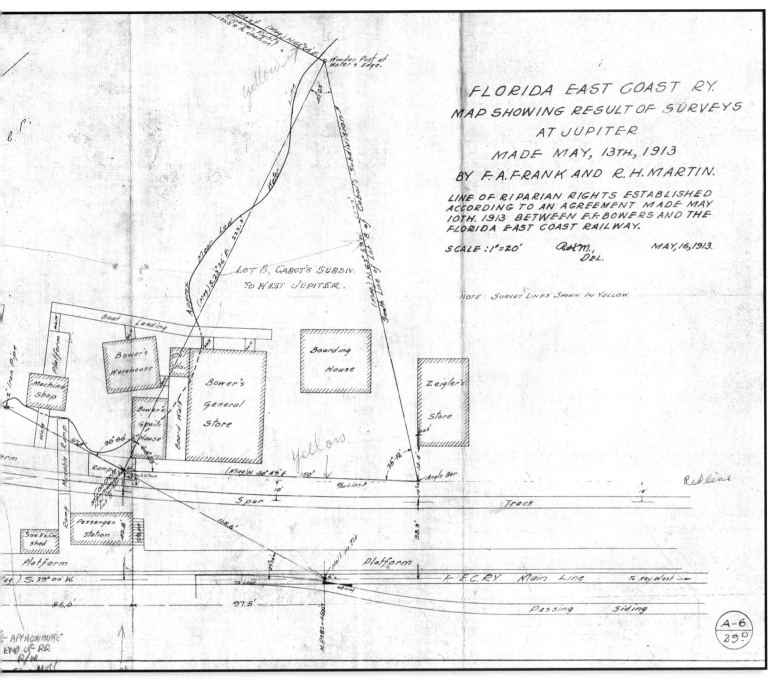

and whatever other birds they could kill for profit. As Mary Carlin noted in her recollections, "A man came down from Boston to kill egrets. He hired Indians and whites to get them for him, paying them low prices. But he told me he sold the feathers in Boston for seventy-five cents apiece. So you never see an egret these days."

One might say the same for tall pines and old cypress. Along about 1900 gangs of itinerant woodcutters began working their way through Florida, typically with five or so white foremen and twenty black workers. They'd set up a portable sawmill, cull out the best lumber in a region, then move on—all without employing a single local.

If anything sustained Jupiter day in and day out, it was of course fish—and the few tourists who came to find them. Jean Hepburn, whose parents settled in 1889, recalled for *The Jupiter Courier* that her father supported his family mostly by fishing— and mostly for pompano.

*Pompano in those days sold for $1 a pound and was shipped to New York markets in barrels packed with ice. When the Royal Poinciana* *Hotel opened in Palm Beach…some were sold there. The pompano abounded in the river then. Dad always fished out of a rowboat and always at night.*

Farming never seemed to get a firm foothold. Along the Indian River, John Grant, the former lifesaving crewman, "raised a beautiful crop of tomatoes and was sure he could make a killing," his daughter Ola May recalled. "Then the heavy rains came. He ended up with a field full of ketchup."

Over on the North Fork, the Young family couldn't always count on receiving cash even when their 66 acres of mixed vegetables brought a decent harvest. Many shipments were on a consignment-only basis. Sometimes, after the Youngs had packed up their produce and sent it north by train, "the commission agent [at the receiving depot] would refuse the shipment and throw away the produce," their daughter recalled. "Farming was and is a hard lot."

Might pineapples be the answer? Pineapple farming had been a success in the Florida Keys, but the plants soon exhausted their

In 1908, their Uncle Will gave Harry and Susan DuBois a ride in his new Cadillac.

*(Florida State Archives)*

shallow soils. By 1890 the industry had re-created itself with a "pineapple belt" that stretched from Miami to Fort Pierce. By 1910 there were more than 5,000 acres in production along the Indian River and the annual crop exceeded a million crates.

But even this briefly blooming business wasn't able to put down firm roots. Citrus growers were rocked by a big freeze in 1894. In 1917 a heavy freeze hit in February, followed by a killer blow in late fall. It happened just as Cuban growers were invading northern ports with pineapples shipped by boat at less than what it cost Floridians to send by rail. Almost at once, Jupiter's growers threw up their hands and quit.

What gradually built Jupiter's infrastructure was stability, diversity and outside capital. Stability, for example, came largely because Jupiter soon became an outpost for businesses that had already been established elsewhere and could afford to lose while they became established. Bowers Grocery was an example. Frank Bowers actually began with a trading post in Indiantown that he ran with his brother Joe. He swapped merchandise with the local Indians for hides and beautiful beadwork. And he must have been esteemed as an honest man because several Indian babies were named for him. He and his brother also bought orange groves near Indiantown and brought in the harvest to Jupiter to sell to locals and ship the rest up north on the Florida East Coast Railway.

Ruby Bowers McGehee, in *The Loxahatchee Lament,* recalled one of her fondest childhood memories: going to meet her Uncle Joe coming to Jupiter from Indiantown and riding with him on the covered wagon. "He used to come half way and camp for the night," she said. "Then Father [Frank] would take me half way to meet him for the ride back."

Another example was Lainhart and Potter. When Flagler was building his Royal Poinciana Hotel in Palm Beach, two of his carpenters proved so reliable that Flagler encouraged them to open their own building materials business. After George W. Lainhart and George W. Potter had proven their mettle in Palm Beach, they set up a lumber supply outpost in Jupiter. They also bought some groves along Indiantown Trail where its primitive wooden bridge crossed the Loxahatchee.

Already the area around today's Riverbend Park was known for producing first-rate fruit, some of it having won prizes at the 1893 World's Fair in Chicago. The first grove owner, it seems, was Augustus F. "Saw Grass" Miller, who bought land directly from the Internal Improvement Fund. He bought the property on the northern half of today's Riverbend Park and the land immediately to the west of the Loxahatchee just north of Indiantown Road. Scattered trees still remain from his groves.

In 1896 Miller sold it to Lainhart and Elisha N. Dimick, the first mayor of Palm Beach and a fishing buddy of Lainhart. Although they bought the land as a weekend getaway, they were also serious about its economic value. They established a packing house just south of Indiantown Road and managed the groves together until Dimick sold his share to Lainhart in 1913.

The Potters also owned nearby land during 1896–1919. Richard, a physician and brother of Lainhart's partner, bought what is roughly the southern half of today's Riverbend Park and immediately established citrus groves, bordering the Dimick/Lainhart groves on the north. By the end of World War I a roughly two-square-mile area—with the wooden Indiantown-Loxahatchee River bridge as its center—was already dotted with groves, packing houses, weekend homes for owners and cabins for workers.

Meanwhile, those who lived back in town gradually began to carve out sustainable specialties. In 1920 Harry DuBois discovered a good income from raising bees. Rex Albertson figured there was a future in the automobile, so he started a garage on the south side of the Loxahatchee between the railroad tracks and the old one-way Dixie Highway Bridge. One reason for the location is that he still had more business fixing boat engines than autos. But as cars took hold, he moved his shop to the corner of Center Street and Old Dixie. In time he employed 15 men in tire recapping, auto painting, engine work and towing.

The real survivor was *diversity* and it came in the form of Pennock Plantation, founded in 1898. Henry Pennock may have been no smarter than his neighbors, but he seemed to have more resources, more staying power and the ability to switch gears quickly once a particular enterprise went sour.

Henry Pennock came to Florida in 1895 seeking the best place to raise *asparagus plumosis*, the fern most commonly used in floral arrangements. His father was already the largest florist in Philadelphia, and Henry had degrees in civil and electrical engineering from Drexel University. He chose Jupiter as a worthy place to raise asparagus ferns, but his ambitions were greater than one crop.

In 1903 Pennock went "west" on Center Street to where the Jupiter Plantation townhouses are today. There he bought 29 acres on the river for $1,000. People snickered that the city slicker from Philadelphia had been fleeced but good.

In time, it would be the base of Pennock Plantation, which would expand to include a large Jersey cattle herd, several fern growing sheds, several crops, 17 windmills, a sawmill, an ice making plant, an electrical engineering plant and Jupiter's only telephone. More importantly, this diversified economic base—Jupiter's only claim to a large "industry"—quickly became the area's biggest employer. It was also a starting point for many young people to learn an array of job skills and save a nest-egg before buying their own farmland or starting a business.

In 1910, if you wanted to drive your new horseless carriage up Dixie Highway (then Route 1), this is what you'd be looking at. *(Historical Society of Palm Beach County)*

ABOVE: Not long after Henry Flagler built his railroad bridge over the river (see cross–ties at right), a one–lane span was built for carriages and pedestrians. It had a wide spot in the middle for those rare occasions when two horseless carriages would cross at the same time. *(Lynn Drake Collection)*

FAR RIGHT: A photo of the same bridge a few years later, looking in the other direction. *(Lynn Drake Collection)*

John DuBois casts his bait net in the late thirties. His home is now
DuBois Park on the inlet's south side. *(Loxahatchee River Historical Society)*

# CHAPTER 5

# 1920-1940: BOOM, NO. BUST, YES.

Folks in Jupiter got tired of the saying, "Mother Nature knows best." All they knew was that people, fish and fowl were healthier and happier when the inlet was open.

In 1921 a delegation from Jupiter prevailed on the state legislature to create a special taxing body, the Jupiter Inlet District. With funds from its first bond issue, the District hired Captain J.O. Webster, a Mainer lately of Miami, to dredge the inlet and install large granite blocks to make jetties on both sides. In the summer of 1922 Webster's tug *Salvor* arrived, soon followed by schooners loaded with granite slabs from his native state. In 1928 Webster strengthened the jetties with more Maine granite, all hauled in boatloads of 800 to 1,400 tons per voyage. The north jetty was extended about 200 feet and the south one by 75 feet.

In 1928 the jetties proved their worth when they held in the face of a fierce hurricane and kept the inlet open so that Loxahatchee floodwaters could drain into the ocean.

More dredging and jetty improvement continued during the thirties, but the three-man Inlet Commission constantly found itself fighting an uphill battle for funds. During several Depression years the Commission scarcely had enough money to pay interest on its bonds. Things would get worse when Martin County was formed and took with it the southern part of Hobe Sound. Even though two-thirds of the land drained by Jupiter Inlet is in Martin County, its taxpayers didn't want any part of the Inlet District. So the inlet again fell under control of shifting sands, and the story of the 1933 hurricane shows how Jupiter paid the price.

ABOVE: Jupiter Inlet gets its first dredging in 1922 as the crew of the *Salvor* arrives to begin unloading slabs of Maine granite for the north and south jetties. *(Florida State Archives)*

MIDDLE: Photo shows the first dredge beginning to cut through the sandbar. *(Jupiter Inlet District)*

BELOW: Two men inspect the newly built south jetty. *(Florida State Archives)*

## PROHIBITION: HOW DRY WE WEREN'T

In January 1919, when the Volstead Act officially closed America's saloons, Jupitarians suddenly found themselves with another short-term opportunity, much like laying tracks for the Celestial Railroad or shoveling shellrock into trucks to make roads. For this they could thank the Jupiter Inlet in the same way that Civil War blockade-runners did. It was sparsely populated and led to twisting waterways and coves where cases of booze could be stashed or off-loaded for rapid highway transport.

Vehicles ranged from trucks the size of moving vans—perhaps destined for Al Capone's speakeasies in Chicagoland—to a Jupiter cracker's old Model–A with enough room under his hollowed-out seats for a profitable run to Indiantown. Some had taken the trouble to install extra springs so that chasses wouldn't sag and alert the authorities.

The economics worked something like this: At West End, some fifty miles across the Bahamas Channel, a handful of well-connected English "merchants" maintained warehouses filled with imported beer, booze and wine. Rye whiskey, for example, would sell at their docks for $10 a case. "Importers" who survived the trip back through St. Lucie or Jupiter inlets could fetch $4 to $5 a bottle, or up to $60 per case.

Once the cases were stacked aboard a boat at West End, the skipper would immediately pluck the bottles from their wooden cases and re-pack them into burlap sacks of six quarts or twelve pints. They were nicknamed "hams" because that's how butchers wrapped smoked hams. It was easier to stuff them into all sorts of nooks and crannies of boats that had been designed, after all, for fishing or sightseeing.

Because none of the boats had been built for high-speed rumrunning, the typical crossing would take 15 hours. Along the way, the two-man crew would cook themselves a meal on a wood fire in a sawed–off oil drum. Their biggest fears were bad weather and government patrol boats. Last on their worry list were local citizens, who mostly saw Prohibition as a nuisance.

In case the authorities should actually materialize, the rumrunners were ready with some pre–James Bond diversions. For example, if a boat approached an inlet and encountered searchlights, it could heave its "hams" overboard to be lighter and faster for the chase that would surely follow. A loaded automobile might be equipped with a small tank of oil near the motor that would drain into the exhaust. When a policeman went around to the rear to have a closer look, the driver would step on the gas pedal,

Composed as if for a family photo album, an unknown arranger took the trouble to track down prison photos of the Ashley gang around 1921. With John Ashley at center as "King and Queen of the Everglades" is his long-time companion, Laura Upthegrove, who took her own life not long after his death. Might the photos have been hers? *(Florida State Archives)*

producing a hot blast of smoke in the face of the law as the car sped off.

When a cargo of hams was tossed overboard, the citizens of Jupiter would be out on the beach with a skill honed by decades of picking apart shipwrecks like Christmas turkeys. As Bessie DuBois reports,

*One winter night a cabin craft, well loaded, started to come in the inlet. A great swell sneaked up, rose to a terrifying height on the bar, and broke over the boat. As it capsized, the men jumped for their lives. Swimming desperately in the strong incoming tide, they watched incredulously as the loaded vessel righted itself with the motor still roaring, circled madly around them, then made a run through the breakers and hit the beach.*

The two "sailors" were taken in by a sympathetic family and given dry clothing. But by then people had spotted the flotilla of hams in the water. At daybreak the smugglers had put out another craft, patrolling just beyond the beach and gaffing hams where they could. But by then most of Jupiter had decided to take a brisk beach walk that morning and visit the now-marooned vessel from West End.

Again, Bessie:

*A tiny elderly Englishwoman, who kept house for a doctor who lived near the inlet, went over to the beach. Going down into the [shipwreck] cabin herself, she found a bottle of her favorite port wine, which she wrapped in her apron before hurrying home. Another visitor, a noted cook and fisherman with a built-in thirst, found a bottle of imported champagne. He displayed it to all, licking his lips in anticipation.*

Meanwhile, the authorities gamely persevered. Here's a smattering from the police blotter, recorded in *The History of Martin County*:

• Two males in a Chevrolet roadster fined $150 for smuggling eight sacks of whiskey, despite their claims that the intended use was personal—not resale.

• The search of a house in Hobe Sound yielding 300 bottles of "home brew" and nine gallons of moonshine.

• 28 barrels of mash and moonshine—and a 300-gallon still—destroyed in a "Christmas present" to the local Women's Christian Temperance Union.

• A raid producing two stills and several bottles of home brew near Stuart. A "Mrs. M," facing charges, swore she made the home brew solely for her own health.

The bigger fish were seldom surprised or inconvenienced. Down in Palm Beach, typical of the beneficiaries of the fleet arriving in Jupiter Inlet were Edward Riley Bradley and his popular, sophisticated Bradley's Beach Club. There, booze was a money-loser set up to attract gamblers, and it flowed like water. Whenever the local authorities conducted an official "raid" (more like a social call), Bradley's casino was prepared. It had been built by carpenters from Jupiter so that the walls would rotate—library shelves on one side, collapsible gaming tables on the other—just

# THE PERILS OF A BACKWOODS DOCTOR

In the early twenties the person living farthest upriver was Albert Daniel Blanchard. He captained the school boat, ran fishing charters, grew pineapples, dabbled at carpentry and was in constant demand—although reluctantly—as a doctor.

"Doc" Blanchard had a love-hate relationship with medicine, and the reason why offers a glimpse at the harsh reality of life in the wilds.

As a young man, Blanchard had been in his third year at Wooster (Ohio) Medical College when his father's death forced him to quit. However, twenty years later found him "unofficially" practicing medicine in rural Michigan Why? Probably because backwoods folks welcomed without questions anyone who could deliver babies and mend broken bones.

One of Doc's patients was a middle-aged, prosperous farmer named Cummings. He had recently married a very young lady named Grace when he died suddenly. The large Cummings clan was surprised to learn that one A.D. Blanchard had been named her guardian. And they were enraged a few weeks later when Grace, 28, said she was marrying her 52–year–old executor.

So ostracized was the new Blanchard family that they used the Cummings largesse to start another life as far away as they could get from Ohio—the untamed Loxahatchee River in Florida. About six miles west of Jupiter Inlet they bought a 150-acre patch of wilderness from lighthouse captain Joseph Wells. It came with a cabin and cookhouse that Wells had built as a family getaway.

The year was 1900 and by then the union had produced two boys, three-year-old Albert Dwight ("Bert") and two-year-old Merle. This handful, plus her starkly different surroundings, soon began eroding the constitution of Grace Cummings Blanchard. Doc tried raising pineapples, but making ends meet meant that he would often be away fishing, hunting or doctoring somebody in distress at a faraway farm. Sometimes Seminole Indians would just appear at the door for medical treatment, and they'd hang around until Doc came home. Meanwhile, Merle and Bert were growing quickly and discovering all sorts of ways to keep their mother on edge.

Soon Grace was rocked by unexplainable headaches. In summertime, when the bugs became unbearable, she was often too weak to manage a swat. None of Doc's remedies worked. Then Grace became pregnant and the headaches grew worse. She delivered a baby boy, Keith, but he soon died. Now the headaches brought crushing pain.

Beside himself with angst, Doc finally arranged for Grace to

Albert Daniel (Doc) Blanchard did his best to care for rich and poor alike along the Loxahatchee, but the wilderness and isolation soon overcame his more delicate wife, Grace.
*(F. Dwight Blanchard Collection)*

stay with friends in Juno. But on May 24, 1902, when Doc was gone, she slipped away. She was only thirty.

Doc always blamed himself. Had he given her the wrong medicine? Had he neglected a brain tumor? Had she deliberately taken an overdose to escape the pain?

Blanchard would continue to raise his boys upriver, but he vowed to give up medicine. He hired out as a carpenter, then ran the school boat when Charles Jackson became a full-time clergyman and moved to Homestead.

But Jackson had also been Jupiter's physician, and now Doc was *it* by default. People didn't care about some diploma on a wall. Doc was good *enough,* dammit, and they headed upstream whenever they had a crisis. Moreover, Doc was *absolutely* the last hope for poor black and Seminole families, who would walk for miles to see him.

One afternoon in 1922 a deranged young man staggered through Doc's front door waving a pistol. Blood oozed from his left shoulder and he demanded to be "patched up." With the gun constantly pointed at his head, Doc tweezed a bullet from the

wound and tightened a bandage around it. No sooner had the young man fled when Doc's door flew open again, revealing two sheriff's deputies. They announced that the Ashley Gang had robbed a bank that day and they had traced bloodstains all the way to Doc's. He told them what had happened—being held at gunpoint and all—but no matter. Off he went to jail for being an accessory to a crime.

Doc got a lawyer the next morning and walked out free. But ever afterwards he would insist that the cops had it in for him. They were sore, he said, because they felt he would treat "colored" and Indians for free, yet had to be coerced to see whites who were willing to pay.

In 1925 Albert Daniel Blanchard, alone in his Loxahatchee preserve, died at age 77. His grown sons would revisit the cabin for an occasional vacation, but over the years it just disintegrated. Today, the foundation of the old home is the center of the amphitheater at the Boy Scout camp. Doc's grandson, Francis Dwight Blanchard, was on hand in May 2003 to celebrate the camp's 50th anniversary.

One of the highlights of life in south Florida was the annual Sundance Festival and parade in West Palm Beach. Groups in Jupiter worked hard to compete for "best in parade" prizes, as shown by this entry in the 1922 Festival. *(Loxahatchee River Historical Society)*

like a set in a George Raft movie.

'Lest the rumrunning be viewed as some sort of gentile sport, one need only recall the calamitous Ashley Gang. The Ashley family hailed from the well-defended Corset Island in Hobe Sound, where they were further shielded by poor locals as modern Robin Hoods because they were liberal in helping families in need. The reason why it was wise to be in their favor is that John Ashley and his five brothers were good at taking other people's money and shooting those who objected.

In November 1916 ringleader John Ashley was sentenced to 18 years in Raiford Prison for bank robbery and manslaughter. Two years later he broke out and, sneaking back to Hobe Sound, decided that Prohibition offered more opportunities than bank robbing, especially because the family home on Corset Island in the middle of Hobe Sound was a smuggler's paradise.

At first the Ashleys were just one of many West End visitors, taking their chances with all the other smuggler boats. But in October 1921, a liquor-filled boat piloted by Ashley brothers Ed and Frank mysteriously disappeared at sea. Word got around that it had set off with an overloaded cargo worth $85,000. Soon afterwards, all too many fellow boatmen were seen in the bars of Jupiter and Stuart spending money, well, like drunken sailors.

John Ashley took a new tack, and from then on bootleggers feared his gang more than they did the revenuers. They would ply the waters just off Jupiter Inlet and board arriving bootlegger boats with drawn guns. If the captains didn't fork out a certain percentage of their take, they'd be scuttled with a blast through their hulls.

It was only after 1923, as the number of incoming boats began to wane, that the Ashleys went back to robbing banks. A year later, when they were camped around the family moonshine still a mile or so southwest of Corset Island, sheriff deputies surrounded them and let go with a thunder of bullets. John and some of the gang survived, but in the inferno the Ashleys killed sheriff Robert C.

Baker's cousin Fred and the posse shot down John Ashley's father Joe.

From then on it became a blood feud between the Bakers and the Ashleys. It came to a violent end on November 1, 1924 when Baker and his concealed sheriff's deputies lay in wait for a carload of Ashleys that was about to cross the Intracoastal in Sebastian. As driver John Ashley approached the bridge, he saw a rope across the right of way. When he slowed to a crawl, the five men inside found themselves surrounded by lawmen with drawn guns. Flushing their quarry out of the car, the officers were reaching for their handcuffs when suddenly John Ashley gave a signal and the others grabbed for handguns they'd hidden in hats and holsters. When the smoke cleared, all of the outlaws lay on the ground dead.

That, at least, was the official rendition. Later, word spread that the fugitives had been handcuffed and marched onto the bridge. There they were shot and dumped overboard. When the undertaker—who doubled as local coroner—examined the bodies, he reported that all had marks on their wrists, apparently made by handcuffs. The sheriff testified that the marks were caused during the undertaker's examination. A coroner's jury agreed.

Congress repealed Prohibition in 1933. But it had been null and void in Jupiter for many years.

## LITTLE BOOM, BIG BUST

Jupiter never experienced the euphoria that engulfed Miami and other large Florida cities in the real estate boom of the early twenties, but there were spurts of optimism that made a local's heart beat faster. Typical was the time when word spread that some big New York financiers were going to buy the old Sperry estate on the lower river and turn it into a high-class winter resort for Manhattan millionaires. Indeed, the story donned the mantle of truth when no less than the *Palm Beach Post* confirmed the rumors. On April 25, 1926, it reported that "Felix D. Doubleday, head of the international banking concern of Doubleday and Company," had bought the hundred acre estate "and will place the property on the market as Palm Beach Point, an exclusive residential park" of some five hundred home sites.

Mr. Doubleday assured the *Post* that "we intend to establish on Palm Beach Point a residential community which will appeal to those who enjoy life in all its phases but who like their homes set apart from too much activity [i.e. the Palm Beach social whirl]. We have neither that ambition nor the land to undertake a 'development' as the term is generally used in Florida" and "shall not offer any plot as a speculative possibility."

The problem was that the globally invested Doubleday was, in fact, dabbling in speculation in this quaint corner of the world. When the Big Crash came in 1929, Palm Beach Point was among the first "fringe" projects he flicked off his balance sheet.

## THE BIG BLASTS

One reason why Jupiter never fully felt the impact of the economic boom up north was that it was already too busy reeling from the impact of some hellish hurricanes. The year 1926 produced nine hurricanes in the South Atlantic, and Jupiter twice swayed to their tune. On July 27 what Nassau radio had called the most severe storm in twenty years slammed into Jupiter at ninety mph and swept away several boats and docks.

People had just raked up the debris when on September 18 more than 300 in Miami died after another hurricane hit from the south and began tearing its way straight north to Lake Okeechobee.

After heavy rains flooded its surrounding fields in 1924, a five–foot earthen dike had been built around the southern rim, stretching northwest almost to Moorehaven. The 1926 hurricane spun counterclockwise at 138 mph. Like coffee swirling in a giant cup, the water sloshed over the earthen rim and surged toward Moorehaven, which had no rim at all. Everything in its path was engulfed and more than 150 helpless field hands were swept away to their death.

Jupiter felt the spillover and the torrents that flowed down the Loxahatchee just when the inlet was precariously near closing again. Why so soon after the dredging of 1922? The Jupiter Inlet Commission lacked maintenance money following its first big splurge on dredging. Moreover, the first jetties weren't nearly the size of the big concrete barriers in place today. So, sand continued to move towards shore, as it had for thousands of years.

All this, however, was but an *aperitif* for what Jupiter experienced two years later. This one had already been named *San Felipe* as it thundered through Puerto Rico and left 200,000 homeless. It hit Palm Beach with a sledgehammer blow the night of September 16 and was soon pitting its strength against the buildings at Jupiter Lighthouse. A barometer reading at 7 p.m. showed 27.42 inches, nearly equaling the lowest on record in the U.S.

The tower began to swing and sway, causing mortar to squeeze out between many of the bricks. The lighthouse had already experienced a setback when in 1927 the assistant keeper's house had been set ablaze after someone left a bag of oily cotton rags in the kitchen after using them to clean the lens. Now the storm claimed another building—the frail old wooden Weather Bureau

*Continued, page 106*

Looking upriver from the lighthouse, probably 1925. Note the Navy's wireless transmission station in the foreground. *(Lynn Drake Collection)*

# HOW WE ALMOST BECAME 'PLUMOSUS CITY'

In 1929 the fernery growers out Pennock Plantation way had pretty much had it with taxes and tickets. The way they saw it, the town councilmen were spending too much tax money on "big city" amenities like schools, sewers and streets in hopes of cashing in on Florida's development boom. But what really galled them was the speed trap run by the state constable who patrolled the area. Since the constable got no pay other than a percentage of each traffic fine, he'd become quite proficient at nailing speeders and charging them a fee for escorting them to the courthouse in West Palm Beach.

Enough, said Henry Pennock, Jupiter's largest landowner. Vowing not to pay taxes to avaricious Jupiter, Pennock and 26 other growers along Center Street (west to Roebuck Road) met and indignantly incorporated a town named after the most popular fern in their bouquet. Plumosus City was run from the office at Pennock Plantation, and monthly meetings were held beginning July 25, 1929. The first mayor was A.R. Roebuck and his five aldermen were W. E. Gibson, Harry Pennock, Herb Pennock, J. H. Freeman and W. T. (Bill) Bogardus, Jr.

During the next two years, the Spartan city's budgets were topped by expenses such as $43.65 on a newspaper ad and $6.77 to re-file its incorporation papers. By the 1931 mayor-alderman election, 13 voters cast ballots. In the 1933 election no one voted.

Still, the phantom city continued on the official records in Tallahassee until 1959 when the legislature enacted a bill officially abolishing the "Town of Plumosus City." But no matter. The fernery business had long since been eclipsed by the Depression and an invasion of plastic greenery. Most of its land had been annexed by the Town of Jupiter anyway.

But even today, many of the deeds and plats for older homes in western Jupiter still list their location as Plumosus City.

Old greets new, 1927. Where the river swings south to become the Intracoastal Waterway, Sam Barfield kept an alligator farm and duck blind. It's almost as if that duck blind were straining on all four legs to see what was up with the bridge being built across Dixie Highway to replace the one blown down by the hurricane of 1926.
*(Loxahatchee River Historical Society)*

# HISTORICAL HIGHLIGHTS

| | |
|---|---|
| **1919** | Jan. 29. States ratify 18th Amendment, outlawing manufacture, sale or transport of "intoxicating liquors." |
| **1920** | League of Nations established in Geneva, Switzerland. |
| **1920** | First commercial radio broadcast. |
| **1921** | Jupiter Inlet District formed; first contract for dredging and jetties. |
| **1924** | Insecticides used for the first time on crops. |
| **1924** | John Ashley and the last of his Hobe Sound gang slain by Martin County posse. |
| **1925** | Town of Jupiter incorporates as municipality. |
| **1927** | May 21. Charles Lindbergh becomes first man to fly solo across the Atlantic. |
| **1928** | Jupiter's most devastating hurricane strikes on Sept. 16. |
| **1929** | Stocks reach all-time high in Sept., then crash next month on "Black Tuesday," triggering worldwide Depression. |
| **1933** | Franklin Delano Roosevelt inaugurated president. Ushers in "New Deal" era. |
| **1933** | 21st Amendment repeals Prohibition. |
| **1933** | Jupiter socked by another big hurricane. Serious flooding at a time when the inlet closed. |
| **1934** | Trapper Nelson establishes camp nine miles upriver. |
| **1935** | State census of "North [Palm Beach] County Area" lists Jupiter at pop. 242 (135 males and 107 females). |
| **1936** | President Roosevelt defeats Alf Landon to gain second term. |
| **1937** | Vince Nelson opens *Trapper Nelson's Zoo and Jungle Garden.* |
| **1938** | Pennock Plantation opens "state of the art" dairy plant near today's Indiantown and Maplewood roads. |
| **1939** | Germany invades Poland Sept. 4. France and Britain declare war on Germany. |
| **1939** | Secret Navy radio transmission unit at Jupiter Lighthouse begins monitoring of German U-boat activity in South Atlantic. |
| **1940** | France surrenders to Germany. |

station.

But the night's priority was keeping the beacon flashing, and here Captain Charles Seabrook faced two problems. The first was that the light had recently been converted from oil burners to electricity. When power lines began snapping, the light went out. The auxiliary generator failed to work. Seabrook just might be able to reinstall the old oil burners, but that would take time. His only immediate recourse was to push the heavy, cumbersome apparatus round and round by hand.

Problem number two was that the captain had been weak with blood poisoning from an infected right arm that was already red from his hand to his elbow.

The rest is a heroic story even if there do happen to be two contested versions. According to the Seabrook family, the captain's sixteen-year-old son, Franklin, saw his father's agony and stepped in himself. After thrice climbing to the top only to be blown back downstairs by the fierce gale, he clawed his way up once more and for the next four hours doggedly pushed the lens apparatus around the watchroom. At one point one of the expensive lens windows blew out, letting in even more wind and creating an eerie whistle.

And yet, the light shone all night; ships at sea stayed their courses and the Seabrooks were officially commended in the *Congressional Record* by Jupiter's representative, Ruth Bryan Owen.

But what about the two assistant keepers? One of them was Ralph Swanson, and his descendants insist there was no way two strong men in their mid–thirties would not stand side by side with the older Seabrook. Swanson's son Raymond says his father helped the captain reinstall the oil lamps and disengage the lens carriage from the electric motor, then—alone—rotated it by hand all night.

Either way, there seems to have been enough jeopardy for everyone to be heroically busy that savage night. Across the water, it was all people could do to scurry to any place that might be dry and secure. The first place most folks—black and white—headed was Jupiter School. It was one of the area's few concrete buildings and it provided welcome security to those who had seen their roofs lifted off and their foundations wrenched as much as ninety degrees off center. Power poles were uprooted and spun around, their electrical wires wrapped around them like strings of Christmas tree lights.

Miraculously, the hurricane seems to have caused no deaths in Jupiter. Then the survivors began hearing reports about the almost unbelievable disaster unfolding to the west along Indiantown Road. As usual for late summer, the waters inside the levied Lake Okeechobee were supposed to be somewhat higher than normal so that some could be drained off in an orderly manner during the drier months. In the three weeks just before the storm heavy rains had already added three feet to the lake's average depth. Now came the hurricane with another ten–plus inches in one evening.

Just beforehand, some people who had heard radio alerts had made gallant efforts to drive around the rim towns warning everyone within earshot. But the great majority of the population was black and poor with no radios, and with houses that sat out in the fields on dirt paths.

Everything was set for the earthen dike to break, and it did—in many places and nearly all at once. Within minutes the water

Down near Jupiter Inlet, the 1928 hurricane swept along the south side of the river, tearing the roof from the small store on John DuBois' dock and ruining all the merchandise inside.
*(Loxahatchee River Historical Society)*

depth in surrounding farms rose four to six feet above ground level. Houses, docks, people, farm animals and walls of dirt were swept off in all directions. It would be three days before the governor of Florida even learned about his state's worst-ever natural disaster.

The lake spill carried well into the groves west of Jupiter. A *Palm Beach Post* article described a rescue truck's hazardous journey from Jupiter trying to reach the Hull Groves, five miles west, with food and clothing "for approximately fifty hungry people held prisoners in torn and battered homes" by the uproarious Loxahatchee River. After fording a rushing creek on a wobbly bridge, the truck arrived at the Hull homestead to find it completely under water.

*From that point back into the interior, for how many miles no one knows, there is no dry land. Out from the practically impenetrable lake that stretches westward through the flat woods occasional farmers, wading for miles, are slowly making their way to the Hull Grove with strange tales and havoc wrought Tuesday night. None of them escaped damage. Few roofs remain on the dwellings. Food gave out. In some cases, houses and barns were swept off their foundations.*

Doris Wehage Ebert was seven at the time and still remembers painfully how severely the hurricane struck the family's hardscrabble potato and watermelon spread in Philo Farms. "You could move by rowboat or you could try your luck by taking a wagon on top of the dirt road that ran along the canals," she says. "By that time we had no dry clothes. My mother was in labor with Jerome. We put her in the rowboat with my little brother Albert and we pushed it along the canal. At one point my brother fell overboard and my Dad had to fish him out."

When a neighbor, George Gawan, saw the pitiful family pass by his property, he ran out and soon had them drying off in a room above his garage. He got a midwife just in time to deliver Jerome Wehage.

As she lay awake that night, Doris would recall the "good smell" of new lumber as her father hammered their new home together a few years before. She remembered her mother unwrapping home-made bread for their picnic lunch, topped off by warm, sweet "sinkers" made from leftover dough. Now it was just a memory. The home was too musty and mildewed for further habitation.

When the hurricane finally expired, the death toll was well over 2,000, ranking *San Felipe* one of the nation's worst natural disasters along with the Johnstown Flood. The number of bodies soon outgrew the available wood for coffins; so most were simply loaded like cordwood and burned or taken away to mass graves at Port Mayaca and West Palm Beach. Roy Rood remembers a gang of men trucking in from the lake area and practically dragooning Jupiter lads into joining them in a roundup of dead bodies. By that time rot and bloat had begun to take their toll. Roy Rood

*Continued, page 110*

The '28 hurricane raged upriver to Pennock Plantation where it ripped off another roof—that of the Pennock residence—and set it down neatly on the front yard.

The rearranged furniture of a room on the top floor. Above the wall, that's not a gray-painted ceiling, but the overcast sky as seen from inside the roofless second story. *(Raymond Swanson Collection)*

# JUPITER'S BYGONE LANDMARKS

Although the inlet remains a visible landmark linking the generations, much of Jupiter's terrain in the twenties and thirties has either vanished or been rearranged beyond recognition. For example, some of the mainstays most folks in town would have known at the time included:

**The Mackay Radio Station.** This commercially-owned shipping communications installation was built in 1927 at the intersection of today's Toney Penna Drive and Loxahatchee Drive. It consisted of a 50-by-100-foot cement transmission building topped by a corrugated asbestos-cement roof. Outside, a half-mile apart, were two 300-foot towers, anchored by thick metal guy wires. It was part of the Postal Telegraph System owned by Clarence Mackay, who happened to be songwriter Irving Berlin's father–in–law. Its purpose: to serve merchant ships sailing from New York to the tip of South America. It did its job so well that when World War II came, the station was commandeered by the Navy as a vital communications link to Allied merchant mariners in the Atlantic.

**Limestone Creek.** Before it was widened and deepened to accommodate the C-18 Canal, Limestone Creek was a shallow Loxahatchee tributary. "The water was so clean we drank it," Wilson Horne would recall from his boyhood. "The wooden bridge on Loxahatchee River Road was the neighborhood swimming hole. The water on the top four feet was warm, brown and fresh and floated atop three feet of cold salt water on the bottom. We would start our swim by everyone jumping off the bridge railing together to create a huge splash to scare away the always nearby alligators."

**Benton's Bridge.** Gone now, this two–lane wooden bridge (also called Fleming's Bridge) on Center Street crossed over a stub canal that ran from the river to Evernia Street on the east side of Loxahatchee Drive. The same canal is now a large culvert running under Loxahatchee Drive.

**The Section Houses.** Located along the Florida East Coast Railway tracks every 15 miles or so were up to ten one–story, yellow and white houses for the black section hands. In Jupiter, they were located just north of Indiantown Road about a hundred feet east of the tracks. Further up, just west of the tracks off Riverside Drive, was a two–story house occupied by a Mr. Chesser, tender of the railroad bridge that crossed the tracks at Riverside Drive.

**Histed's "Garden of the Gods."** Before Florida had its first tourist gardens or parrot jungle, the Histed family maintained a profusion of exotic plants and trees in a park–like, 15–acre plot west of Shuey's Inn and trailer park on the east side of Dixie Highway. Today it's mostly occupied by Jupiter Cove condominiums. "It wasn't a commercial venture," says Wilson Horne. "It was just a labor of love by the Histeds that sort of got out of hand. It was open to all who just wanted to come and enjoy it—and it was spectacular. But it was all bulldozed down later by developers."

**Brooker's Point.** Just off Center Street, from Town Hall Avenue west to Loxahatchee Drive was a large saw grass swamp (long since filled in). To the north it met the river and an oyster bed, forming a point that was handy for seining (netting) fish. William ("Mullet") Brooker, eldest of nine Brooker brothers, had a fishing shack there until the hurricane of 1933, when he was shot dead on the lighthouse grounds by a deranged youth. The spot was then occupied by M.H. Yohey just when seines (or weirs) were outlawed. Game wardens made Yohey's life miserable by paying surprise visits and dumping acid on his nets. Somewhere during the catharsis, Yohey became an avid evangelist, even building his own church. Mrs. Yohey kept the ministry afloat by working as janitor of Jupiter School.

**Bozeman's Welding.** They called him "Dadblame Bozeman" because he couldn't finish a sentence without using the word. Jim Bozeman and his family lived in a wooden house with cypress shingles that rose above a field of junk parts near today's Dixie Café on Old Dixie. Anytime someone needed a spare part, chances are he'd find it somewhere in the yard and weld it to whatever you wanted. But Mrs. Bozeman may have yearned for a real garden with a pretty white picket fence. It was said that she ran off with the iceman.

Out west in Philo Farms, Albert Wehage and his all-important mule plow the boggy turf around 1924. At left, four–year–old Doris Wehage (Ebert) plays in front of their newly built home with her two–year–old brother, Albert. The home would be flooded out by the 1928 hurricane. After starting over in a rented house, the Wehages again lost everything when the 1933 hurricane tipped the place on its side. *(Doris Wehage Ebert Collection)*

remembers his brother–in–law going west in one of those trucks and returning many hours later, bowed and ashen faced. He could barely speak of what he'd seen.

At each mass gravesite, steam shovels usually dug two trenches—one for whites, one for blacks. Just hours before, many of them had clung together to a branch or saved each other's children or clasped hands helping one another climb to higher ground.

## WHEN JUPITER NEEDED NOAH'S ARK

The storm that hit September 3, 1933 was one of 21 that swept across the Atlantic in a record year. After the usual snapping of utility poles, the eye of the hurricane passed over Jupiter Inlet for a calm forty minutes before the 125 mph winds returned. They dissipated inland soon enough, but that was just the problem. A tropical downpour hung over the area for days, ruining the citrus crop from Jupiter to Fort Pierce.

In Jupiter Susan and Rex Albertson lived in a little three-room house across from the original Town Hall. Their daughter Mary Albertson Ryan recalled the hurricane years later to the *Jupiter Courier*:

*The inlet was closed at the time. It rained so hard that the Loxahatchee River overflowed into the surrounding areas. The water was three to four feet deep in our yard. Mullet were swimming under and around the house.*

*Mama could both knit and throw a cast net. She cast the net under a nearby mango tree and caught some big mullets. Then she put them*

*in a No. 3 washtub filled with water. When I asked why, she replied, "Because your daddy would never believe me if I just told him about this."*

Wilson Horne was only five in 1933, but already trying to help his mother and five siblings run a twenty–acre farm after his dad left to join the Civilian Conservation Corps. "It rained for 18 hours," he recalls. "The water was lapping at the bottom of the railroad bridge which crosses the Loxahatchee River and into the front door of our one–room house. My Mom, three brothers, Kenneth, Jack and Neil; two sisters Ramona and Vera, were marooned. No neighbors, telephone, tractor, bicycle, car or boat."

The next morning Horne's Uncle Edwin [Raulerson] arrived by rowboat. "It wasn't big enough to fit everyone, so Uncle Edwin pulled the boat," wrote Horne. "I was amazed to see every fence post, wire, tree and bush loaded with billions of ants, roaches, lizards, snakes and an endless variety of insects."

And now, back to the Wehage saga.

After its 1928 disaster the family from Philo Farms had started all over on the edge of Jupiter in a rented frame house on Loxahatchee River Road. The hurricane of 1933 leaned hard against the little house and tipped it on a 45-degree angle. Doris was twelve by then and was helping her mother keep a spotless home. Suddenly, she remembers, "all the things on our shelves came tumbling down—all my mother's wedding cut-glass shattered."

This time the Wehage children were whisked to West Palm

Beach and deposited in a second story hotel room for safekeeping. They'd never been in any such place. "They left my brothers and me there and told us not to open the door," she says. "We screamed in panic. Finally we tried to crack the door open and the wind came rushing in so hard it blew out the back windows."

In the aftermath, Albert Wehage Sr. vowed to build a house no hurricane could take down. All the Wehage kids had tasks on the project, Doris recalling that her specialty was mixing concrete. The third Wehage house still stands on Loxahatchee River Road (albeit under different ownership).

## PENNOCK PLANTATION: AN OASIS OF STABILITY

High water or low, Jupiter increasingly came to rely on the steadily expanding, invariably profitable Pennock Plantation as a source of strength—a place one could brag about and where those in need could probably find some form of gainful employment. Judson Minear, whose father headed the dairy operation, remembers it like this in the twenties:

*The Pennocks owned most all the property from Sims Creek on the west all the way to the Railroad on the north side of Center Street, plus all of Pennock Point where Fort Jupiter stood.*

*South of the Plantation (now Jupiter Plantation), the property extended beyond Toney Penna Drive then west to include all of Section Eleven. It included all that lying from Pennock Lane east past the present apartments to nearly Douglas Drive. That acreage was fenced cow pasture. The ownership also included most of the land from*

LEFT: One of the large dairy barns at Pennock Plantation in the 1920s.

ABOVE: Seen partially at right is "The Old House," which Abraham Liddon Pennock II built in 1905 on the river off Center Street. It's still occupied by a Pennock today. The structure to the left of the original Pennock home was a large shed, since torn down.

BELOW: "Pete" Pennock, aged three, tries his hand at priming the pump. *(Ramona Horne Pennock Stark Collection)*

Indiantown Road south to Section Eleven where we now have Home Depot and all of Pennock Industrial Park. About where the entrance to the Industrial Park is today Mr. Pennock built three or four tenant houses for some of the black families employed by the Plantation. That settlement was known as "Bama" back then.

To the east where Pennock Lane crosses Indiantown Road (on the southeast corner) he built three tenant houses for white families. Also along the east side of Pennock Lane across the street from the Freeman property were four or five more tenant houses for white employees.

The heart of the Plantation, where most of the farm buildings sat, extended over fifty acres from Center Street to the river. Separate buildings housed pregnant cows, breeding bulls, an equipment repair shop and a shed just for brushing insects from livestock. Pennock was one of the first farms to use high voltage fly zappers. One building had a bottle washer and sterilizer. Inside another building was a huge, 10,000–gallon, wooden water tower, which captured all the rainwater from the roof. The same tower had a gravity pump that fed water to various cow watering ponds. The main residences had solar panels, making Pennock Plantation one of first enterprises in Florida to provide hot water.

Founder Henry Pennock died suddenly at age 53 in 1932. By that time he had established a fine–tuned business. Amos Bassett headed the nursery. Lloyd Minear managed the dairy while George Sweet headed cattle breeding operations.

The dairy was probably the steadiest profit producer. The Plantation's label, "Certified Milk," began selling in 1922 and enjoyed a thirty–year run, with deliveries from West Palm Beach to Fort Pierce in its heyday.

Judson Minear, whose father Lloyd managed the herd, writes in a memoir,

*Management of the dairy was anything but easy. In those early days before man learned how to control insects, many cows died when swarms of mosquitoes were known to actually suffocate the animals. Also, a major problem experienced was known as "Salt Sickness." With help from the University of Florida, the problem of proper salt and mineral balance was fully solved, but only after many cows died.*

*The isolation of South Florida made it fairly easy to remain free of tuberculosis and brucellosis, but insect-transported diseases were deadly and difficult to combat. Once a group of Seminoles with oxen camped on Plantation property, only to leave the ground infested with Texas Fever ticks. It took many months of dipping cows into large vats and spraying the infested ground before all the ticks were eradicated.*

*The biggest scourge of all was anaplasmosis, which destroyed the cow's red blood cells, caused abortions and depleted the immune system. With help from the University of Florida, we shot cows intravenously with several sodium derivatives for years until the antibiotic tetracycline came along and stopped the disease.*

The high point in the Plantation's life came in 1938 when, despite the Depression, it opened a new facility just southeast of

It wasn't as fancy as Carlin House, but John and Bessie DuBois' Jupiter Inn and Restaurant became a friendly gathering place in the 1930s. Both fishermen and diners tied up at its dock. *(Loxahatchee River Historical Society)*

today's Don Carter bowling lanes. "The new milking parlor was considered one of the most modern facilities of its day," recalled Judson Minear. "The same vacuum used to operate the milking machines also pulled the milk through a pipeline into the milk room where it was then cooled and run into a holding tank. Never being exposed to air assured its purity."

The glue for the whole Pennock operation was supplied by Harry P. Jackson, its chief financial officer for 33 years. Jackson was the grandnephew of the physician–preacher–farmer Charles P. Jackson, who had been the first of his clan to settle in Jupiter. Young Harry had come south from New Jersey in hopes that warm weather would cure a severe case of double pleurisy, and, like his great-uncle, he was captivated enough by the North Fork of the Loxahatchee to build a home there. Jackson must have been someone special, because he was quickly snatched up by Pennock to be its secretary–treasurer, and when he joined the Congregational Church he served as its chief layman for 28 years.

Pennock Plantation was also a black-white melting pot. In a typical year it had ten white and 25 black employees. Although each were housed in different corners of the property, blacks and whites worked side by side every day. After work they'd play baseball in the pasture at Pennock Point, using dried cow chips for bases. On the south side of Indiantown Road, about where Wal-

ABOVE: She didn't exactly own a business, but Rebecca Simmons worked as hard and long as anyone in town. Widowed in 1926 with seven children, she grew food for the family table on her sixty acres on Riverside Drive while also cooking and cleaning for the Carlins, Seabrooks, Roods and other Jupiter families. On Sundays Mrs. Simmons marched her children, all scrubbed and impeccably dressed, eight miles to their church by Limestone Creek. And she made sure they arrived that way. Simmons' children encountered the same grim determination when all were gathered inside the Jupiter School during the hurricane of 1928. Recalls daughter Idella, "Mother suddenly decided that we were going to ride out the storm in our own house. We didn't want to leave because they were just starting to hand out free sandwiches. But off we marched, walking all the way home through the howling wind."
*(Idella Simmons Harris Connaway Colleection)*

LEFT: Don Lainhart sells tomatoes from a truck on the family's groves along Indiantown Road.
*(Lainhart Family Collection)*

Mart stands today, was a cluster of black homes with Lettie Gaines' general store, which people of all colors found handy for bread, beer and cigarettes like convenience stores supply today.

## OTHER BUSINESSES GAIN A FOOTHOLD

Gradually, others started to find business niches that built stability for their families—many with skills learned at Pennock Plantation itself. No better example exists than the family of Homer Harlow Rood. After toughing it out in Philo Farms for a few years, the Wisconsin native landed a job at Pennock Plantation and soon moved his wife Sophia and their eleven children to a five–acre plot on County Line Road.

Eventually, it would become headquarters of the prosperous Rood Landscape Company, but that's getting ahead of the story.

In 1923 Homer Rood had learned enough and saved enough money from his job at Pennock to begin raising ferns on his own. In the same year he was struck dead in an auto accident on Center Street and Old Dixie. It might have destroyed Sophia as well, but instead she and the children began the slow climb back from hell. The house they'd moved into was still only half-completed, and the neighbors "were all a big help during our time of trouble," her son Harlow would recall. "Mr. Lainhart sold us the lumber at cost and Ben Holmes, a local carpenter, supervised the building."

Harlow, the eldest son, dropped out of school and found a cash paying job as a carpenter's apprentice in West Palm. But he also ran the family fernery and lightened his load by giving each sibling a specific task of weeding and watering. Soon afterward, thanks to a sympathetic postmistress, Ethel Sims, Harlow also landed the mail run contract from Jupiter to Indiantown—a full day's trip in a government Model–T Ford.

Sophia Rood went to work as a substitute teacher and held that post for over twenty years. Despite eleven mouths to feed and umpteen garments to wash and iron, she would walk—the family had no car—to Sunday school in the morning, to church service that night and to Wednesday night Bible study. Unable to pledge to the church, she served instead as its unpaid charwoman for over twenty years.

Other breadwinners discovered success for themselves. Harry DuBois, after years of seeking that one reliable cash crop with mixed success, found it in beehives. By 1920 he was overseeing 600 colonies of bees in a dozen locations from Deerfield Beach to Hobe Sound. DuBois' secret was in finding friends and other property owners who would agree to let him keep colonies of bees—ranging from fifty to a hundred—on an out–of–the–way corner of their land.

After collecting honey, Harry and his sons would pile the barrels on their dock until they had enough to barge up to the Jupiter railroad dock. They were then rolled into a boxcar, sent to Jacksonville and shipped by sea to New York. "They went on consignment," added John DuBois. "Sometimes six to eight months passed before Dad ever saw his money."

Meanwhile, Harry DuBois was fighting the onrush of pernicious anemia. No one knew how to control it at the time, and the head of Jupiter's second "founding family" passed away in 1924 at the age of 53—the same age that had spelled the end for his fellow pioneer, Henry Pennock.

Neil DuBois, Harry's second son, took over the bee business and would shortly expand it to 800 colonies. But he also added a business that sustained many Jupiter families for years. Planting about two acres of asparagus ferns on a place the family called "Banana Point," DuBois would harvest, mow the plants down, fertilize new beds and watch them grow back in three or four weeks. "Ferns were prepared for shipment in sprays," he explained. "Each bunch of fifty sprays was wrapped at the cut end with an old newspaper and soaked in water. Then they were packed in cases of about thirty bunches each. The thirty bunches were packed in fifty pounds of ice, half of which was chipped."

Out around today's Riverbend Park, Robert Handy Hull made a game stab at becoming a regional grower-baron. In 1919 he bought out what is now the Reese property (just east of Riverbend Park) as well as George Potter's groves in the same area. In 1925 Potter's lumber supply partner, George Lainhart, sold out to Hull as well. Thus, from 1925 until 1934 Hull owned all of the groves along the upper Loxahatchee east of today's Jupiter Farms.

But the story ends there. The Great Depression took its toll on Hull like everyone else. Actually, his "purchases" of the Reese and Lainhart properties had been installment sales, and in 1934 both families found themselves reluctantly repossessing their old groves.

## EKING OUT, MAKING DO

For the majority who didn't get a steady paycheck or find that special business niche, feeding a family by fishing or farming was a crapshoot in threadbare Jupiter. The trouble with trying to make a living fishing was that there were so many fish. You can feel the frustration in this account by Roy Brooker for the *Loxahatchee Lament*.

*We got 3 cents a pound for the fish we brought in. Finally one time we came in and the man* [at the wholesale dock] *said, "The price of fish has gone down. I'll pay you two cents a pound."*

*I told my brother: "If we're going to give them away, let's just give them away. We took what was in the scales and the rest of our catch and went to each family in Jupiter handing out fish. We had about 250 pounds that day. There were about 25 pounds left when we went to West Jupiter and gave those to Lettie Gaines.*

The small family farm faced so many obstacles one hardly could list them all. In the year 2000 Wilson Horne sat down at his typewriter and pecked out a few thousand words recalling a life that began "kicking and screaming" on December 12, 1928.

*Life was primitive on the farm. No radio, refrigeration, newspaper, magazines, electricity, car, store, doctor, dentist, neighbors, Spartan clothing and furniture.*

*We tried to live off the land with a cow, chickens and a garden. Our diet leaned towards poke greens, swamp cabbage, huckleberries, wooly berries, palmetto buds, rabbit, turtles, gopher tortoise, cornbread, fish and grits.*

*The mosquitoes, sand flies, deerflies and horseflies made our and the animal lives miserable. We made smoke smudges for the animals, but*

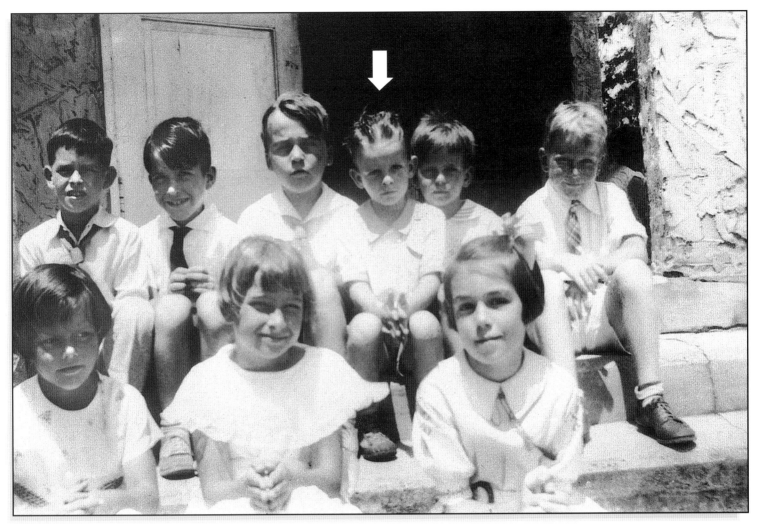

chickens would still fall off the roost, weak from loss of blood. Florida sores, boils, hook worm (ground itch) and ringworm were a constant source of misery. Rattlesnakes, cottonmouth moccasins, raccoons, opossums, skunks, owls and chicken hawks were a constant menace.

Due to our inadequate diet, most of us kids suffered from respiratory infections. We ended up having our tonsils out. I was around nine years old and for the first time, I had Cream of Wheat in the hospital and a woman gave me a whole pack of chewing gum—my first. Other than that, we did not go to the doctor. We either got better or we died. None of us died.

We killed every rattlesnake we saw to protect ourselves, the dog (one killed him) and the cow. We would cut off the rattles as a trophy and hang them on a string from the wall. One night my mother woke up to the rattle of a rattlesnake in the house. We knew that if you killed a rattler, his mate would seek him out. Mom's dilemma was she did not know exactly where the rattler was, so she was afraid to put her feet on the floor. She had no light and was afraid if she did nothing the snake would get one of the small children. With great trepidation she stood up in the bed and managed to light a kerosene lamp. There on the floor was a mouse with the string of rattles, eating them and creating the noise.

The Jupiter school was about a three-mile walk twice a day by way of dirt car ruts. Snakes, bugs and rain were a problem. On the way we passed an abandoned homestead that we called the "big mango trees" and an abandoned cemetery. A rutted road through the sand was nearby and we would pick the green turpentines and bury them in the hot sand to speed their ripening. Nearby was a big patch of

Wilson Horne says he has no photos of his childhood because "we were too poor to have a camera." But a shot of his Congregational Church Sunday School class captured this pensive eight-year-old in 1936 (top, third from right). *(Wilson Horne Collection)*

Ten-year-old Raymond Swanson, son of the assistant lighthouse keeper, spears a stingray in the shadow of the pier that served the reservation.
*(Raymond Swanson Collection)*

115

ABOVE: Jupiter School. Built in 1911 next to the original Town Hall, it housed grades one through eight. A windmill in the back provided power for indoor plumbing.
*(Florida State Archives)*

RIGHT: Some kids wore shoes to school, most didn't.
*(Florida State Archives)*

*huckleberries and wooly berries. Along with palmetto buds this was our after school snack. The big trees, by the way, are still standing in a yard east of South Loxahatchee Drive. They must be over a hundred years old.*

*After the flood [of 1933] Mom had enough. She moved us into a small Pennock [Plantation] house on Center Street that rented for $15 a month. It was built on a filled swamp of beach sand. Dogs slept under the house and caused a real flea problem. We were only a mile from the Loxahatchee River so us boys spent a lot of time on Brooker's Point gathering oysters, crabs and fish. This did not last. Dad was discharged from the CCC and back to the woods we went.*

*Dad tried farming on the twenty acres but lacked money, knowledge, fertilizer and just about everything else. I remember we saved the urine from the slop jars to sprinkle on the young plants to keep the rabbits from eating them. He leased my uncle Horace Raulerson's hammock farm and planted velvet beans. He made a beautiful crop, but these*

*were Depression years and he couldn't sell them for the price of picking. We kids harvested part of them and we ate them till they came out our ears and fed them to the chickens and cows.*

*Then he tried raising chickens on Horace's farm. Again, lack of funds, knowledge and bad luck with disease turned it into a money losing deal.*

*After this my Dad took on the job of janitor of Jupiter School, and we got to ride on the homemade bed of his 1928 Overland. For our lunch he kept peanut butter, bread and sometimes spiced luncheon loaf and our cow's milk, as he couldn't afford the 35 cents that the school cafeteria charged.*

*Around 1939 Dad received a World War I veteran's bonus, so he paid Amos Bassett Sr. $600 for a cottage on the corner of Indiantown Road and Loxahatchee Drive. It had been a two story but the top had blown off in the 1933 hurricane and it was patched up into a one story with one bath and one bedroom. So the eight of us moved in. Crowded*

When everyone knew everyone. Teenagers in 1926 pose with their "wheels." From left to right: unidentified, Ruth Rood, Hally Jackson, Ralph Brooker, unidentified, Beth Malcolm, seated Denison Van Vleck, seated in car Karla Bassett. *(Loxahatchee River Historical Society)*

*as we were, we thought it was great. Dad bought an electric pump from Sears so we could flush the toilet. And we had running water in the kitchen lean-to and the bathroom. We had 120 volt electricity, a kerosene stove, a Maytag wringer washing machine and for the next few years one of my jobs was building a fire under the #2 wash tub to heat water with wood to fill the washer and to fill the rinse tubs with cold water. There was no hot water heater or water softener, so we tried to catch as much rainwater as possible.*

Horne's boyhood was a blur of chores. Staking out the cows. Milking twice a day. Leading cows to good grass. Preparing their food. Building smudges in summer to smoke away the mosquitoes. Feeding chickens and ducks. Gathering their eggs. Cutting off chicken heads and scalding them with hot water to make feather plucking easier. Picking up manure and spreading it in the garden. Digging garbage holes and burning trash.

During summer vacations, it was work wherever one could. Horne weeded ferns for Henry DuBois at 25 cents an hour and dug sandspurs from the church yard at ten cents a bucket. He did odd jobs at Pennock Plantation, sold clovering salve and delivered the Miami *Herald*. He picked huckleberries, pried oysters loose and speared crabs—then sold them door to door. On some summer days Louis Freeman, Ray Bassett, Emanuel Yohey and Horne would walk over to the Woods' Bridge that led across to Jupiter Island. There they'd help the widowed Mrs. Woods crank the turning draw span across the Intracoastal. In between cranks, they'd scour the sandy scrub for turtle eggs, wild grapes, rose apples, mangos and "anything else in season we could bring home."

"It takes a lot of food to fill nine mouths," Horne wrote. "It's too bad that people can't realize this before they start reproducing like rabbits."

## TARZANS IN THE WILD

Louis, Ray, Emanuel, Wilson. In their spare time, they were also real-life Huck Finns or Tarzans, depending on the day. They swaggered about with homemade hunting knives in sheaths, some with ivory handles that Wilson's big brother Jack made from sea cow ribs on the Pennock Plantation grinding machine. One year, said Horne, the gang decided to create a secret clubhouse on the west side of a half-mile wide pond just south of today's Jupiter Medical Center. Its waters were clear and fresh. It had a sandy beach all around.

*We carried all of our building materials on wagons and bicycles. We pulled up a pitcher [water] pump on the old Miller house on A1A and drove it at our camp. We cleared the area for fire protection and planted trees. We dug boat slips for our little homemade tin boats, which we used to get across from A1A [Old Dixie Highway] after ditching our bicycles in the palmettos. This was all done in secret and remained so for years. The shack was three feet off the ground—because of flooding—with a trap door in the floor. This protected us from insects and varmints. We had a fire pit for cooking and a toilet.*

*We would take some flour, lard, salt, tea, sugar and milk and spend many days and nights boating, swimming and living off the land. We ate every animal that walked or flew except for snakes and skunks. Entertainment was going down to ponds and ditches that were drying up and chopping up the garfish and moccasins with machetes.*

When Louis Freeman and Gene Wehage were around twelve, they found a moonshine still up on Limestone Creek. "The runoff went into the creek," remembers Wehage. "We filled up a mayonnaise jar and brought it home to Louis' father. But we had a nip or two beforehand."

The Freemans and Wehages ate snook when tourists snubbed it as "trash fish." Today, when mullet still equals bait to most residents, Roy Rood still calls it his favorite fish. "Charlie Carlin, Ben Evans and I used to smoke them in an old refrigerator with the top cut out," he says. "We'd lay fish on the grilled shelves and light a fire in the bottom. Back then we didn't think we were eating so high on the hog."

Over on the lighthouse side of the river, the Seabrook kids and their friends would tie a rope to a bicycle, then ride the bike as fast as they could off the end of their dock. Then they'd pull hard on the rope and dredge up the bike. At night they'd coast the shoreline with a fire suspended from a frame on the bow of the boat. When a curious fish would follow along, the boys would spear it.

Shirley Floyd, one of the Pennock daughters, used to somersault into the river from the family dock. "We children also used washtubs for boats," she wrote later. "We'd take them out on the river and they'd maneuver surprisingly well. Across the river the Girl Scouts had a camp at Anchorage Point, where the swimming was great. Sometimes we'd hang onto a rope and let a motorboat tow us real fast. No water skis—just hanging from a rope."

For sheer ingenuity one might nominate Raymond Swanson and Harry DuBois for their homemade "diving suit." The boys

A growing fruit business along the upper Loxahatchee didn't stop the Lainharts from fishing on a leisurely Sunday afternoon. Here, Donald Lainhart and his father George W. try their luck from a fallen log on the river while a family friend, identified only as Mrs. Koenig, suns herself.
*(Lainhart Family Collection)*

found an old hot water heater and sawed the top off. Then they carved a window into it and connected it to a garden hose and bicycle pump. "With sixty pounds of lead weight attached, it was kind of hard to keep your balance," said Swanson, "but you could walk around for about a half hour, as long as the guy on the other end kept pumping, until the water eventually seeped up to your nose. It didn't smell too good inside, but it worked fine."

When the rest of the south was segregated, Jupitarians didn't quite fit the mold. True, one wouldn't find African–Americans owning car dealerships or attending dances at the Women's Club, but whites and blacks intermingled daily because they lived alongside each other. Yes, this was mostly because blacks worked as farm hands and/or domestic helpers, but the nature of their jobs put them close to each other and meant that their kids played

together as well. Typical was the Simmons family with their sixty-acre homestead on Riverside Drive. Idella Simmons Harris Connaway notes that when her mother Rebecca worked at the lighthouse for the Seabrook family, "I'd spend my days there. We'd race up the lighthouse steps barefoot—always careful never to touch anything when we got up there. Then we'd fish all afternoon. I can even remember hiding under the dock when my mother would call me to come home for dinner."

The Simmons saw a lot of the Roods, who lived nearby on County Line Road—perhaps because Rebecca was a widow with seven children and Sophia Rood a widow with eleven. Rebecca was always helping Sophia, which meant having to police the rambunctious Roy (who would one day found Rood Landscape Co.). One day, it seems, "Buster" (as he was known then) climbed

up a tree and defied Mrs. Simmons' orders to come down and tend to his chores.

"Buster, you come down here right now!" she ordered.

Buster sassed her back.

"Oh yeah?" said Mrs. Simmons. She grabbed an ax and started whacking at the trunk. Buster Rood felt his tree start to wobble and quickly shinnied down.

The same Mrs. Simmons would dress up her children each day and walk them the eight miles from their place on Riverside Drive all the way to the dirt-floored Rosenwald School that fronted Limestone Creek Road. After one day off on Saturday, she'd get up on Sunday morning, dress her children in even more formal finery and walk them that same eight miles to the Mt. Carmel church on Limestone Creek Road.

ABOVE: On Center Street, just west of the railroad tracks, a new "commercial center" evolved in the 1920s. At left, Albertson's Garage and, a little beyond it, the grocery store run by Henry and Elma Aicher. *(Ramona Horne Pennock Stark Collection)*

RIGHT: The Women's Club, Jupiter's only claim to avant-garde architecture, soon became the town's center for dances, bridge parties and other social events. It stood at Orange and Evernia streets, a block off Old Dixie and just behind today's Lainhart and Potter store. *(Loxahatchee River Historical Society)*

## FINALLY, A 'REAL' TOWN

After decades when education was handed up from the Carlin and Ziegler houses and the strange little "Octagon" school, Jupiter finally had a "real" school with a front door, principal's office, classrooms, lunchroom and—that icon of any learning institution —a janitor. A windmill provided power for indoor plumbing. But Jupiter parents still bristled at the fact that when their charges reached high school age, they faced a grueling two–way trip to West Palm Beach five days a week.

Thus, in 1927, one of the first milestone achievements of the young municipality was spending $150,000 to build a new Jupiter School. The new institution would serve all grades through high school—even if some of the age groups were so small that several "classes" had to meet together and share one teacher.

Mildred Carlin Shepherd, the oldest daughter of Charles and Addie Carlin, recalled being given the job of "driving the so–called school bus. It wasn't a real school bus; it was an old truck," she said. "But it served the purpose."

Mildred was also a dancer, and "we taught the boys in school how to dance, too. In fact, we even taught the principal, for he didn't know the first thing about it. We used to enjoy commuting

to the dances held down in the West Palm Beach school. Then, when the Jupiter Women's Club was built, we didn't have to go so far to trip the light fantastic."

In fact, the Women's Club would soon eclipse Carlin House and the school as the center of community culture, be it plays, dances or speakers on the Chautauqua circuit. Built in a garish combination of what one might dub "Moorish-Alamo" the building just off Dixie Highway resembled a CCC project gone amok. But no one seemed to remember the Alamo and all were grateful for a meeting place with a spacious ballroom and a volunteer staff of enthusiastic ladies.

Another proud women's achievement was the founding of a Girl Scout camp on the North Fork of the Loxahatchee. Originally called "Camp Schaum–A–Hatchee," it was located on three acres donated by Otto W. Schaum, a Philadelphia philanthropist who actually let the girls use all of his several hundred acres for hiking and nature study.

During the early years, however, the Girl Scouts often had to share their preserve at night. As Claudet Benton recalled in her history of the camp, "the river shore was shared unwillingly with a

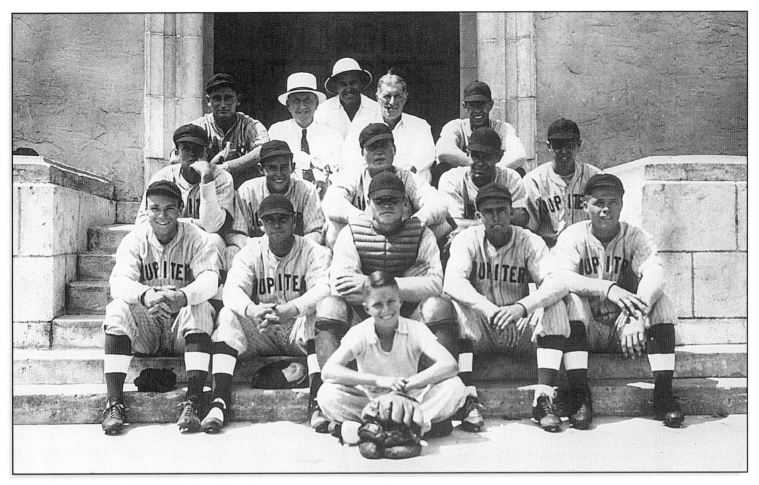

When Jupiter's semi-pro team played at home, scarcely a store remained open. In 1936-37, the team consisted of (first row) Dennison Van Vleck, Ben Penny, Ernie Histed, Roy Brooker, Roy Rood and batboy George Brooker. Middle row: Ralph Brooker, Jerome Hightower, Charlie Ridenour, Pete Pennock and Joe Floyd. Third row: Coach Mike Brindle, team sponsors Goerge Bingham and Bob Wilson, William T. Bogardus and son Bill Bogardus Jr. *(Rood Family Collection)*

bootleg ring. The men would deposit their forbidden booty there to be later collected by some amiable confederates in a large Packard automobile from which the seats had been removed. The bootleggers didn't mind sharing the camp with the girls—they simply explained that 'Our hours are different.'"

The first Girl Scout camp came to an abrupt end in 1928 when the hurricane tore its buildings apart like matchsticks. A guardian angel, however, soon appeared in the form of Mrs. Margery Durant Daniel, a New York-Palm Beach socialite who had a long-time interest in Girl Scouting. Thanks to Daniel, a new $10,000 building for fifty girls rose on the same site, and, understandably, the camp got a new name: Camp Margery Daniel.

Mostly the camp served girls from West Palm Beach—but not all of them. On one occasion a colored scout troop arrived at the camp and were turned away because "rules are rules." Somehow, word of two-dozen disappointed girls reached the ears of Rebecca Simmons, whose sixty-acre homestead was nearby on Riverside Drive. "Buster" Rood and his family heard about it, too, and today, Mrs. Simmon's eighty-year-old daughter Idella remembers that the Rood boys suddenly descended on her property, using axes and mowers to clear a patch suitable for camping. "The girl scouts pitched their tents and we all had a grand time," says Idella. "And we never forgot Buster Rood's kindness."

## HELPFUL HOLES IN THE OUTFIELD

For hours on end, boys would drop their Huck Finn mantles and become Babe Ruths. "Jupiter was a real baseball town," said Roy Brooker whose family of nine kids could have fielded a team all by itself. "Our high school baseball and basketball teams played to a packed crowd. The two grocery stores in town closed when the baseball team played a home game. Most of the enthusiasm was due to Mr. Henry Pennock, who had four boys himself. He always saw to it that kids had bats and balls and a field to play on."

When West Palm Beach High came to town, upwards of 200 people would show up at the field behind the Town Hall. "I remember how West Palm Beach used to complain about coming here," added Brooker. "They alleged we had gopher holes in our outfield, but we insisted on home games here."

## STEPPING OUT

A special treat was splurging on a trip to West Palm Beach, which had four movie houses and whose retail stores offered eye–popping window displays. Wilson Horne's older brother, Jack, drove a the Pennock Plantation milk truck every afternoon to the Alfar Creamery in West Palm, and when he'd make his Saturday run, Wilson and his buddies would pile in and head for the big city. Mostly they'd see a movie, but they'd always try to hit the new Montgomery Ward store. "Jupiter had no air conditioning," said Horne, "so it was a big thrill just to walk around Montgomery Ward and feel cool." Afterwards, they'd take the Florida Motor Line bus back to Shuey's Inn (fare: 55 cents), then walk the two miles home.

## TRAPPER NELSON: JUPITER'S OWN TARZAN

During the thirties hundreds of hobos wound their way through Florida in freight cars, jumping off wherever gossip promised a day job, a slot in a migrant work gang or maybe just a quiet beach where a fellow could rest and clean up a bit before the next train whistled. The few who found hope in tiny Jupiter would wait until the train began a crawl south across the river, stopping at the small depot along Old Dixie long enough to snatch the mailbag or pick up a load of lumber for Miami. Most would probably stop at Bowers' store for smokes or sundries, then gravitate towards Jupiter Beach.

One of them was a 23–year–old from New Jersey. He was different from the others because he fell in love with the Loxahatchee at first sight and would spend the better part of the next 37 years building a unique homestead.

Vincent Natulkiewicz was born in Trenton in 1908 to parents who probably had been smuggled into the United States from war-ravished Vilna, Poland, just a few years before. One of five children, young Vince had been a bright student, but his formal education stopped after the eighth grade when his mother died and his father remarried—all too quickly for him, apparently. Vince and his brother Charlie—older by eight years—soon found many excuses to stay away from home. Usually it was living in the woods, which led to hunting and trapping. And when the state offered a bounty on muskrat hides, the brothers found they could actually make money in the fur business.

The "Wild West" offered many more challenges to a budding trapper, so before long Charlie and Vince were riding the rails through Colorado, Oregon, Arizona and Texas. They'd play in boxcar poker games for cash, learn to walk atop a speeding train and how to roll off a slow-moving train when they fancied a good spot for trapping.

In September 1931, it was well before Florida's hobo season, but Charlie and Vince had already seen the leaves turning in Trenton and were eager to test their traps in the tropics. This time they took with them John Dykas, a boyhood chum of Vince's who had lived next door. They'd figured on maybe riding all the way to the Keys, but when they crossed the Loxahatchee and saw the picture postcard scene with the blue water, lighthouse and mullet jumping all about, they jumped off at the depot without a second thought.

For three months they lived in a lean-to down at today's Carlin Park, not far from the pavilion the town had built for public picnics. Elsewhere, the hammock behind the dune line was wild. Beachgoers would recall seeing skins hung out to dry all along the shelter, and every week or so the trappers would bundle up their hides and take them to the depot for shipment to waiting wholesalers in New York. Otter, fox and other furs were all the rage in women's wear, and the pay was good.

All was well financially, but not socially. Charlie Nelson—the brothers had adopted a new name because everyone garbled *Natulkiewicz*—thought Dykas was a lousy trapper. He was irritated that the two younger men kept taking sides against him, even insisting that young Dykas keep their money. Here Charlie was, eight years older. Hadn't he practically raised Vince? Saved his hide out West more times than he could count? Now this interloper was coming between two brothers.

One morning when Vince was out checking his trap line, Dykas was stirring some eggs in a skillet over a campfire. Charlie came out of the lean-to and told Dykas he'd decided to strike out on his own. He wanted his share—$75—from the pot and the old jalopy they'd bought with their first sale money. When Dykas didn't even answer, Charlie got steamed. He said he blow the kid's head off in 15 minutes if he didn't get his money.

Vince had told his friend never to "get into it" with Charlie, who had a bossy streak to begin with. Maybe Dykas thought Vince would come back and resolve the whole matter. But he didn't. And when 15 minutes passed, Charlie picked up his shotgun and without another word pulled the trigger at point-blank range. Then he calmly put the gun in the car, drove to the West Palm police station and matter-of-factly announced that he'd just killed a man over in Jupiter.

The trial of Charles Nelson in February 1932 had been big news from Trenton to Palm Beach. In the weeks before, *nonchalance* was Charlie's credo as he tantalized newsmen as to whether he would or wouldn't plead guilty. He did plead not guilty, but on the last day he broke down sobbing, admitting that he had killed the man who had come between two brothers. This, after Vince calmly testified that Dykas had in fact been a hard worker and honest treasurer.

Charlie Nelson was sentenced to life in Raiford prison, and as he was being led away, he pointed at Vince and Judge Curtis Chillingworth, threatening to escape and kill them both.

Vince Nelson found himself alone and broke. He tried trapping by himself on the wild other side of the inlet where Jupiter Inlet Colony would sprout thirty years later, but by 1933 he was back in New Jersey working in a thousand–head dairy farm.

Sometime in 1934 Nelson took the train back to Jupiter. This time he'd saved up enough to set up a homestead. He was six foot two, a well-chiseled 220 pounds, and he feared no one. He bought a large heavy rowboat, stocked up on tools and nails, and rowed nine miles upstream. When he rounded a bend and came upon the foundation of a long–collapsed hunter's cabin, he went to work.

Each morning around five Vince Nelson would rise and set his trap lines. Later on, he'd chop a cord of wood. Then it would be time to build: a hundred–foot dock, boathouse, cabin, large chickee hut and a water tower that fed an irrigation network of underground pipes. He needed the pipes because he had planted a grove to last a lifetime: guava, Surinam cherry, bamboo, Java plum, key lime, orange, grapefruit—with rings of pineapple plants at their base.

Once a week Nelson would row that heavy boat into town for supplies. Tarzan movies were all the rage at the Lyric Theater in Stuart, and when this tanned Adonis would emerge from his boat at DuBois' fish camp, people would start getting the connection. He was now called "Trapper Nelson" by most, and he played the part. Usually he'd be wearing a pirate's bandana, no shirt, skimpy shorts with a hunting knife in the belt and big hunting boots. By the time he'd polished off a box of candy bars and a quart of Neil DuBois' honey, girls would be standing on their front porches to watch him walk to the post office. "Kids and dogs would follow

Vince "Trapper" Nelson
in his mid-thirties—the
prime of his unique life
and a time when Tarzan
movies were all the rage.
*(Richard Little Collection)*

ABOVE: Once Vince Nelson opened *Trapper Nelson's Zoo and Jungle Garden* in the late thirties, his photos (like his talks to visitors) took on a more theatrical tone. *(Celmer Family Collection / Jonathan Dickinson State Park)*

LEFT: Trapper Nelson in perhaps the earliest photo on record (1935) of his first surroundings some nine miles upriver. His first cabin had to be burned down because it hadn't been built on concrete and bugs quickly took over. Note the Tarzan-like waistcloth. *(JoJo Hicks)*

behind like he was some kind of Polish pied piper," was how one wag would put it.

Before long people would wonder what Trapper Nelson was doing up there on the river. There was no other entertainment in town, so boats of picnickers would begin appearing at his dock, asking if he wouldn't mind they tied up long enough to eat lunch…and maybe walk around a little. Trapper was always cordial. By now his appetite was legendary and people had learned that bringing an extra sandwich—or three—could make him downright gabby.

Soon tourists who usually chartered boats for deep sea fishing were instead asking captains to take them up to this trapper fellow's place so they, too, could see for themselves. One day Vince Nelson put two and two together, and before long a large sign appeared on his water tower: *Trapper Nelson's Zoo and Jungle Garden.* A parking lot was hewed out behind his cabin and signs listed admission at a quarter for kids and fifty cents for adults. At dockside he had racks of plants for sale, and just behind were cages full of alligators, otters, foxes, wildcats and skunks de-scented by Dr. Trapper himself. The breathtaking main attraction was a barrel of rattlesnakes, collected mostly by paying teenagers a dollar a foot if they caught one.

As the thirties drew to a close, Trapper Nelson was already becoming famous well beyond Jupiter. Wealthy families from Palm Beach and the Jupiter Island Club would boat their houseguests upstream and the result was a "multiplier effect" in terms of word-of-mouth publicity. As Jupiter Island's Nathaniel Reed explained it: "Our home had five bedrooms and they were always full of guests when I was growing up. These people didn't fly in for the weekend like they do today. They would arrive with trunks and stay for two or three weeks.

"As a result, my father developed a sort of routine for keeping them entertained. One morning each week we'd go fishing in the wide part of the river, then stop at a clearing above Kitching Creek where we'd grill the catch. After lunch came the highlight of the day. To these people from up north, this was already an exotic experience like they'd always imagined the Amazon to be. But now we'd twist along the river, round a bend, and there would be Tarzan himself standing on his dock with a big Indigo snake draped around him!"

Others had similar entourages of guests, and it's no exaggeration to say that when those visitors returned to their homes in New York or London or Paris, they would regale dinner guests with tales about their exotic Tarzan. Indeed, Vince Nelson had become Jupiter's first and only celebrity.

And he was well on his way to acquiring more riverfront property. County law allowed anyone to bid on a parcel if its owner had failed to pay taxes on it for five years. Trapper watched the property tax rolls like an osprey eyeing a school of mullet. One can get a glimpse of how this Polish peasant's son used his saved up quarters and fifty–cent admission fees from a postcard (below) the author found in Trapper's scrapbook. It's addressed to Vince Nelson from the clerk of Martin County, and was answering his query as to how much he had to bid on two forty-acre parcels on the river.

In other words, the land was valued at an average of $9.37 an acre in 1932. Trapper got it for $2.34 an acre.

*(Celmer Family Collection / Jonathan Dickinson State Park)*

Jupiter Beach Bridge

Jupiter Beach Bridge led across the estuary that begins in today's DuBois Park. Below, someone has penned in vistas looking north from the bridge. *(Loxahatchee River Historical Society)*

Mangroves

Jupiter Light

N

Jupiter River

Jupiter Beach Bridge

Jupiter Beach Bridge - Looking North.

RN UNION
BLES
ANCHOR

427

Parking by the south jetty at Jupiter Inlet, early 1920s.
*(Loxahatchee River Historical Society)*

# SHORTY'S GOLD

One of Jupiter's most conspicuous characters—conspicuous because his fish shack and ice house stood out on the railroad dock—was Elbert C. "Shorty" Root. Although Shorty's main business was buying fish for shipment up north, he was more famous for his cooking. Locals as well as yachts from Palm Beach used to tie up at the dock to savor his gopher tortoise stew and mullet gizzard casserole. He also made first-rate fish hash and served a delicious honey ice cream for dessert. And when the children trooped down to the railroad dock to wait for the school boat, Shorty would often treat them to cookies and doughnuts (both made with tortoise eggs)

Shorty's shack was always spotless, with fish nets festooned from the rafters. Out in back was a pen kept full of live gopher tortoises. People would tell about the time when the *Palm Beach Post* reported that a new state tick eradication program mandated that owners of food animals drive them to Indiantown to be dipped in vats. Shorty wrote a letter to the editor complaining of how difficult it would be for him to drive his herd of "gophers" to Indiantown.

After the railroad dock was torn down, he moved to a houseboat in Sawfish Bay. Just after Shorty and his houseboat rode out the hurricane of 1933, he asked a friend who ran a small grocery if he could go "on credit" for a while. He confided that he had been saving coins in an old iron kettle with a cover on it. The kettle handles were attached to a wire that was suspended from the houseboat below the water line. Seems that whenever Shorty wanted to make a deposit to his "savings account," he just lifted up the kettle and plunked it in.

But as Shorty had emerged the morning after the hurricane, there was no trace of the wire. He dove for the kettle, but no luck. He figured it was carried far downriver. Shorty died in 1937 at age 76, still mourning his lost savings.

By then his doctor, known now only as a "Dr. Body," had heard about it. Dr. Body loved diving as a hobby, and one Sunday morning he showed up in Sawfish Bay with a professional treasure hunter from New Jersey who had equipment that could locate metal objects underwater. Within an hour or so, the "pro" had found a heavy wire sticking out of the sand. After scraping away the muck and pulling hard, out popped the old iron stew pot, with its coin collection intact.

The treasure hunters counted it up that day: 6 fifty-dollar gold pieces, 309 ten–dollar gold pieces, 388 five-dollar pieces, 217 silver dollars and 306 fifty-cent pieces. The grand tally: $7,920.

LEFT: The big plunge. Noel Rood remembered it well. "I was still in school [Feb. 13, 1935] when the Florida Special to Miami went off the railroad bridge. It hit the draw with such force that the engine went into the river. The engineer and fireman jumped to safety. A hobo hitching a ride also jumped. Luckily, no one was killed. Twenty-nine people were injured, though. Some ambulances were sent up from Miami to take care of them."
*(Loxahatchee River Historical Society)*

Today it's Carlin Park. Then it was just "Jupiter Beach," and these boys are hanging about while their parents build Jupiter's first beach pavilion. From left to right: Harlow Rood, Jack Wilson, Howard Cromer, Judson Laird, Robert Hepburn, Frank and John Shuflin. *(Loxahatchee River Historical Society)*

In the twenties, everyone knew the parking area at Jupiter Beach simply as "The Turn-Around." The new beach pavilion is behind trees at left. At right, a beach view of the open pavilion. *(Loxahatchee River Historical Society)*

Jerry (age 12) and Ed Seabrook (15) show off some turtle shells found on the beach around 1935. *(Seabrook Family Collection)*

When kids at Jupiter School went on a special beach outing, their teachers did, too. This group poses during a picnic around 1927. *(Florida State Archives)*

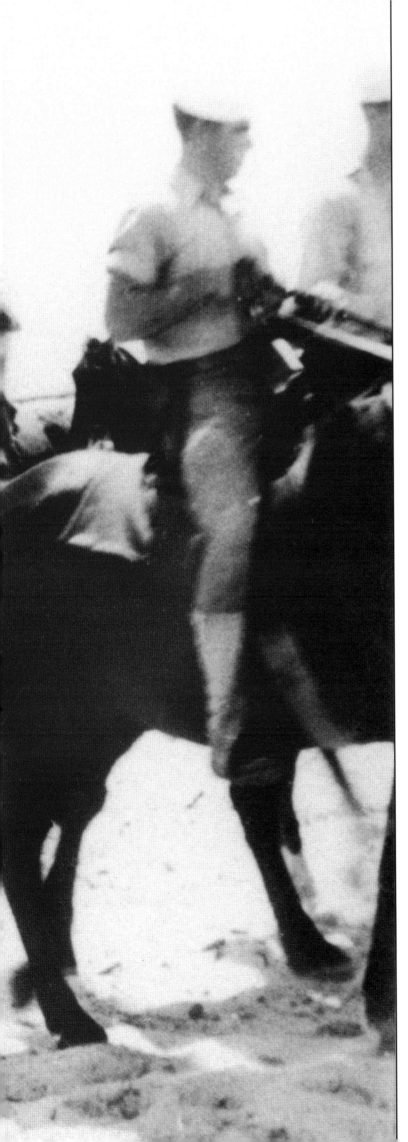

# CHAPTER 6

# 1941-1945: A VERY PERSONAL WAR

Leo Albert (Al) Kuschel Jr. was just 16 in the spring of 1943, working weekends as a mate on a 36–foot charter boat. They were trolling just off Juno Beach when they spotted a *Vee* in the water being made by an obviously big fish.

"In a few seconds we could see something like a pipe sticking up," says Kuschel, now a retired police detective. "Then we could see it was the tip of a tower atop a long gray shadow. We knew what it had to be, and luckily we had a radio we could use to alert the Coast Guard station in an emergency. We called in and said we thought we were right next to a submarine. They said they would radio Washington for the latest on enemy sub positions, but meanwhile we should get the hell out of there fast.

"I remember nearly losing my balance as the captain gunned the engine for all it was worth. We headed south towards another reef opposite The Breakers [in Palm Beach]. In about 25 minutes or so two military aircraft roared right over us towards where we'd seen the submarine."

Kuschel never learned if the planes found their target, but one could say that the captain had just jumped from the skillet to the frying pan. It was later discovered that a broad reef ledge off The Breakers was a frequent hangout for U–Boats. They'd hover under the wide ledge by day, then surface at night to prey on Allied ships.

Al Kuschel's experience was not unusual in Jupiter during World War II. Although the war for nearly everyone in continental America mostly meant rationing and scrap drives, it was often personal and even violent for the 200 or so souls who remained in Jupiter.

The reasons why were much the same ones that had made Jupiter Inlet a communications and transportation hub at the turn of the century. Before the war was over Jupiter would be the center

Beaches along Florida's entire east coast were patrolled by mounted Coast Guardsmen, often with trained attack dogs. In Jupiter they worked in close radio contact with the Civil Air Patrol, which flew daily roundtrips between Lantana Airport and an air base in Melbourne. *(Historical Society of Martin County)*

of a vital lighthouse, two sea-traffic monitoring stations, a busy beach patrol unit and a super-secret army base that taught a breakthrough technology called radar (for *radio detecting and ranging*).

Jupiter, in fact, got a bad taste of war well before it was even declared in North America. On Nov. 3, 1939, *The Palm Beach Post-Times* ran this page one story:

*Seas of heavy fuel oil blackening the beach, covering trees and cottages with filmy slime and turning waves into "blackcaps" for hundreds of yards offshore have convinced residents of Jupiter that a ship went down near there last night.*

*Thousands of gallons of unburned fuel oil cover a large area of the ocean.*

*Coast Guard and Radiomarine officials said today that no distress signals have been reported recently. But on the beach at the Surf Cottages four miles south of Jupiter is a heavy ship's door with newly–shined brass fittings and nails still unrusted by the salt water. Strewn along the shore are dozens of direct current light bulbs, still in good condition, of the vibration type seamen say is used in ship's engine rooms. The beach is covered with reeking black slime.*

*Among the debris are personal belongings including a shaving brush marked, curiously enough, with a swastika trade-mark….*

The swastika, of course, was the clue. Three days later, scores of local beachcombers had pieced together what happened. A bottle marked *Soda Wasser*, a lifeboat with German insignias and shaving brushes adorned with more swastikas told experts that a German submarine tender had been sunk by an enemy vessel (probably English) in U.S. waters and that neither party cared to report the episode. Frank Bound, owner of the Surf Cottages, told the press, "No fewer than 3,000 persons had stopped there Sunday to view two life belts, a ship's door and other miscellaneous pieces of the wreckage."

It was just a preview of what would hit Jupiter three years later. Shortly after the U.S. officially entered the war the Germans launched an operation called *Paukenschlag*, or "Drumbeat." More than seventy U–Boats crossed the Atlantic, attacked shipping along the coast of Canada, then spread south until they preyed throughout Florida and the Caribbean as well.

The most favored targets were merchant ships that had loaded up at the Port of New Orleans, bound for Europe with fuel, heavy equipment and other supplies for desperate Allied nations. As ships rounded the Florida cape and entered the Gulf Stream to gain six or so knots of speed going north, U–Boats would be lined up ready to pick them off like a ducks on a pond.

Shortly after the war ended, the navy would report that 111 Allied ships had been attacked off south Florida and the Caribbean, with 882 men killed or wounded.

The first U–Boat attack happened off Cape Canaveral on February 19, 1942. In the five months that followed, the slaughter–at–sea continued unimpeded. The entire U.S. military had but six small ships on the Florida coast, four of which were laid up for repairs. Its three B–18 bombers were so old that it would typically take two days' notice to get any one of them airborne.

During February–May 1942, eight merchant ships were lost directly off the coast of Palm Beach County and six within sight of Jupiter Inlet. All the people of Jupiter could do was paint black over the top of auto headlights and reduce the wattage in the lighthouse from three 250-watt lamps to a lone 60-watt bulb in hopes that the U–Boats wouldn't have as much illumination for their night targets.

Ironically, Jupiter was already home to two very special radio stations that could have greatly aided an anti–submarine force had there been one. The Mackay station, at what is now Toney Penna and South Loxahatchee Drive, had already been upgraded before the war. Taken over by the Coast Guard, it played a big role in linking commercial shipping traffic between New York to the tip of South America.

An unidentified tanker burns just off Jupiter Inlet in March 1942. It may have been the *Republic*. *(Florida State Archives)*

Even more critical was an installation on the lighthouse grounds known only as "Station J." Not even Coast Guard or lighthouse employees were allowed to ask what it did. It wasn't until many years later, when retired army colonel David S. Meredith III wrote a little-circulated monograph entitled *Spy Station Jupiter,* that the public got an inside look.

Today, electronic monitoring is the backbone of the U.S. intelligence gathering system. In 1929, when staff members handed Secretary of State Harry L. Stimson some decoded wireless messages from a potential adversary, he gruffly tossed them into a wastebasket. "Gentlemen do not read each other's mail!" he huffed.

But ever since the navy had acquired 8.4 acres of the Jupiter Lighthouse reservation in 1929, its wireless radio station had just that type of capability. It was improved over the years—but always

under the guise of "training"—until war broke out in Europe in 1939 and the Coast Guard assumed the duties of the old Lighthouse Service. In July a high frequency direction-finding radio was shipped to Jupiter and the official taboo on listening to one's potential foes began to dissolve. In September 1939, when Germany invaded Poland, Station J had eight men engaged in what bureaucratic mumbo jumbo called "neutrality enforcement." Within a few months it was ordered to cease all civilian communications. It was now called a "strategic tracking station."

By late 1941, just before Pearl Harbor, Station J was as primed for its wartime mission as any military facility in the U.S. The grounds had been expanded to twelve acres. It included thirty men and two barracks (each with its own signal intercept room at one end), two sets of married quarters with eight families each, a cottage

On the eastern horizon off Jupiter Beach, a tug begins towing the freighter, *DeLisle,* disabled by U–Boat torpedoes. On the beach is a life raft, that stayed afloat despite being riddled with machine gun bullets. The reason: it was built atop 55-gallon drums filled with fiber from Kapok trees. Locals used it to stuff pillows. *(Raymond Swanson Collection)*

for the officer in charge, a power house, garage, dispensary and ship's store. In fact, in 1942, when Washington sent twelve Marines to serve as security guards, station commander L. Alfred Newberry complained that there was nowhere to put them. Author Meredith confides that Newberry's real objection to the new arrivals was that they were too scruffy a lot to mix with his well-educated intelligence technicians. But the Marines got the best of it anyway: the Pentagon arranged for them to be housed at the swank (by comparison) Shuey's Inn just a stone's throw from the station.

The unit had nine receivers attuned to six line-of-sight radio frequencies used by German submarines. Monitoring soon became rather routine because the methodical Germans would surface just after dusk to charge their batteries and broadcast their positions and weather conditions to their home base. As Colonel Meredith noted, "These reports were always in ten groups of five letter code. The frequency was predetermined depending on the sub's location. The frequencies changed each month but went on a regular cycle that the intercept stations could easily determine."

Surrounding the buildings of Station J were three sets of doublet antenna arrays—each 500 feet apart. The term "doublet antenna" means that four antennas, linked in a group, each "aimed" at specific frequencies and interacted to pinpoint the location of a vessel engaged in radio transmissions. All messages were then relayed to and decoded by the Office of Naval Communications in Washington.

Thus, when war was declared, Station J was already in full swing. The only problem was a big one: the U.S. military had no way to

do anything about its constant stream of reports. Station J could pinpoint the name and location of a given U–Boat and could warn an oil tanker that a sub was so many yards away. But that was all. Jupiter was reduced to watching and rescuing.

### RESCUES AT SEA

On February 21, 1942, the oil tanker *Republic* was riding high on the Gulf Stream, returning empty to its port, when German torpedoes tore into its engine room, instantly killing five crewmen. The *Republic* quickly sank in about forty feet of water, three and a half miles northeast of Jupiter Inlet.

As ever, Bessie DuBois was quick to preserve a dramatic moment in local history:

*In Hobe Sound dishes were broken and windows cracked. In Jupiter almost everyone reported running into bedrooms to see if some family member had fallen out of bed. Telephones rang frantically. On Hobe Sound Beach two lifeboats came ashore. From them, men dripping oil were received into two exclusive residences, the Scranton's and the Bartlett's. Here they were received with the greatest hospitality. Dry clothing, food and drink were provided.*

*The* Republic's *captain, Alfred H. Anderson, later arrived. He reminded the men of the casualties, and sobered by the situation, they filed out to the waiting navy trucks and were taken to a hotel in West Palm Beach.*

Another account adds that when the men boarded the bus "they were elegantly outfitted in Mr. Scranton's expensive jackets and trousers—all except one sailor who was too large to fit into any of the donated clothing. He left wearing one of Mrs. Scranton's robes with a feather boa."

The day afterward, two Jupiter men, D. Leonard Smith and Kenneth Myers, ventured out toward the *Republic* in Smith's 25–foot boat. They found it wallowing in the waves, lying on its side. "Water hissed through her hatches with a fearsome sound," Smith said. "Clothing and wreckage of all sorts drifted back and forth, and the ship groaned as she moved. We found a small wire–haired terrier that had been left aboard."

After wrenching loose a lifeboat and a large quantity of rope for salvage, the two and their overjoyed dog (later reunited with its owner) headed back for the inlet and managed to get a push from a wave over the sandbar that had closed it to bigger boats. Little did they know that they'd been observed by the Coast Guard the entire time. Their salvage prizes were impounded and Smith was summoned before the district naval commander. He might have done time, but when the commander learned that Smith was due to enlist in the army the next day, he quietly dropped the charges.

The day after the sinking of the *Republic,* people driving along the ocean road at sundown were horrified to see a tanker on the horizon go up in a great sheet of flame. The victim was the *W.D. Anderson*, an Atlantic Refining Company tanker. Thirty-five men had been sitting down to their evening meal and all 35 perished.

One didn't. Frank Terry had been sitting on the ship's fantail. After being picked up two days later, covered with oil and numb from cold, he told the *Miami Herald:*

*I was sitting on the fantail with my buddy drinking a cup of coffee when I saw a torpedo coming. He saw it at the same time. I dove straight from my chair, but he paused to put his hands on the rail. I never saw him again. I swam under water as long as I could away from the ship, but when I came to the surface there was gasoline all around me. I went under again and swam until my lungs were ready to burst. When I came up again I was clear.*

Terry's legs were so numb he had to be reassured that a shark had not bitten them off.

The *W.D. Anderson* sank in 240 feet of water, not to be seen again for over fifty years. The *Republic,* however, was deemed salvageable, so a lighted buoy marked its place in purgatory.

On May 13, 1942, just after torpedoes hit the
*Potero del Llano* and its cargo of 35,000 barrels of
diesel fuel oil, a Civil Air Patrol plane filmed the
attacking U–Boat as it dove to escape detection.
*(Historical Society of Palm Beach County)*

CONFIDENTIAL
→ (013-6IOM-3M)(5-16-42-3:30P

ABOVE: In the spring of 1942, Camp Murphy, a U.S. Signal Corps radar training base, sprouted in just ninety days along nine miles in Hobe Sound. At its peak, it encompassed more than 800 buildings serving some 6,000 radar students from all service branches. Arrow shows U.S. Highway 1 northbound along Intracoastal Waterway.
*(Loxahatchee River Historical Society)*

RIGHT: The more that newsreels credited radar for a wave of successful Allied air victories, the more trainees at Camp Murphy were warned to keep their mission a secret. Their job was to operate and maintain a technology that was becoming more sophisticated month by month.
*(Jonathan Dickinson State Park)*

RESTRICTED
REGARDLESS OF CURRENT PUBLICITY—
The Discussion of
RADAR
outside the Classroom is
FORBIDDEN!
TELL YOUR FRIENDS YOU'RE STUDYING RADIO—
TRANSMITTERS—RECEIVERS—SUPERHETS — NO MORE!
IF PEOPLE ASK YOU ABOUT RADAR....
TELL THEM TO READ THE NEWSPAPERS
IS RADAR Bzzz---?
WUXTRY— ALL ABOUT RADAR
CLASSROOM
RADAR MEGS
FREQUENCY
DON'T TALK ABOUT RADAR TO ANYONE OUTSIDE THE CLASSROOM
REPORT ANY PERSISTENT QUESTIONERS OR ANY VIOLATORS OF RADAR SECURITY TO THE POST INTELLIGENCE OFFICER.
KEEP SILENT!
RESTRICTED

A month later a Bull Line freighter, *DeLisle,* was headed for the Virgin Islands with a cargo of general merchandise when a torpedo tore a forty-foot gash in her side. When the ship came to rest near the partially exposed *Republic,* authorities decided it could be towed and repaired. Soon tugs appeared with barges. While some men patched compartments to make it tow-able, others used swing booms to offload crates of shoes, lingerie, liquor and other merchandise. Meanwhile, other crates could be seen on the sea bottom through the clear water, and soon townspeople were circling the wreck in their skiffs, diving or trying to gaff a treasure from the sea.

Crews worked all day, but at night a single watchman remained on aboard. For five nights the lonely, scary job belonged to young Ernest Histed, who would later become a commercial photographer and take some of the pictures used in this book. Each night the wind would rush through the vessel's wound and it would groan as if in great pain. On the second night, as Bessie DuBois wrote, "Ernest stood looking down into the vitals of the vessel [and] saw something white floating back and forth with the motion of the ship. It was the body of one of the engine room crew. Another body was recovered from the engine room the next day. It was the sad duty of Captain Seabrook, keeper of Jupiter lighthouse, to deliver these bodies to the Martin County coroner."

All through 1942 the slaughter continued. In May alone Bessie's personal log showed:

May 6. The freighter *Amazon,* loaded with coffee, sisal, orange peel and oil burners, sank in 13 fathoms and marked for later removal by the Coast Guard.

May 6. The *Halsey,* a tanker from Delaware, was destroyed with a cargo of 80,000 barrels of fuel oil, gasoline and naphtha.

May 8. *The Ohioan,* loaded with manganese ore, licorice root and wool, disappeared in 550 feet.

May 8. A Cities Service tanker, *Empire,* fully loaded with 92,437 barrels of Texas crude, broke in two and sank in nearly 800 feet.

May 13. The *Potero Del Llano,* with 35,000 barrels of diesel oil, went down in 1,800 feet.

Curiously, there is no record—nor even recollections of residents—that any of these sinkings produced the kind of shoreline ecological damage that might have been expected. It's all the more puzzling because locals were in the midst of the action. Many went out in their own boats seeking survivors at great personal risk. As Bessie recounts: "Pleasure yachts patrolled the ship lanes rescuing survivors of the torpedoed vessels. One captain boasted that he would ram a submarine if the opportunity offered, but when one day a 200-foot submarine arose before him, he became completely unnerved."

Still, acts of heroism and kindness were too numerous to report. Rescue often meant pulling aboard a sailor completely covered with flaming oil. A Danish survivor remembers being blown into the water as a torpedo tore his ship in two. When he was spotted by volunteers, sharks were circling all around. As the rescuers were about to lift him up the U–Boat surfaced and shelled them. When he was finally brought to Good Samaritan Hospital in West Palm

A daily flag raising at Camp Murphy in 1943.
*(Jonathan Dickinson State Park)*

Beach he had a broken arm and leg as well as deep burns that required skin grafts and three months of hospitalization.

Mrs. Grady Stevens, the night supervisor at Good Sam, told her friend Bessie DuBois of nights when as many as fifty men were brought to the emergency room. Her first task when arriving for duty each night, she said, was to assemble as many cots, blankets, spare sheets and oxygen tents as she could find to be ready for the inevitable arrival of U-Boat victims.

Other wartime phenomena were the constant mounted patrols of Coast Guardsmen along the beach. At the war's outset four saboteurs from a U–Boat had been captured at a beach town near Jacksonville (some say their smell gave them away: they'd spent several weeks inside a stifling tube). The military reacted by dotting the Florida coast with a series of outposts and airfields. Each morning a Civil Air Patrol (CAP) plane would fly north from Lantana Airport, about a hundred feet over the beach, looking for signs of enemy activity. If the crew spotted anything fishy, they'd mark the spot on their chart and call the Coast Guard outpost in today's Juno Beach. All day long, mounted Marines and Coast Guardsmen would roam the shoreline with dogs. By then, the flight crew would have turned around in Melbourne, making the same beach-spotting trip back to Lantana by dusk.

The soft sand wore down the horses and the horses' hooves were tough on vegetation. J. Alden DuBois, son of John's brother Henry, remembers ruts atop the dune line where the patrols had cut a swath through the sea oats.

DuBois, who still lives along the tidal basin that runs through DuBois Park, hasn't forgotten a nighttime encounter he had as a teenager:

*We had two acres of asparagus ferns. One of my jobs was to pick worms off them, which I'd do by going out there at night with a milk bottle and a miner's light strapped around my forehead. One night I was out there when all of a sudden a jeep pulled up and a guy in uniform jumped out. I took two steps and ducked behind a tree. The guy hollered, "Halt!" and I recall thinking that "halt" is a German word and there'd been rumors afoot that Germans had come ashore from a submarine. When I peeked around the tree, the soldier was American all right, but he was waving a heavy [Colt] .45 and telling me I hadn't been very smart. He said if he wanted to shoot me, the bullet would go right through the tree.*

People growing up in wartime Jupiter still have sharp vignettes seared into their memories. Judy Seabrook Wehage was a small child who often slept out on the lighthouse balcony on hot nights while her grandfather

Knowing how to handle a rifle was no idle exercise at the base. Despite their "technician" image, Signal Corpsmen often went into combat ahead of regular troops and sustained a higher rate of casualties than most service branches.
*(Jonathan Dickinson State Park)*

Charles was on duty. She can still hear the unmistakable thud of torpedoes hitting their mark, the phones ringing in the tower and her grandfather's footsteps as he scurried down the stairs towards a rescue boat. Raymond Swanson, whose father was an assistant lighthouse keeper, saw or heard six ships hit during the war years. Alden DuBois remembers 8 p.m. on February 21, 1942. He was opening a door in his home near the inlet and suddenly felt the knob tremble in his hand. The *Republic* had just been hit three miles away.

## THE TIDE TURNS

The first ray of hope came in late 1942 when blimps began tracking the gray shadowy forms of submerged U–Boats. A call would go to Morrison Field in West Palm and planes would take off twenty or so minutes later with their own arsenal of torpedoes.

And by this time ships had learned to travel in convoys. As Bessie DuBois recalled, "It was a moving sight to stand on the shell mound overlooking the inlet and see one of the great convoys pass by. The long line of gray ships, the absence of sound, and the light gray mist that veiled them gave the whole scene a ghostly aspect and an awesome majesty."

Except for one local tragedy, 1943 literally brought a sea change in the "Florida war" as the U.S. military tooled up its infrastructure. By mid–1943 Station J had expanded to 24 receivers and 72 men—52 of them engaged in U–Boat sleuthing. Americans were beginning to catch and crush more German subs than they could count. But for Jupiter, the worst was saved for last. On the night of October 20, 1943, the tanker *Gulfland* had just passed Jupiter Inlet headed north with a full cargo of gasoline. It was running under blackout conditions, and as seaman first class Joseph O'Brion later told the *Palm Beach Post:*

*I was on watch about 10:50 p.m. Suddenly I spotted another ship bearing down from the north. It appeared to be 75 yards away. It* looked as if it was going to pass us, but as the ship approached I saw it was going to be close.

*I turned and started for the telephone to report it to the bridge, shouting as I ran to Walter Atkinson, another member of the gun crew. Before I got to the telephone, there was a crash.*

*A terrific explosion followed and I was blown about ten feet across the deck. Regaining my feet, I raced through the flames and jumped off the stern. I guess I was the first one off the ship. I swam as fast as I could for a while until I thought I was safe. Then I stopped to look back.*

*Waves of flame were coming toward me on the water and they almost caught me. Burning gasoline covered a wide area. I could hear a lot of screaming and yelling from the direction of both ships and I knew a lot of boys were trapped. It was awful!*

O'Brion was picked up clinging groggily to an overturned lifeboat. Of 116 men aboard the two ships, 88 had perished. Ironically, the *Gulfland* had been rammed by its sister ship, *Gulf Belle*—an unprecedented occurrence in the marine insurance world. Navy and Coast Guard vessels tried to extinguish the

Looking up the tall signal tower that stood atop Hobe Mountain. *(Jonathan Dickinson State Park)*

flaming cauldron but finally gave up. The *Gulfland* drifted northward and finally burned out seven weeks later off Hobe Sound, where it finally settled in thirty feet of water near the carcass of the *Republic.*

## JUPITER'S BIG SECRET

In June 1942, the lighthouse reservation with its hundred or so men would be quickly overshadowed by another facility that sprouted on the sand along Hobe Sound to include 11,364 acres, more than 800 buildings and some 6,600 men and women. Its name was Camp Murphy and locals were allowed to know only that it was a training facility for the Army Signal Corps.

Anyone interested enough in learning more might have looked into the life of Col. William H. Murphy, for whom the camp was named. Besides being the highest–ranking U.S. army officer to have been killed in action at that point, Murphy had been a pioneer in the development of radio beams and equipment for military aircraft. His main contribution had been the refinement of radar technology. The camp named for him was created to train people from all service branches in equipment operations and repair so that American forces would have the edge in spotting enemy targets and troops at distances far beyond the realm of the

human eye. Radar was already beginning to be credited with a big role in Allied victories, and a classified student's handbook saw fit to proclaim that "Years hence when the history of World War II can be written without giving aid and comfort to the enemy, radar will come into its own."

The first courses were actually taught in a converted warehouse in Riviera Beach as construction crews began bulldozing the permanent campsite between U.S. 1 and the railroad tracks in Hobe Sound. At the same time, a continuous convoy of dump trucks hauled shellrock and oyster shells scooped from the banks of the Loxahatchee. They'd be packed into roadbed for a network of streets and trails over nine miles.

Within ninety days the new complex—a city of mess halls, barracks, offices, shooting range, officers' club, theater, bowling alley, post office—was sufficiently completed to stage an opening ceremony with brass from Washington and no less than RCA Chairman David Sarnoff as keynoter. The camp historian took time to crow a bit:

*The ground renders itself admirably for its purpose, since the school is built along camouflaged lines, and natural camouflage in the form of vegetation makes the center of the post and school activities practically invisible from both the air and the ground.*

*Great care was taken in clearing the jungle on the fringe of the Everglades upon which the camp rests in order that none of the dense, semi-tropical growth of cabbage palmetto, swamp maple, Australian pine, palm, live oak, cactus, mangrove or other shrubbery was removed unnecessarily. All buildings were painted dull green to blend with the surrounding landscape.*

*Instead of making a large clearing and arranging buildings along company streets, as in most camps, Camp Murphy is laid out in an irregular pattern…with streets and buildings facing in every direction. The natural protection offered by the surrounding foliage and terrain was utilized to the utmost.*

The instructional packets given to arriving soldier-students didn't mention the fact that snakes regularly slithered along barracks floors at night, that black widow spiders infested the mess halls and that more men went to the infirmary with bites from a collage of critters than all the other causes combined. And newcomers may have been surprised to read that radar classes usually began at 6 p.m. Reason: there was no air conditioning and the classrooms would make a cucumber sweat.

Nonetheless, a manual for camp officers gamely extolled the post library, barber shop, post exchange, and the "well known, famous resort area" surrounding the base. In the section on officers' club rules, it attempts a little radar humor when discussing proper attire: "Your girl may be high 'amperage' in shorts or slacks, but someone may take her for a chorus girl if she is seen in them at the club after [seven o'clock]. "

As for nearby shopping, it advises going to Stuart or West Palm Beach because "there are practically no shopping facilities" nearby.

Unsaid by any manual was an unofficial "perk" that no other military base could boast. Joseph V. Reed, founder of the exclusive Jupiter Island Club just across the water, had managed to get himself appointed captain at Camp Murphy. As Special Services Officer, Reed made himself in charge of camp "morale"—which he saw as everything from the mess halls to the camp theater to recreational facilities.

Even if it meant paying the cost personally. Captain Reed bought a used boat and regularly ferried soldiers over to the Jupiter Island Club's beach pavilion, which he'd retrofitted as an *ad hoc* R & R facility. There, he dragooned some of society's most elegant matrons into serving as hostesses. They served refreshments and often helped kids with scant schooling write letters to their families. And when officers were invited to golf, it was at one of the nation's most exclusive clubs.

One of Joseph Reed's pet projects under his imaginatively defined mandate was Vince "Trapper" Nelson. As the local draft board was busily processing more than eighty eligible males, the only military interest Jupiter's finest physical specimen had shown was when Captain Reed offered to pay him $50 a week from his own pocket to become Camp Murphy's "predator removal" officer. For weeks a diligent Nelson could be seen plunking snakes and black widow spiders into gunnysacks. This was pure synergy because Trapper would take his conquests to his Loxahatchee River camp and sort them into various exhibits for visitors.

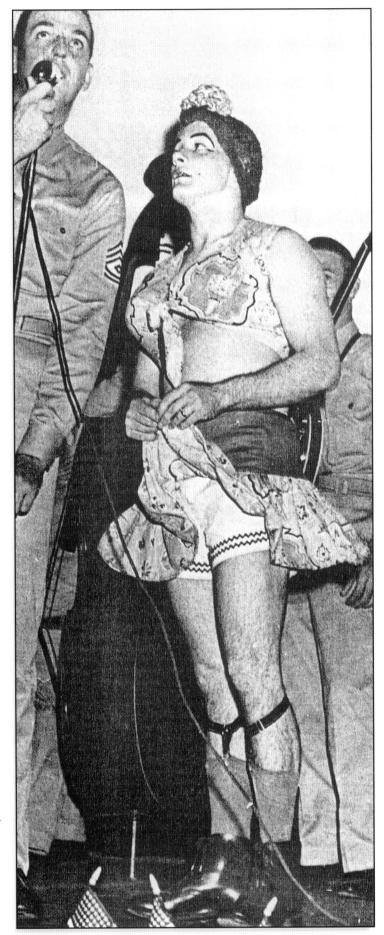

In addition to its bowling alley, officers' club, and other amenities, Camp Murphy boasted a theater that came alive under the wing of Special Services Officer Joseph V. Reed. Captain Reed, who founded Jupiter Island Club, had already backed numerous Broadway productions and knew how to spark a show that would further his mission as "officer in charge of troop morale."
*(Jonathan Dickinson State Park)*

As the war intensified in the spring of 1942, Nelson thought he might bob and weave past the draft board by marrying a barkeep named Lucille from the *Nineteenth Hole* down in Lake Park. Alas, he was soon snared and dispatched to a boot camp in Texas.

Woe was Trapper. Rumors soon came back that his bride enjoyed entertaining soldiers more than feeding snakes and alligators. Shortly thereafter, Nelson somehow sustained an injury to his thigh doing calisthenics. An officer and a gentleman like Joseph Reed would never confirm such audacious gossip, but some believe that the camp's Special Services Officer got a desperation call from his old friend Vince Nelson. In any case, Trapper was soon transferred to Camp Murphy. He was made an M.P., issued a jeep and told to patrol the base boundary in search of suspicious intruders.

Since the boundary bordered extensively on the grounds of *Trapper Nelson's Zoo and Jungle Garden,* one could truly say that Br'er Rabbit had been flung back into the briar patch.

### 'SOLDIER, SOLDIER WILL YOU MARRY ME?'

Although "downtown" Jupiter—at that time the cluster of stores around Center Street and Dixie—was five miles south of the main Camp Murphy gate, the two couldn't help but impact one another.

For the locals, still seeking that economic thrust that would propel them above subsistence, the exchange was largely salubrious except, perhaps, for the aggressive way the War Department snatched up land for its radar training base and shooed off dozens of squatters. In early 1942, for example, a friend from Virginia sent John DuBois a letter complaining that the War Department was offering a mere $2 per acre for 120 acres he owned along Kitching

Creek. "I replied," he told DuBois, "that the price was confiscatory and that I would not accept less than $5 an acre for the high ground and $3 an acre for the swampland next to your property."

DuBois, who owned 17.5 acres on Kitching Creek, must have filed the information in his head and laid low. Later that year the War Department paid him $1,000, or about $57 an acre.

The DuBois family also offers an example of how locals blended into and benefited from the Camp Murphy largesse. At a time when rationing severely hampered the family's ability to run a restaurant, the camp furnished Bessie with flour and sugar. In exchange, she baked forty pies a day for the mess halls. Meanwhile, John DuBois was a camp carpenter, son Harry worked in the dining room, daughter Dodie was an office secretary and sister Susie worked in the camp tailor shop.

Back in town, cash registers were jingling. Bowers Store (behind today's Economy Tire on Dixie) gave way to a bar with a pool table (which would have mortified its founder, a teetotaler). The open–air civic center at the end of Jupiter Beach Road became a bar complete with a line of tabletop slot machines that could be lowered beneath the counter if someone spied a cop car. Even the DuBois restaurant became more of an off-base soldier social center, with a jukebox and ping-pong table. And way upriver, Vince Nelson would host barbecues and poker games for Camp Murphy, with transportation courtesy of his handy army jeep.

But lest history record wartime Jupiter as a sin city, Saturday nights would find most of its young people at the wholesome U.S.O. dances at Camp Murphy or the Jupiter Women's Club. Alden DuBois' mother Dorothy was president of the club's U.S.O. and his sister Marion still has the book in which men signed up to dance with the girls who volunteered. Marion was "underage," she says, but closely chaperoned by her mother. She vividly remembers the strains of the band playing Glenn Miller's *Pennsylvania Six Five Thousand.* She remembers the cakewalks: if the music stopped and a soldier stood in front of a winning number, he won a cake baked at home, perhaps by the apple of his eye.

When Marion was pursued by a young Marine, Jack Hughart, her courtship strategy was a bit unorthodox. First she beat him at ping-pong. Then the next day she beat him at tennis. Suddenly shipped out, he proposed in a letter. But Marion wasn't bowled over: she'd already had seven proposals and she was barely 16.

Mrs. DuBois wasn't bowled over either. She sent Marion off to college for a year's seasoning. When she returned, so did Jack Hughart, with another proposal. This time Marion's mother kept him waiting for three months by sending him down to Homestead to work in her brother's TV shop. "But she was also using the time to make all my wedding and bridesmaids' dresses," says Marion. The couple was married in 1946.

Other Jupiter romances didn't take quite as long to consummate. Of the twelve Marines who were assigned to the lighthouse grounds as security detail in 1942, five married local girls and settled down to raise families.

## WAR OR NO WAR

Meanwhile, despite the torpedo explosions and horse patrols on the beach, kids went to school, made mischief and took advantage of opportunities that could come only when able-bodied adults were absent or preoccupied with wartime concerns.

Wilson Horne was 13 when war broke out. As he described Jupiter in a family memoir, "There were two churches and four gas stations. No doctors, dentists, movies, drug stores, fire or police stations, red lights or signs with street names. No Tequesta, [Jupiter] Inlet Colony, Salhaven, or Jonathan Dickinson State Park. And most roads were shellrock."

Here are some "lasting impressions" Horne recorded in that memoir 55 years later:

*Working a summer job at Camp Murphy as a cafeteria bus boy, a clerk in the hospital PX, at a filling station with Albert Wehage simonizing cars and finally with his dad tearing down the* [Camp Murphy] *recreation building.*

*The school being a gathering place for a permanent scrap drive for everything from cars to silverware.*

"I got married once; couldn't get unmarried fast enough," Trapper Nelson would later tell his visitors. He wed Lucille Gee, a Lake Park waitress, in May 1942. Several weeks later he was drafted and sent to boot camp. Lucille, not fond of caring for Trapper's snakes and alligators, melted away, later married four more times. *(Celmer Family Collection, Jonathan Dickinson State Park)*

By the forties, it was a ritual for anyone in Jupiter with out–of–town company to visit *Trapper Nelson's Zoo and Jungle Garden.* And everyone wanted a photo taken with Jupiter's own "Tarzan" (in pith helmet). *(Celmer Family Collection, Jonathan Dickinson State Park)*

*Finding a short road at Camp Murphy paved with lead toothpaste tubes.*

*Tramps climbing up into the attic space of the train depot and living there on the Q.T.*

*Volunteering at an airplane spotting tower that was built east of the Center Street R.R. crossing on Kenneth Myers property. It was manned 24 hours a day by volunteers and reported by telephone all aircraft seen or heard. I still have my spotter's identification book dated Sept. '42.*

*Finding an old double-barreled shotgun with a broken stock. It was decorated and had external gooseneck hammers. I made a stock for it and sawed off the barrels. I shot a woodpecker on a tree. Nothing was left but a few feathers and drips of blood. I never fired it again.*

*Hitchhiking. Everybody would stop and pick you up, no crime in those days.*

*During the winter after Boy Scout meeting, lying on a warm Indiantown Road and looking up at the stars.*

*Rabbit hunting in Pennock's south pasture.*

*Shorty the Negro handyman buying us kids Bugler tobacco so we could roll our own or smoke our homemade pipes.*

*The 6'2" rattlesnake I killed that had a full-grown marsh rabbit inside and the fur was still dry.*

*Finding our cow that had been lost for a week in quicksand in a swamp. She lived.*

*Being hit by a car crossing the street in W.P.B. and having my head stitched up.*

*When I ran into a butcher knife at the big pond and cut open my thigh 4" long by 2" wide. I applied a tourniquet of one dirty sock and two pieces of wire. Was carried on a bicycle two miles home and caught Jack Pennock's milk truck to W.P.B. for 12 stitches.*

*Finding what looked like silver ore along the RR track and burying it at the big pond camp.*

*Playing kick the can and hare & hounds at the school in the evenings.*

*Mowing with the plantation's whirlwind mowers.*

*Painting the house screens with kerosene. Making smudges of rags sprinkled with bee brand insecticide and covering my head with the sheet to avoid the sand flies and mosquitoes.*

*Fighting ground itch (hookworm) with kerosene, iodine, Neuzo and turpentine.*

*Visiting Trapper Nelson with the Boy Scouts and hearing Trapper tell why he cut off his thumb with a hatchet after a rattler bit him.*

*Watching my pet cat Toby die in my arms after eating toad [puffer] fish guts.*

*Making cigarettes with a rolling machine and Bugler tobacco and putting them into empty packages. Smoking rabbit tobacco, coffee, grape and pine twigs and homemade pipes.*

*Crawling under Shuey's Inn deck to recover coins dropped thru cracks.*

*Stopping at Kelly's Grocery store on the way back from the beach and pouring Pepsi in 5-cent cups of Alfar vanilla ice cream to make sodas.*

*Seeing and smelling the two huge hog farms that were established in Jupiter to consume the Camp Murphy garbage. One was about two miles south of town and the other on Loxahatchee River Road just past Center Street. The hogs, in a feeding frenzy, would bite off each other's ears and tails—and swallow silverware accidentally dropped in the garbage and pass it badly chewed.*

The one land swinging bridge from the lighthouse area to Jupiter Island was "Woods Bridge" before the war and "Cato's Bridge" thereafter—both for the names of the families who lived in the tender's house. When not carrying cars and people, the span pivoted towards the water to let boats pass. *(Lynn Drake Collection)*

*Gathering wild butterfly orchids from the swamp and selling them to a local nursery.*

*Harvesting sphagnum moss from a pond near our house, drying it and selling it to a local nursery. The war had cut off our northern supply.*

*Smelling fresh baked bread coming from the school cafeteria. Buying candy there. Getting immunizations from Mrs. Howell the county nurse. She would give us a toothbrush from China made of bamboo and hog bristles.*

*Mom and Mrs. Yohey trading surplus food. We would give them milk and they gave us USDA surplus flour, raisins, peanut butter and fresh fish.*

Horne. Freeman. Yohey. Swanson. The gang of four, by then in their teens, did what boys do regardless of what swirls about in the adult world. One of the favorite attractions was a sawmill just off Indiantown Road between Jones Creek and today's Dodge–Mazda

dealership. "The piles of sawdust and wood chips were enormous," says Horne. "People bought the stuff for gardens and hog pens. For us they were great for climbing and rolling down."

Raymond Swanson remembers the time when his buddy Horne wore "special" shoes to school. "They used to ship raw rubber from South America," he says. "To cure it they would light the rubber on fire, dip a stick in it and rotate it in the smoke until it became a big ball. Wilson found some of the raw stuff and used the same method to re–sole his shoes. The first day he came walking into the schoolroom, there was this tremendous stink. Wilson must have gotten used to it because he just sat there without saying anything. When the teacher found out what it was, she made him go barefoot and put his shoes outside."

Swanson also recalls the nights in the Pennock's feed barn in what one might then call an "extreme" sport for bored boys. "First, we'd go over there in the afternoon and whittle a plug to fit every rat hole. We'd sit each plug beside its proper hole. Then we made sure

each guy had a club. A couple of hours after dark we'd sneak in there real quiet like. One guy would stay beside the light switch while the others plugged up all the rat holes. Then we'd flick the switch, grab our clubs and beat the hell out of the rats."

Sometimes the game plan went awry. "I remember one time a rat ran between someone's legs and another guy whacked him right across the shins," laughs Swanson.

Other capers sometimes backfired as well. One day Swanson and friends spotted a barge being towed by a tug up the Intracoastal. As the big rusty barge rounded the bend by the lighthouse the boys swam out, hoisted themselves aboard and walked around to see what they could see.

"I was absorbed in examining something or other," Swanson recalls. "When I looked up, I saw that everyone else had already jumped off the barge. In order to catch up I ran to the back and took a dive.

*Continued on page 150*

Weekends found lots of locals like Gracie Wehage and son Albert Jr. dancing to the jukebox at Ralph's open-air beer, burger and fish house on the water north of the Dixie highway bridge. *(Wehage Family Collection)*

Blanche and Ralph Crooks. After the war, they would leave their fish camp and open Ralph's Package Store on Center St. *(Wehage Family Collection)*

RIGHT: J. Alden DuBois, age 14, shows off at the beach while his father Henry snoozes. *(Alden DuBois Collection)*

BELOW: The senior class of 1945 wore bizarre getups to start their annual "skip day." From left, Richard Bassett, Ray Swanson, Louise DuBois, Eloise Brooker, Judson Minear (in back), Bertha Benton, Frances Floyd, Billy Jenkins, Marion DuBois. Jenkins was actually a junior—the entire class, in fact. *(Raymond Swanson Collection)*

Seniors on the beach. From left, Ray Swanson, Mrs. Mary Helen Weeks (teacher), Marion DuBois, Louise DuBois, Richard Bassett, Bertha Benton, Frances Floyd, Judson Minear. *(Raymond Swanson Collection)*

149

"Roxie" hogs the lens in front of two–year–old Judy Knight (Wehage) as her grandfather, Capt. Charles Seabrook, lowers the flag.
*(Seabrook Family Collection)*

"As I was in mid-air, I saw that I was headed into a churning mass of water caused by the slipstream. It created a rotating cyclinder effect, and in an instant I was inside the thing turning cartwheels. I'd go five feet underwater, then back up to the surface—over and over. I had already sucked in seawater and I knew I'd be dead in two seconds. I just managed to wrench myself loose. If I hadn't, I knew my body would have gone around and around in that thing until it finally stopped at it's destination."

Mostly, wartime presented a youngster with many reasons to stay *out* of trouble. Swanson, for example, worked at Shuey's Inn doing everything from topping trees to stocking the bar and cleaning the twenty tourist cabins. "There just weren't any adult males available to work there," he says.

## DISAPPEARING ACTS

People who lived through it are still amazed as how quickly wartime fixtures sprang up and then shriveled away. The first to shrink was the secret Station J. During April 1943 it was helping track 230 enemy subs in the Atlantic. The next month thirty were destroyed, then 37, and more in each succeeding month. By 1944 France was liberated, Germany lost its Atlantic U-Boat bases in Bordeaux, and Station J was clearly winding down. Equipment was gradually transferred to other navy installations, and on July 15, 1945, hardly anyone was at Station J to salute at the formal decommissioning ceremony. Ownership of the remaining buildings reverted back to the Coast Guard, but a bit late for lighthouse keeper Captain Charles Seabrook, who would retire not long

By the not–then–so–big banyan tree at the foot of the lighthouse in 1943: Captain and Dora Seabrook at right. At left are their daughter Bertha Knight with her daughter Judy (Wehage) and the Seabrook's son Jerry.
*(Seabrook Family Collection)*

afterwards.

Camp Murphy, which had thrown up 800 buildings in ninety days, also disappeared at breakneck speed. Radar training was consolidated at Fort Monmouth, New Jersey in 1944 and by October the base was formally decommissioned. A bomb shelter, now used as state park headquarters, and a barracks building housing park rangers are all that remain inside the boundaries. Outside, one can still find some buildings that were bought as government surplus and moved to sites from Hobe Sound to Stuart. Look closely at some of the service buildings on Jupiter Island and you'll see that Captain Joseph Reed was also a shrewd buyer of surplus property.

Today, the only written reminder of a base that held 6,000 is a train shed by the tracks inside Jonathan Dickinson State Park. *Camp Murphy North,* reads the little sign on the roof.

## POSTSCRIPT

As the war had wound down, Raymond Swanson, just out of high school, dreamed of joining the Marines. Living on the lighthouse grounds, he had hobnobbed with the dozen or so Marines who served as security guards for the lighthouse reservation. All had seen intense combat in the early South Pacific campaigns and Jupiter was deemed a safe haven for these battle-scarred survivors.

Says Swanson: "Two or three of them were standing around one day when I was giving this big speech about how bad I wanted to go and fight for my country. Suddenly, out of nowhere, a leather boot with a foot in it smacked me in the butt so hard I almost fell over.

"The guy who did it looked at me with a glare I'll never forget. He said 'Look at us. We're all supposed to be war heroes and there isn't a one of us who's worth a damn anymore. You'll go only when you're called.'"

Swanson stayed, for the time being. When he turned 18 he joined the navy.

By 1946 Wilson Horne's brother Ken had enlisted in the Army Air Corps and brother Jack the Marines. Wilson enlisted in the Army and stayed nearly twenty years, retiring a major. Brothers Neil and Roger would become Marines in the fifties, making five Hornes who saw military service.

It wasn't all work. The memories of blue water and ocean breezes inspired hundreds of GIs to settle in Jupiter after the war. *(Historical Society of Martin County)*

# CHAPTER 7

# 1945-1980'S: SNAPSHOT OF A TOWN IN TRANSITION

Enough was enough. The inlet had been closed all during the war. The Loxahatchee, which ordinarily drained some 270 square miles of river basin, was swollen and stagnant. People missed the ocean fish and the Caribbean-blue tides. The Jupiter Inlet District was too broke to hire a dredge, so local folks went to lighthouse keeper Charles Seabrook and asked for his advice. Could they do it themselves?

Recalls Raymond Swanson: "Captain Seabrook consulted his charts and meteorological reports and picked a time when conditions were most favorable. We had recruited a gang of young folks with shovels, and we started to work during the outgoing tide. After a few hours we had dug a trench from the west part of the inlet almost through the sandbar that sealed off the ocean. The current took care of the rest. The water flowed out so strongly that from the lighthouse you could see brown water surging out nearly a mile into the ocean."

Postwar Jupiter had officially begun.

In the spirit of liberation right after the war, a group of mostly unidentified youths turned out with shovels to dig a channel through the sandbar that had been allowed to block the inlet. After a morning's work, the pent-up Loxahatchee waters were streaming a mile out to sea. Leaning on her shovel is Louise DuBois, with sister Dodie bent over at immediate left. *(Dodie DuBois Hawthorn Collection)*

## 'AN AWESOME PLACE TO GROW UP IN'

"I didn't appreciate what an awesome place Jupiter was to grow up in until I was an adult," says Skip Gladwin, now a successful building contractor. He was six in 1948 when his parents moved down from New Jersey. They rented the same house on Jupiter Inlet that Harry and Susan DuBois had built in 1899.

"We had no roots here," says Gladwin, "but the DuBois family opened their doors to us. And so did the other 'established' families. Pretty soon we found ourselves being immersed in the heritage of Jupiter.

"The difference between kids then and today is that everything we did revolved around the river. Today, the idea of one's 'rite of passage' is to get the keys to a car. Mine came at age eight when I got a little boat that I could take to Pennock Point or Cato's Bridge or anywhere I wanted."

As Gladwin became a teenager, Pennock Point was the place to be. "We'd spend all weekend swimming and skiing there. To this day I can't believe how wonderful families like the Pennocks, Minears, Floyds and Liebs were to us kids. You were welcome in their homes any time of day or night."

And the plantation was a special feast for a lad who would become an engineer. "They had acres of maintenance sheds with all sorts of drill presses, forges and the like," says Gladwin. "My closest friend was Steve Floyd [today a Jupiter veterinarian]. The two of us put a go-cart together from an old engine and wheels from a discarded mower. We drove that thing all over the back streets of Jupiter."

Attorney William S. Wood, who recently marked his fiftieth year in Jupiter-Tequesta, came along just a few years later. "My dad was chief of staff at Good Samaritan Hospital and we lived in Lake Worth," he says. "On weekends the family headed north, and we always had the same routine. We'd spend the day at Blowing Rocks beach, swimming, fishing and using the dunes for target practice. Then before driving home at night we'd have dinner at Shuey's Inn.

"One day Dad said, 'This is just too nice up here. We've got to buy a place.'"

In 1953 Dr. Wood paid $14,000 for a cottage on a .8-acre lot on Riverside Drive, just down the river from Shuey's dock. On weekends and all through their summers, Bill Wood and his brother Ed became regulars with the Pennocks, Catos, Minears and other Jupiter kids. They formed a club called the Beachcombers, fishing and diving off Cato's Bridge. Or they might water-ski off Pennock Point, where the Liebs had built a ski jump.

On weekends the Beachcombers would go to dances at the Women's Club, or to outdoor movies, which were shown on the back of the Jupiter Elementary School on S. Loxahatchee Drive. "We'd drive to Riviera Beach for roller skating, and one time we even went in a boat-a-cade down to Miami Beach and stayed in a fancy hotel on Key Biscayne," says Wood.

Little did he realize at the time that he'd one day buy that first home from his parents and raise his own children there.

The Jupiter Bill Wood remembers in the mid-fifties was clustered mostly around Dixie and Center streets. Ruby's, the main grocery, stood on the corner where a consignment furniture store is today. Across the street was Jupiter Sundries, which had an inside

*Continued on page 158*

"Central" Jupiter as seen from the sky in 1946. *(Lynn Drake Collection)*

155

# SLAMMED AND SLIMED IN '49

In August 1949, Jupiter got slammed by a hurricane that compared with the legendary blows in 1928 and 1933.

Although the wind velocity at the lighthouse measured 167 m.p.h., seven-year-old Skip Gladwin slept through the whole thing at the rented DuBois house just across the inlet. "When I woke up and looked out, I almost got sick," he said. "Everything was green. Every building in sight was covered with a green ooze from the rooftops to the foundations. What had happened was that leaves of all kinds had been plastered onto windows, walls and screen porches with such a force that they simply pulverized like they'd been in some giant blender."

Down by the beach, Mayne Reid Coe had just retired and bought the old Seahorse Ranch, a motel on what was then U.S. 1. "The day we bought the motel we raised the insurance on it," he said. "It turned out to be a very wise move. The hurricane arrived and blew down our motel. It was completely demolished."

Over at the bridge leading to Jupiter Island, the Cato family had just moved into the caretaker's cottage on the west side. Daughter Shirley, then in her teens, remembers: "We stayed in the Coast Guard station because we were afraid to stay in a house that hung out over the river. But all the shutters blew off the house we had run to. When we got back to our house by the bridge, it was completely unharmed. It

hadn't even been boarded up."

Meanwhile, back at the Seahorse Ranch, Coe used his insurance money to rebuild bigger and better. He named the new place the South Seas Motel.

LOWER LEFT: The yard at the DuBois home looking toward the lighthouse prior to the 1949 hurricane.

UPPER LEFT: The same yard just after the big blow.

ABOVE: That's young Dodie DuBois (now Hawthorn) by the fallen tree. *(Dodie DuBois Hawthorn Collection)*

## HISTORICAL HIGHLIGHTS

| | |
|---|---|
| **1949** | Jan. 20. Harry S Truman sworn in for 2nd term. |
| **1949** | Jupiter-Tequesta Chamber of Commerce organized. |
| **1953** | Jan. 20. Dwight D. Eisenhower sworn in as 34th president. |
| **1953** | Juno Beach is incorporated. |
| **1957** | Village of Tequesta incorporated. |
| **1959** | Jupiter Inlet Colony incorporated. |
| **1959** | Assistant lighthouse keepers' house, built in 1883, is demolished. |
| **1959** | Centennial celebration held to mark completion of the lighthouse in 1859. |
| **1961** | Jan. 20. John F. Kennedy becomes 35th president. |
| **1961** | First black student enrolls in Jupiter High School. |
| **1962** | July. LORAN (Long-Range Aid to Navigation) station activated on lighthouse reservation by Coast Guard. Later moved six miles north on U.S.1. |
| **1967** | Dedication ceremonies held to plant lighthouse marker sponsored by the Florida Chapter of the National Society of Daughters of the American Colonists. |
| **1971** | Loxahatchee Historical Society founded. |
| **1973** | Coast Guard renovates lighthouse tower and oil house. Includes sandblasting, painting and covering iron roof of tower with copper sheeting. |
| **1975** | Jupiter Lighthouse placed on National Register of Historic Places. |
| **1977** | Jan. 20. Jimmy Carter becomes 39th president. |
| **1977** | Spanish galleon discovered two miles off coast of Juno Beach. Dates back to late 1500s. |
| **1979** | Jupiter's 156-bed hospital reorganized as Jupiter Medical Center. |
| **1985** | Federal government designates the upper portion of the Loxahatchee a "Wild and Scenic River." |
| **1987** | Lighthouse automated. Thousand-watt electric bulb shines 24 miles out to sea. |
| **1988** | Loxahatchee River Historical Museum opens to the public. |

Shuey's Inn, Cottages and Marina straddled the northeast end of the U.S. 1 (Dixie Highway) bridge. *(Lynn Drake Collection)*

At Jupiter Sundries, on the south side of Center Street, you could get anything from prescription drugs to a cherry Coke at the fountain. It also had an inside connection to its next-door neighbor, the post office. *(Loxahatchee River Historical Society)*

Returning veterans infused Jupiter with new enterprise. Roy Rood had learned landscaping at Wilson Palm Gardens before the war. In 1949 at age 30, he poses in front of the new Rood Landscaping headquarters with his secretary and sister, Margaret Small. *(Rood Family Collection)*

connection to the post office next door. Add the Florida Power & Light building and the Volunteer Fire Department station, and that was about it.

Lynn Lasseter Drake's perspective was younger and further east. She was six in 1959 when her parents moved into Suni Sands while their permanent home was being built. "I'd never been around water," she says, "and suddenly my whole life was bait and hooks. We kids would lie for hours on Suni Sands boathouse dock catching sand perch on hand lines and feeding them to the pelicans.

"When we went to the beach, Alternate A1A [then U.S.1] took a lot different path than it does today. Just after it crossed Suni Sands it took a wide swing to the left and cut all the way to where Jupiter Ocean Grande condos are now. It went in front of the civic center and right up along the dune where the Loggerhead Café sits today. The A1A we know today came much later."

If the Lasseters went to the store, it would probably be on Indiantown or Center streets. Although they were linked by Dixie Highway, people were more apt to use Loxahatchee Drive. Dixie Highway's (now Alternate A1A) handful of eateries, gas stations and motels were more for tourists in transit. Says Drake: "On Indiantown Road [between Dixie and Loxahatchee Drive], we had Miller's Market, Goodner's Five and Ten, and Greene's Dry Goods store on the corner. Over on Center Street the Kwik Serve had replaced Ruby's and Jupiter Sundries was now Stine's Fountain. Further out was Michael's Meat Market where Robinson Citrus is today. If you wanted to buy clothes, you went to Sears down in West Palm Beach."

Indeed, Jupiter was literally an oasis in the middle of the sand. Juno Beach, incorporated in 1953, was like a tiny moon to Jupiter with a mini–motel strip, a gas station and a few homes. Bulldozers were busy in Jupiter Inlet Colony, which was just incorporating in 1959. Hobe Sound, the closest neighbor to the north, consisted of the FEC Railway line, a few fruit stands and Algozzini's souvenir store (which may well be the area's oldest continuous retail business). Across the water, the Jupiter Island Club was insular in the height of the season and a ghost town in the summer.

Yet there was a new vitality in Jupiter. Despite the disappearance of Camp Murphy and the radio station at the lighthouse, there was more money as servicemen returned with their mustering out bonuses. Others from up north had fond memories of their military training in Jupiter and returned with families to raise. Between 1957 and 1958, eleven developments, three new churches and 17 businesses got underway. Population had already doubled from the 250 during wartime.

Two more reasons for the optimism were the arrival of air conditioning and the departure of bugs (at least a lot of them). Ditches were dug along the salt marshes in Juno and other areas and keeping them flushed (because mosquitoes lay their eggs on a receding water line) did wonders. Edwin L. (Ed) Seabrook, a son of the lighthouse captain, became an entomologist during the war and later played a role in combating the insect problem back home. He opposed those who would have filled in the ditches and eased up on pesticides. "I think we should use every tool at hand, including biological and chemical control," he would say. Jupiter did, and some of the effects still linger in the sediment below the Loxahatchee.

# JUPITER, FLA.

For Instructions on How to Use the Dial Telephone See Opposite Page.

## TELEPHONE SERVICE AND EMERGENCY CALLS

Long Distance _____Dial "Operator"

Information—Numbers Not Listed in Directory
             Dial "Operator" and ask for "Information"

TO REPORT DIFFICULTY
    With a Local or Long Distance Call_____Dial "Operator"

To Report a Telephone Out of Order—
             Dial "Operator" and ask for "Repair Service"

Business Office—Telephone Company
             Dial "Operator" and ask for "Business Office"

To Report a Fire_____Dial 3444

Sheriff—West Palm Beach_____Call Long Distance (Dial Operator)

For the Telephone Number or Address of the Nearest Federal Bureau of
     Investigation Office_____Dial "Operator" and ask for "Information"

---

## ALPHABETICAL TELEPHONE DIRECTORY

Aicher Harry F County Rd----------------------3011
Albertson Susan C U S Hwy 1-----------------2161
Albrecht Theresa Mrs Hwy A1A----------------2672
Alexander Dale Hood Rd----------------------3936
Alexander H R Center------------------------3091
Anderson Clarice Mrs Jupiter Heights---------2243
Arline T G Riverside Blvd---------------------2181

Baird A V Old Dixie Hwy----------------------2411
Bassett Amos E Indian Town Rd----------------2131
Bassett James A Center-----------------------2141
Beau's Service Station U S Hwy 1-------------9141
Belcher Oil Co Jupiter------------------------3951
Bender John C Pennock Point Rd---------------3734
Benton Alice Mrs Centr-----------------------2641
Bieger Mary Center--------------------------2641
Blocker Mary A Mrs State Rd A1A--------------3431
Boss Edward F Riverside Blvd-----------------2001
Brewster Warren H E Center-------------------2941
Brooker David C 4th-------------------------2441
Brown Ted & Son rl est Centr-----------------2481
Bryce James Loxahatchee Rivr Rd--------------2851

Casey Emil S Hood Rd------------------------3935
Catlin George B Riverside Blvd----------------2061
Christensen N T Loxahatchee Rivr Rd-----------2271
Clark L B Indiantown Rd----------------------2531
Clemones W M Suni-Sands Motor Court----------3681
Coe Mayne R Center-------------------------3822
Colwell C A Old Dixie------------------------2151
Cone Paul Mrs State Rd A1A-------------------3431
Cooper A A U S Hwy 1-----------------------2541
Crandall Perry B Pennock Pt------------------3751
Cross Marie K Old Jupiter Beach Rd------------3601
Cushing Milton L Mrs Loxahatchee River Rd------3731

Daily Jas Y State Rd A1A----------------------2671
DeBussey Richard R Centr---------------------3791
Derrick Albert W Federal Hwy------------------2651
Dickson David H Jr U S Hwy No 1---------------3721
Driskell Hollis B Center----------------------3821
Driskell James F Pinewood Dr------------------2971
Du Bois Fishing Camp Du Bois Rd---------------9151
Du Bois Henry S Du Bois Ln--------------------2051
Du Bois Neil 3rd----------------------------2581
Dunham & MacQueen Market State Rd A1A--------9121

Farish Jos D Point Rd-------------------------3041
Fernsell Farms S Old Dixie Hwy----------------3931
Fife M C Riverside Blvd-----------------------2041
Fire Dept Jupiter Volunteer Center-------------3444
Fisch E W Radio Station Rd--------------------3861
Florida Power & Light Co Center---------------2471
Florida State Road Dept
     Bridge No 5----------------------------2921
     Bridge No 60---------------------------3771
     Bridge No 83---------------------------3761
Floyd Shirley P Center-----------------------2492

Gainey Louis F Pine.-------------------------2571
Gardiner Stuart Center-----------------------3051
Gay R E 3rd-------------------------------3541
Gehr Edw R Jr U S Hwy No 1-------------------2872
Gibson B H Loxahatchee Dr--------------------3811
Gladwin Ransom F Jr Point Rd------------------3732
Gladwin Richard A Riverside Dr-----------------2362
Gould Howard U S Hwy No 1-------------------2931

Gregg Ashton Mrs Center----------------------2231
Gus's Fishing Camp U S Hwy No 1--------------9281

Hammock J T Sr Hood Rd---------------------3933
Hammock Jas T Jr Hood Rd--------------------3934
Haymond R W Center------------------------2621
Haymond W E Railroad Av---------------------3001
Heath G W MD Vesta Dr----------------------2551
Hubbell Frank J River Bend--------------------2111

Jackson H P Riverside Blvd--------------------2011
Jaeger William Loxahatchee River Rd-----------2031
Jakra Carrie Lou Mrs U S Hwy No 1------------2301
Jenkins Earl Center--------------------------3851
Jenkins Eugene Center------------------------3611
Jenkins Richard Center------------------------3621
Juno Ranch Motel Federal Hwy Juno Bch--------★2371
Jupiter Beauty Shop U S Hwy A1A--------------2461
Jupiter Food Store Center---------------------2881
Jupiter Lighthouse Restaurant U S Hwy 1--------2261
Jupiter Public School Loxahatchee Dr-----------2331
Jupiter Realty Jupiter Hgts-------------------2241
Jupiter Tourist Stop U S 1---------------------2242
Jupiter Town Of
     Mayor Old Jupiter Bch Rd-----------------3601
     Clerk Center--------------------------3611
     Fire Dept Volunteer Center----------------3444

Kegg W O U S Hwy No 1---------------------3551
Kindt C R Du Bois Rd-------------------------3031
Kleiser Bob Riverside Dr----------------------3881

Ladner Luther Old Jupiter Bch Rd--------------3671
Laird Frank J Center--------------------------2481
Lanier Elzie 1st-----------------------------2561
Lanier J S Loxahatchee Dr---------------------3871
Leary Wm U S Hwy No 1----------------------3071
Ledford T W Loxahatchee Dr-------------------3691

MacQueen Robt B State Rd A1A----------------2801
Martin George H Eganfuskee-------------------3021
Mayo M E Federal Hwy-----------------------3781
McCluer Jas S Centr-------------------------3791
McDade Emily A Mrs Hood Rd------------------3932
Mc Gehee Lester Pine Av----------------------3651
McGrath John E Radio Rd---------------------2811
Meden G Riverside Blvd-----------------------2281
Miller Harry M Center------------------------3061
Miller Roy Mrs Riverside Rd-------------------2741
Minear L V Center---------------------------2511
Minear N Laird Center-----------------------3461
Moores H C Center--------------------------2521

Nagel J P The Point-------------------------2091
Niemi Victor Bridge Rd-----------------------2961
Nowling J C MD Riverside Blvd-----------------2101

Ocean Side Restaurant Hwy No 1--------------9131
OCEAN SOUND VILLA U S Hwy 1----------------9101
Osborne George 4th-------------------------2421

Patterson K C 3rd---------------------------3891
Peeler Stanley Loxahatchee Rivr Rd------------2121
Pennock A L Center-------------------------2491
Pennock H S Rivrsde Dr-----------------------2701
Pennock Herbert Mrs Center-------------------2191
Pennock Plantation Center---------------------2321

Pietsch Kurt Point Rd------------------------2451
Plog Helen McKay Radio Rd--------------------3841
Porter Robert A U S Hwy 1--------------------2871
Pullin P B Rev School------------------------3561

Raby Jas H Mrs Rivrsde Blvd-------------------2363
Ralph's Fishing Camp State Rd A1A-------------9111
Ramige Eldon A Dr Center---------------------3641
Rigg Benj H Capt Rivrsde Dr-------------------2952
Roberts Robert Riverside Blvd------------------3521
Roebuck L A Loxahatchee Rivr Rd--------------2841
Rogers Margaret Miss Center-------------------2861
Rood Landscape Co County Rd------------------2791
Rood Roy S Riverside Dr----------------------2792
Rousseau J Ford Hood Rd----------------------3938
Ryan Dan T Loxahatchee Dr--------------------2251
Ryan Milton J U S Hwy 1----------------------3631

Sauter Lodge U S Hwy 1----------------------9231
Savage Mary Evelyn Mrs Center----------------3661
Seabrook Frank 4th--------------------------2431
Shock Alvin R 6th---------------------------3451
Shock F A Mrs Indiantown Rd-------------------2691
Shook Perry L Old Dixie Hwy-------------------3081
Shuey's Inn U S Hwy 1-----------------------2351
Simmons J Homer County Line Rd---------------3591
Skeen Howard Indian Town Rd------------------2501
Smith W W Rivrsde Blvd-----------------------3701
South Seas Sundries U S Hwy No 1 Juno Bch-----9341
Southard George E Hooley Pt-------------------2081
Stalls Richard School-------------------------3531
Suni-Sands Motor Court U S Hwy 1-------------9221
Suni-Sands Service U S Hwy 1------------------2311
Swint Roger J Mrs Cemetery Rd-----------------3471

Thomson Wm U S Hwy No 1--------------------3411
Tommy's Restaurant & Cocktail Lounge U S Hwy 1-9181
Townes C C Centr---------------------------2781
Turner J F Jr Center-------------------------2611

U S Government
    Air Force Dept of
      Missile Test Center
        Subdivision No 2 Jupiter Fla-------------2211
    Coast Guard Light Sta U S Hwy 1-----------2911

Van Gorden Motel U S Hwy 1------------------9261
Vaporette Corporation insecticds
             Loxahatchee River Rd--2031
Volk Adolph Center-------------------------2171

Webb Shelton R N River Rd--------------------2951
Weeks Mary Helen Mrs Pine Grove Av-----------3401
Wegner Julius Riverside Blvd-------------------2821
Wehage Albert J Loxahatchee Rivr Rd-----------2201
Wells H E US Hwy 1-------------------------2652
White W W 3rd-----------------------------3791
Wieking Johanna Eganfuskee-------------------2681
Wilkinson H J Cemtery Rd---------------------2071
Wilson John R Point Rd-----------------------2291
Wilson Palm Gardens Loxahatchee Rivr Rd-------2761
Wolf T C Mrs Indiantown Rd--------------------3711
Wood Katherine Mrs Rivrsde Dr-----------------3741

Ziegler John atty U S Hwy 1-------------------2351
Ziegler John Sr A1A Hwy----------------------2401

## WHY IT'S NOT CALLED 'JUPITER' STATE PARK

For about three years after the war, the nation heaved a collective sigh of relief that almost cost Jupiter its most valuable real estate asset.

As millions of soldiers shed their uniforms and hundreds of ships were mothballed, Florida's many military bases were among hundreds around the country that simply lay fallow. Camp Murphy became a no-man's land, its dunes littered with spent rifle bullets and the chickweed already growing back over shellrock roads.

All this was before 1947 when the Soviet Union put a wall around East Berlin and the West realized it was in for another military buildup and a long war of nerves. In that brief period of euphoria before the Cold War, the federal government laid plans to sell off most of the lands that it had commandeered for training bases.

At one point the government used the former Camp Murphy facilities as a temporary "processing center" (and living quarters) for new immigrants. Then on June 9, 1947, the Florida Board of Forestry and Parks officially obtained title to a 7,871-acre parcel to be known as Jupiter State Park.

But an actively managed park it wasn't. In fact, eight years later the state was all but ready to lease 3,720 acres of it along U.S. 1 to Broadway producer Eddie Dowling. Somehow Dowling had evangelized the park board into granting him a six-month option to rent the land for $10,000 a year. What for? Dowling had experienced an epiphany and a vision. Holy Land U.S.A., a replicated Jerusalem-in-the-dunes theme park, would beckon to every tourist headed into south Florida on U.S. 1. All Dowling needed was a little time and $5 million in investor financing to build it.

Wow! It was the spring of 1955 and members of the Hobe Sound Chamber of Commerce loved it. They sent Dowling and park officials a letter expressing their unanimous support.

One can imagine Mrs. Joseph Verner Reed in her Jupiter Island waterfront villa, gagging on her morning coffee as she read her newspaper. To the wife of the Jupiter Island Club's founder and its unchallenged guardian of civility, throngs of tourists, garish displays and visions of motel row on U.S. 1 were not at all what the staid settlement needed sprawling across lovely Hobe Sound. Her son, Nathaniel P. Reed, picks it up from there:

*Mother flew into action. First, she called on her brother. Samuel Pryor Jr. was the senior vice president of Pan American World Airline and was the chief lobbyist for Juan Trippe, the airline's president. My Uncle Sam knew everyone in state and federal government. He had been awarded medals from our government and from many Central and South American governments for managing airfields that had developed into the southern flyway to North Africa.*

*Uncle Sam had a twin-engine plane flown by an expert pilot. They made a date with the then-governor, Spessard Holland, and then flew in that plane to meet him in his office in the old capitol building.*

*Mother and Sam were very persuasive, especially as a team. They explained the potential impact of the theme park and urged the governor to request that the 3,720 acres instead be incorporated into*

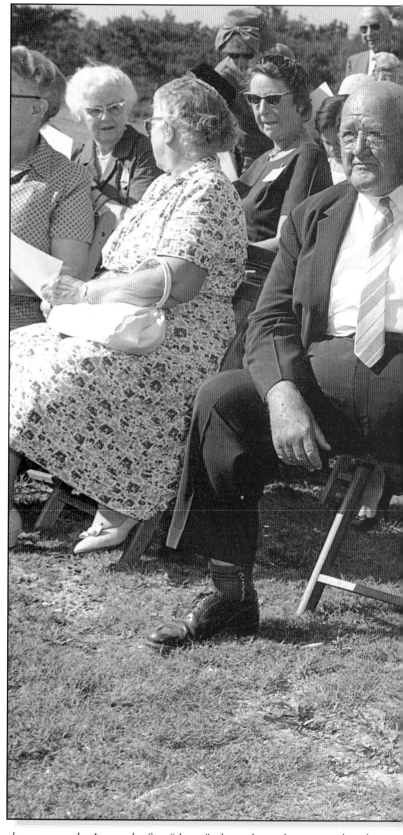

*the state park. In need of a "theme" themselves, they remembered Jonathan Dickinson's shipwreck on Jupiter Island and urged that the state park honor his name.*

The Hobe Sound Chamber never found out who blew up the project until after Dowling announced his withdrawal. "Please reconsider!" they begged. "We endorsed it *unanimously*."

Furious, they suspected a stealth bomber from Jupiter Island. They prevailed on the Martin County Commission, which summoned the town manager of Jupiter Island Club to an investigative hearing.

Billy Bowlegs III (second from right) attends dedication ceremonies for Jonathan Dickinson State Park in 1955. It was his great grandfather who led the last band of Seminoles into the Everglades, refusing to be transported west after the Second Seminole Indian War. *(Loxahatchee River Historical Society)*

Had he, Ret. Admiral Richard Tuggle, or any town officials, opposed the deal on behalf of Jupiter Island? Well, no, he said, he had only attended park board meeting with Permelia Reed.

So, what had he said?

Nothing, said Admiral Tuggle. Mrs. Reed had done all the talking.

Too late for Holy Land. Dowling's option expired. Shortly thereafter, Jupiter State Park was renamed for a man whose ship had grounded on the beach at Jupiter Island. Its new name would be Jonathan Dickinson State Park.

A few years later, the landowners on Jupiter Island donated 967

161

Penn Park (top) and Eastview Manor (Middle) were among the very first housing developments in Jupiter.

BELOW: A crane-mounted barge works at filling in the wetlands on the corner of Center Street and Whitney Road. *(Loxahatchee River Historical Society)*

Gladwin-Bassett built many of the individual homes in early Jupiter-Tequesta, then went on to specialize in commercial buildings. From left, breaking ground for a new First Marine Bank building, Art Stanley of Rood Landscape, County Commissioner Bill Van Kessel, Jim Bassett and Bud Gladwin. *(Skip Gladwin Collection)*

acres to be preserved as a National Wildlife Refuge—five hundred of it coming from the Reed family. Some of it borders the west shore of Hobe Sound, the rest comprising 3.5 miles of beach bordered on the north by the St. Lucie State Reserve.

The donors made only two conditions. The secluded beach was a popular nudist bathing area, which Mrs. Reed did not find at all charming. The reason the "naturists" flocked there was that the beach was shielded by towering Australian pines, which meant that one's tender parts didn't fricassee as fast in the broiling Florida sun. When the Australian pines went (in the cause of native habitat restoration), so did the nudists. Any diehards could be now spotted easily in the binoculars of local policemen and, one must assume, quickly dispatched on their way.

## NEW ECONOMY MEETS OLD ECONOMY

In prewar years, land ownership in Jupiter hadn't changed much. The Pennocks, Histeds, Zieglers, DuBois (and Trapper Nelson out west) owned big chunks of it. But that didn't necessarily make them rich because one doesn't become a "land baron" until developers want to buy and subdivide it. And there were precious few in the forties.

Instead, the first wave of land sales was created by another force. Dozens of young men were returning from wartime service with savings in their pockets and a need either for land on which to build new businesses or business capital to be derived from selling land. Suddenly, Jupiter's "first families" faced pressure—from within—to carve up their holdings.

And the first to feel it was the Pennock family. After all, Pennock Plantation now sprawled from the river on the north to well beyond Toney Penna Drive, and from the railroad tracks west to Pennock peninsula. However, the four Pennock offspring faced a dilemma: none had enough money to buy out the others and all, truth be known, had different ideas of what they wanted to do with their lives. In 1954 they commissioned Ted Brown & Son, registered real estate appraisers, to survey the Pennock domain from the cattle pens and worker cottages to trucks, office equipment and pitch forks.

The entire valuation of Jupiter's largest employer came to $239,840. The tally included $137,225 for the land, $50,430 for ten enclosed farm buildings, $48,507 for 26 sheds and greenhouses, $1,987 for a potpourri of tools, $1,275 for eight trucks and $416 for office equipment.

The assets were divided among the four Pennocks and a gradual sell-off began. The dairy farm property went to Boutwell's Dairy of Lake Worth. Lloyd Minear, who had managed the dairy for many years, bought the herd and sold its milk to Boutwell's. But in 1959 he bought 211 acres in Martin County and moved the herd there. The pastures were ready for sale to developers.

If they built it, would people come? Among the first to test the premise in postwar Jupiter were Jimmy Bassett and Ransom F. (Bud) Gladwin. Skip Gladwin, the latter's son, describes a company that would pervade Jupiter construction in the postwar years. "Jimmy Bassett started as a mason in 1947, making his own cinder blocks. My dad started as a carpenter. They wound up cooperating in so many projects that they ended up forming a partnership.

"You couldn't get two more opposite personalities. Jimmy Bassett was a hard-driving, tough, cracker, smart as a whip. Dad was a refined Rutgers grad. Yet they had deep respect for each other and they were completely honest."

Gladwin-Bassett began building homes for people who had just bought real estate lots. Soon they would become Jupiter's first commercial construction specialists. As First Marine Bank and Community Federal Savings spread along Palm Beach and Martin counties, Gladwin-Bassett would build virtually all of their branch offices. Same for office buildings and many of the retail stores that now line U.S. 1.

As homebuyers proved developers right, other businesses sprouted from the basic infrastructure. Lainhart and Potter opened a branch office in Jupiter and became the city's premiere building supplier. Roy Rood turned the family homestead on County Line Road into Rood Landscape.

Rood was typical of the veterans who came home full of ambition for Jupiter and how they could make it better. He'd taken a temporary job in a local nursery while waiting for the next school term to begin at Purdue University, where he'd begin studies as an engineer. But it took the job in Jupiter to make him realize what he really enjoyed. So, with $300 in "mustering out" pay he'd received on leaving the navy, Rood went to Fort Pierce and bought some used shovels, axes, hoes and saws and pronounced himself a landscaper.

Yet, the surge in development was never far removed from Jupiter's economic roots. Tourists got their first taste of Jupiter in the motels and restaurants along U.S. 1. Stressed-out urbanites moved in because of the sun and water and fishing. Nothing represented those essential ties—and the clash between old and new Jupiter— better than the Jupiter Marina.

It straddled the southeast side of the Dixie Highway Bridge over the river, paralleling the railroad tracks. This narrow rim of riverfront probably embodied more Jupiter history than any site save the Carlin-DuBois stretch along the inlet's south side. It was there where the school boats landed, where the railroad spur had run onto a wharf for loading railroad cars. And alongside was the same road that had run by landmarks like Bowers Grocery and Ziegler's store at the turn of the century.

In 1971 all that was left was a rundown marina that Matthew and Lorry Bressler mortgaged their souls to buy.

In the fall of 1970, Bressler, a product designer with RCA Computer Systems, found himself transferred to the company's Palm Beach Gardens plant to help build mainframe systems. A

Many of Jupiter's oldest families clung to river life, but also took advantage of the "new" economy. Dave Brooker (above) painted houses but also ran weekend charters from Shuey's marina (below). And Saturday night parties on his boat (right) were something locals looked forward to. *(Agnes Brooker Collection)*

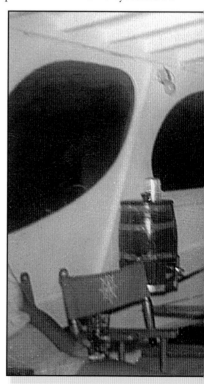

year later RCA's board decided to back out of the computer business. Five thousand employees were laid off, and Bressler, a suit-and-tie executive, found himself stranded in Florida with scant prospect of any comparable job. When he announced to wife Lorry and the kids that he'd found something in Rochester, N.Y., they nearly mutinied at the thought of going back into snow country.

What to do? Bressler and Don Pothier, another out-of-work RCAer, had fished at rundown Jupiter Marina and knew it could be bought. "We borrowed a $25,000 down payment from some relatives and took a mortgage for $150,000," he says. "We figured that if you had good general business experience, you could run any business."

Bressler learned otherwise on day one. The same night the deal closed in January 1971 the seller invited the Bresslers to a farewell party for his employees and the commercial fishermen who rented boat slips. "Two of the fishermen were playing pool with another guy and they started arguing over a woman," Bressler recalls. [He won't name names because they're both alive today "and just as mean."]

"One guy jabbed his cue at the other one and pretty soon the bigger fellow had the other one in a bear hug and was probably cracking some ribs when the second guy managed to reach in his pants pocket. He pulled out a knife and stabbed the other one in the stomach several times. The bear hugger was bleeding all over the place, but he kept chasing the stabber around the table, threatening to kill him. Finally, his friends made him lie down and they packed him with ice—just like a fish—to slow the blood flow until an ambulance came."

When Bressler and his partner took over, their anticipated revenue stream looked something like this: fishermen would pay monthly rentals for slips. Boaters would buy gas and supplies. Pinder's seafood company, which bought fish from commercial boats at dockside, would, in lieu of rent. pay the marina a penny for every pound purchased. Meanwhile, fishermen and passers-by

would both patronize the waterfront eatery, which offered hamburgers, chili and other simple fare.

The reality was captured in a memoir Bressler wrote, "so my grandchildren would know something of our life."

*The monies we collected barely covered the mortgage payments and operational expenses. But since we could eat at the marina, use marina supplies and gas for our cars and staff our operation with wives and children, we managed to survive.*

*My partner and I were working seven days a week. He opened the restaurant at 5 a.m. for breakfast and prepared lunch. I came in to help at lunch and prepared for dinner. Then I worked till the ten o'clock closing. After six months I opened and he closed. Our wives worked opposite hours so we could take care of our children.*

The biggest drag on the operation was the commercial fishermen.

*These fishermen had the run of the marina before we bought the property. They would walk in the back door before daybreak and draw their own coffee from a large urn. They usually didn't buy any food other than perhaps a doughnut to go with their coffee. Then they'd use our telephone to make local calls. They also expected the fuel dock to open at 5 a.m. so they could gas up before heading out to fish.*

*I changed all that! I told them to gas up in the evenings when they came in. I no longer let them come behind the counter for coffee and doughnuts or to use the phone. I served them the coffee and doughnuts and collected the money when I did.*

*This didn't go over well with these rugged individualists. One morning I came in and found two bullet holes in the back door of the restaurant. When I got a pretty good idea of who did it, I didn't confront him directly because I had no real proof. I just told him he'd have to dock his boat elsewhere after the end of the month. He blew his top, saying that there wasn't any marina nearby that accepted commercial fisherman (I wonder why). Then he let it be known that if he had to move, I might just be found shot. The only threat I could make good on was to have the Marine Patrol evict him. These fishermen weren't afraid of the local police, but the Marine Patrol could harass and delay them with all sorts of inspections. That's why the Marine Patrolmen ate at my restaurant for half-price.*

*Even so, it was after that episode that I received a permit to carry a concealed weapon. I gave my wife a snub-nosed revolver and I carried a German Luger. I realized that I was not working with professionals at RCA anymore and that I had to act accordingly.*

After too many struggles and long hours, the two partners had to concede that there just wasn't enough income to sustain both families. It was Lorry Bressler who offered a solution. The Bresslers would buy out the Pothiers and start a full-menu seafood restaurant on the same site. After all, the commercial fleet was bringing in a million pounds a year at their dock. Wouldn't people flock from far and wide to dine on the freshest, finest seafood for miles around as the moon cast its shadow over Jupiter Lighthouse?

Bressler went to Clint Pinder with an offer he couldn't refuse. The new restaurant would have the right to pay market price for

RIGHT: During its heyday in the seventies, a million pounds of commercial fish were brought into Jupiter Fisherman's Marina in a typical year—most of it bought by Pinder's seafood. *(Skip Gladwyn Collection)*

FAR RIGHT: By the late eighties, Jupiter Fisherman's Marina had been torn down and the site offered for development as "Harbour View Plaza." The realtor's promotional photo gives a good look at the waterfront strip that at the turn of the century supported stores along a rail spur. It's where the old school boat dropped off kids who lived on the river. The site is now a public park. *(Matthew Bressler Collection)*

the pick of each day's catch. Otherwise, Pinder could find himself another commercial marina (which didn't exist).

With that, in 1974 Jupiter Fisherman's Marina Restaurant was born, and family fortunes changed quickly. On any day the menu featured over two hundred dishes—twelve kinds of shrimp and four chowders (60 cents a cup, $1.20 a bowl). People drove up from Palm Beach and from Jupiter's budding developments. Perry Como and wife would putt-putt upriver from their home in Jupiter Inlet Colony. Profits were good. Bressler was elected to the Town Council and became vice mayor. Lorry was greeter (when not filling in as waitress) and the Bresslers knew everyone in town.

The only downside at that point was that it was often difficult to offer Pratt & Whitney executives dining ambience with scruffy fishermen guzzling beer at the bar and guffawing around the pool table. "They were a rough crowd," says Bressler.

The roughest, toughest of all was Guy Freeman, eldest brother of a family that had been fishing and hunting in Jupiter longer than anyone could remember. Writes Bressler:

*One day Guy Freeman came in and said something had just been stolen from his boat. Somebody said that he thought he knew who did it and would try to get in touch with the person. Before he had finished, Freeman knocked him flat. He got his hands around the guy's neck and said he'd kill him if the perpetrator wasn't there in five minutes. He was.*

*Another time someone who Freeman had gotten the best of in a fight appeared at the marina with a karate expert. The karate guy assumed the standard pose you see in the movies and told Freeman to get ready for a trashing. Before he made a move, Freeman grabbed a two by four*

*off the ground and started whacking hell out of the guy. The last I saw of them was Freeman whacking the karate man down the street with the two by four as the guy begged him to stop.*

By 1978 the Bresslers were tired. Lorry developed a heart condition. Lawyers at The Florida East Coast Railway had materialized out of nowhere, saying that most of the marina was on FEC property. After an exhausting legal battle, the Bresslers agreed to pay the railroad $72,000, adding another burden to their overhead. They sold to a New York restaurateur, whose eatery up north soon went bust and prevented him from rejuvenating the marina restaurant in Jupiter. It lay fallow for a dozen years. Eventually, the Town of Jupiter saw a chance to preserve one of its most historic properties. Now called Harbor View Park, its scenic markers will explain all of the many early Jupiter sites that occupied it over more than a century.

## TEQUESTA: THE 'OTHER' SIDE OF THE TRACKS

When lighthouse captain Charles Seabrook retired just after the war, he picked a place so unpopulated that he could name his street anything he wanted. Their retirement home on Seabrook Road was (still is) located barely more than a mile west of the lighthouse reservation. The Seabrook's most conspicuous neighbor on the north side of the river was Shuey's motel and cottages on U.S. 1.

Anyone heading for Jupiter Island would have to cross Cato's Bridge, perhaps waiting for the tender to crank the "swing-span" into place after he'd opened it for a passing boat. The tender for ten years dating from 1949 was Avon Charles Cato, who lived in a cottage on the west side with his wife and three teenage kids.

Labels on image: JUPITER ISLAND, JUPITER INLET, US 1, LOXAHATCHEE RIVER, INTRACOASTAL, HARBOUR VIEW PLAZA SITE, ALT A1A, NORTH

"Dad rented rowboats for $1 a day," recalls daughter Shirley, who now lives in Clyde, N.C. "He also caught mullet and sold them five for 25 cents wrapped in newspaper. When the tide was coming in, we'd go under the bridge and catch shrimp and sell them for bait.

"A bridge tender's salary wasn't much with three teenagers to raise." She adds. "We ate fish and beans, and I thought when I grow up I'll never eat another fish or bean. Truth is, they're still two of my favorite foods today."

In 1954 a visitor from Springfield, Mass. poked his head inside the bridge tender's cubicle and asked if Cato could show him around the south part of Jupiter Island that borders the inlet.

"I can't," he said. "There's no roads, no nothing."

So Cato took him on a boat tour. The visitor was Charles Martyn, and within a few years he would almost single-handedly transform the north side of the river (it had no name) into a symbol of the elegant, sun-and-surf lifestyle that would magnetize thousands of northerners to postwar Florida.

Charlie Martyn was a good-looking, gregarious, one-man-band of a residential developer. In 1954 he bought 86 acres on the north side of Jupiter Island for $294,000 from socialites Jock Whitney, Joan Payson and Mike Phipps. The first newspaper accounts trumpeted that Martyn planned "a complete community" of 240 homes with a yacht club, 200-unit apartment-hotel, shopping center, and marina for forty large boats. Moreover, an 18-hole golf course community would be built two miles west on the Loxahatchee River.

Martyn's first brochure in December vowed that his development wouldn't "spoil" Jupiter. No indeed: "Quiet and privacy will still reign. And if the rising tides of Jupiter Inlet occasionally echo to the laughter of sun-browned kids, well, old Jupiter hands will agree it's an improvement."

Across the river, old Jupiter hands cast a wary eye on the seductive ad claims—but not for long. At the time, budget shortages had caused the town to delay a long-pending project to build a water tower for its growing population. Generous Charlie Martyn quickly agreed to form the Jupiter Water Co. and built a 60,000-gallon tower to serve both the town and the new development.

By 1955 the place had been named Jupiter Inlet Beach Colony, and 27 homes were under construction. Waterfront lots were going for around $12,000 and interior sites in the $3,000 range. But what attracted the most attention was the hotel, estimated to cost $3 million. Gushed the *Miami Herald*: "Ground clearing for the ultra-modern 200-unit hostelry was begun last week by the Gateway Construction Company of Springfield, Mass. If the architect's drawing is even a reasonably exact facsimile, it is destined to be one of the fanciest hotels in South Florida, complete

Brimming with optimism in 1954, Lloyd Turner, Charles Martyn and Tom Daly look like they can't wait to get back to work on building the infrastructure for Jupiter Beach Inlet Colony.
*(Martyn Family Collection)*

BELOW: One of the earliest aerial shots (1957) of the Colony after about two years of development.
*(Martyn Family Collection)*

FAR RIGHT: This, the first sales sheet Martyn produced for the Jupiter Inlet Beach Colony, indicates how much an original investment would have paid off today for those who stayed.
*(Martyn Family Collection)*

with swimming pool, cabanas, floral gardens, 27 penthouse apartments, central air conditioning and all the other incidentals which make for top-flight luxury living."

The intrepid reporter also noted: "Apparently this southeastern tip of the peninsula is part of an Indian mound, for more than the usual items of Indian history are being turned over in quantity by the construction work. Jonathan Swift, in his travel narratives, told of being captured at this spot by Tequesta Indians."

Jonathan Swift, the London literary lion, wouldn't have been caught dead on a beach in the colonies, and the Tequesta Indians dwelled around Miami. But the part about Indian artifacts was accurate. Charlie Martyn was fascinated by his finds of tools and jewelry and promised to display them in the hotel lobby. And he was captivated by the name *Tequesta* ("Jeaga" didn't sound very marketable).

Across the Intracoastal, just north of Jupiter Inlet Beach Colony, Martyn parlayed his land sale revenues into money for a second development. In 1956 a large newspaper ad announced the debut of "Waterway Village and the planned Village Square Shopping Center."

Martyn hardly stopped for breath. The same year he opened Tequesta Country Club, with 600 home sites bordering two miles of Loxahatchee riverfront and an 18-hole golf course designed by Dick Wilson. Almost on its heels, he took a $630,000 mortgage to acquire the 340-acre Roebuck tract lying between the north and west forks of the Loxahatchee. It would become Tequesta Hunt Club Colony. Martyn loved to bowl, so one day, almost as a brief break in a busy schedule, ground was broken across the river for the new Jupiter Bowl.

"Charlie Martyn was a genius," says attorney Bill Wood. "They say he could sit down and sketch out a complete subdivision, price out the lots and tell you just how much the value of the lots would rise."

Indeed, Jupiter Inlet Colony was performing even better than Martyn's estimates. As 1957 rolled in, lots had doubled in value and were now averaging $17,500 each (the whole of Jupiter Island had been sold by Eusebio Gomez in 1821 for $8,000). Only one of the new lot owners had sold out, and that was to trade up for two larger lots. Tom and Virginia Daly, who served as exclusive real estate agents for Inlet Colony, had begun with a rattletrap jeep for their office. Now, in one year, they had racked up over $500,000 in property sales.

Life was sweet in what was a unique settlement. "Dad was a reformed alcoholic," says son Charles "Punch" Martyn III. "His closest associates tended to be AA members as well. That led to lots being sold to other AA people. They had lively parties, to be sure [Charlie

always kept a set of drums in his living room], but alcohol wasn't at the center of them."

The only problem with this happy story was in the way each new project was financed. Martyn would use the proceeds from home and lot sales on one project as a down payment on the next parcel. Each new development would spawn the next.

It worked until the recession of 1963-64 slammed into the Florida economy. The extra money people had been using for land speculation and winter homes suddenly dried up. Martyn couldn't pay his mortgage on the new Hunt Club Colony because he hadn't sold enough lots and homes on the previous development. As mortgage holders called in their notes, each domino toppled over the next one. The 200-room hotel never got beyond the blueprint stage.

Martyn tried to hang on. He fell off the wagon for a while with a couple of binges and his wife left him. Throughout the ordeal, says their son, Punch, "he refused to declare bankruptcy because he felt he'd never land another development project. What he did was go to California and work with Litton Industries as a real estate consultant. The rest of us stayed in Tequesta and tried to muddle through [Punch was barely out of high school]. In retrospect, if Dad had just held on to his unsold lots in the Colony and Waterway Village, he could have enough cash to weather the recession. But with the Tequesta clubs he was just too vulnerable."

Charlie Martyn did make a comeback, returning to Martin

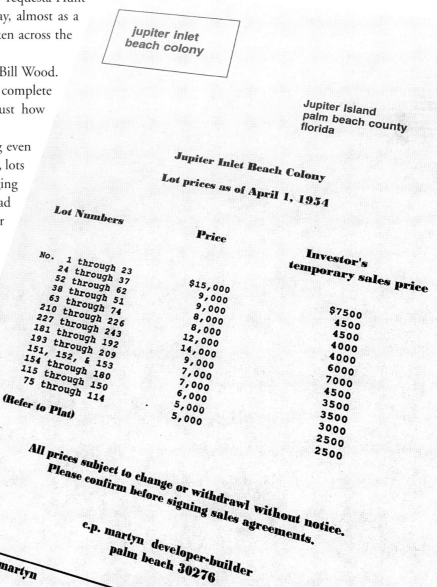

jupiter inlet beach colony

Jupiter Island
palm beach county
florida

**Jupiter Inlet Beach Colony**
**Lot prices as of April 1, 1954**

| Lot Numbers | Price | Investor's temporary sales price |
|---|---|---|
| No. 1 through 23 | $15,000 | $7500 |
| 24 through 37 | 9,000 | 4500 |
| 52 through 62 | 9,000 | 4500 |
| 38 through 51 | 8,000 | 4000 |
| 63 through 74 | 8,000 | 4000 |
| 210 through 226 | 12,000 | 6000 |
| 227 through 243 | 14,000 | 7000 |
| 181 through 192 | 9,000 | 4500 |
| 193 through 209 | 7,000 | 3500 |
| 151, 152, & 153 | 7,000 | 3500 |
| 154 through 180 | 6,000 | 3000 |
| 115 through 150 | 5,000 | 2500 |
| 75 through 114 | 5,000 | 2500 |
| (Refer to Plat) | | |

All prices subject to change or withdrawl without notice. Please confirm before signing sales agreements.

c.p. martyn developer-builder
palm beach 30276

charles p. martyn

Looking east across the Cato bridge to the yacht basin in Jupiter Beach Inlet Colony around 1962. *(Loxahatchee River Historical Society)*

County to develop successful properties in Stuart and Palm City. Meanwhile, the people who *had* bought homes in his Tequesta developments continued to see their property values rise.

Other developers stepped into Martyn's shoes (Hunt Club Colony, for example, became Turtle Creek).

When Pratt & Whitney brought Bill and Patricia Magrogan to Jupiter in 1961, "Tequesta was where everybody wanted to be," says Pat. "We couldn't wait until we could afford something on the other side of the river."

And therein lies the Charles Martyn legacy. When the town of Tequesta was incorporated June 4, 1957, nearly everyone there lived in a Martyn-inspired property. In fact, the first official village meeting on July 10 was held in the office of his long-time realtor, Tom Daly. The first budget called for $8,100:

| | |
|---|---|
| *Municipal dock* | *$1,000* |
| *Police department* | *1,500* |
| *Fire department* | *300* |
| *Legal fees* | *1,800* |
| *Secretarial* | *2,500* |
| *Miscellaneous* | *1,000* |

By 1964, fast-growing Tequesta was approaching parity with its neighbor across the river. On September 3, *The Beacon News* reported that Vacation Homes Inc. had donated a 63,000-square-

foot site on Tequesta Drive to the town. With that, the Village Council approved a bond issue to cover the $148,000 construction cost of a village hall and administrative offices.

## THE CHAMBER: 'ANSWER EVERY LETTER'

Jupiter had maintained a "Board of Trade" in the twenties and thirties. In 1949 business people decided to become more aggressive. They formed the Jupiter Chamber of Commerce and levied annual dues of $5. By the end of 1950 the new organization was in full swing. Frank J. Laird had become president, and began a ten-year habit of answering every inquiry about Jupiter with a personal letter. Later, businesses and people who moved to Jupiter would say that it was Laird's personal, folksy responses that had made them fall in love with Jupiter.

During that first full year the Chamber counted among its achievements getting speed limits along U.S. 1, advocating controls on netting in the river ("it has ruined sport fishing," said the Chamber), and obtaining channel markers for the river. By December the Chamber had 71 members and sponsored the first Town Christmas Tree, with Santa passing out treats to children.

Pop Laird, as they called him, was infectious with his enthusiasm. By April 1951 membership had grown to 118, largely because Laird urged everyone he met to join and refused to take no for an answer. Notes a Chamber history:

Aerial photo looks north across river from Pennock Point to the roads that have been carved out of the landscape. They'd soon become Tequesta Country Club and the Tequesta Hunt Club Colony. (Loxahatchee River Historical Society)

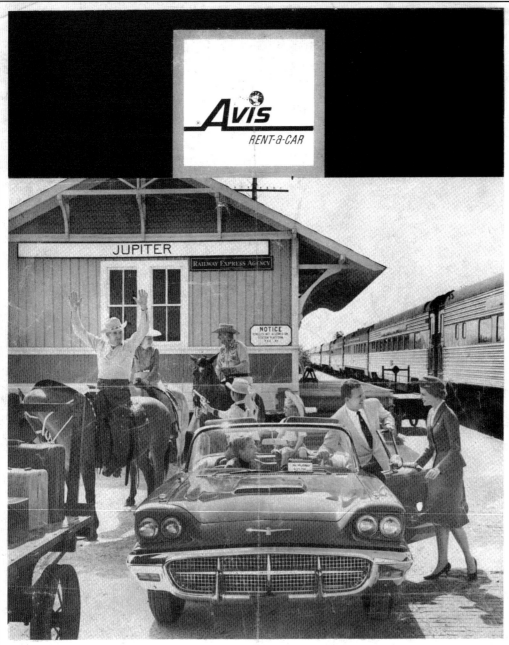

## Wherever you go Avis "minute-saver service" waits for you

Go West . . . go East . . . go anywhere in the world! Avis is there to greet you with new "minute-saver service." A call to your local Avis office will send word on ahead over the Avis Teletype Network so

that you're expected. When you arrive, Avis has your car ready and waiting . . . your name on it, too! You're off in a minute in a smart new Ford or other fine car. No one but Avis saves you so much

time in so many places. Next trip, let us help you make it more enjoyable. Call your local Avis office or your Travel Agent. Ask for "minute-saver service"—the extra service at no extra charge!

Charge Avis Rent-a-Car services with Avis, American Express, Diners' Club, or Carte Blanche cards. Sheraton Hotel, air, rail, and other accredited charge cards are honored. ©1960 Avis Inc., 18 Irvington Street, Boston 16, Mass.

TIME, JULY 11, 1960

Jupiter got its first taste of fame in 1960 when Avis Rent-A-Car used the old train depot in a national ad campaign. Local folks even got a moment in the limelight, too. That's Lige Mayo on horse at left and son Beau mounted at right.
*(Loxahatchee River Historical Society)*

He was a familiar sight wherever there was any activity, opening the trunk of his car and getting out brochures to give members and prospects for distribution. Hundreds of brochures were sent to automobile clubs and chambers of commerce. As soon as welcome stations were opened along the northern border of the state, he supplied them with brochures.

In 1956, one of the Chamber's main goals bore fruit when the last few miles of State 706 (Indiantown Road) and U.S. 98 were opened between Indiantown and Jupiter. Said a Chamber history:

*Replacing a sand trail where one had to wait for six-foot alligators to mosey across the road, the new highway marked the opening of the way west from Jupiter to Tallahassee to New Orleans and Seattle. The event brought state and national officials to the area and was ushered in by a motorcade of a hundred cars, most of them from the Jupiter area.*

[After a ribbon cutting ceremony,] *the motorcade then proceeded to a point 5-1/2 miles west of Jupiter where the new section of SR 706 began.*

By 1957 Chamber membership had risen to 155 and dues were increased to $10. The minutes noted that, "Mitzi Stieper [founder of *Highlights,* a mimeographed advertising circular that later evolved into the *Courier-Journal*] was admitted as the first woman member."

In 1960 a progress report showed the Chamber working for creation of a public park and insisting that railroad crossing gates be installed on County Line Road. A big event that year was the opening of the Pratt & Whitney Aircraft plant near Indiantown, an occasion that brought out another motorcade of Jupiter luminaries, a tour of the plant and a luncheon at its cafeteria.

The Chamber's biggest regular event was probably its annual Stag Barbecue. Says a former president: "We had these down at the civic center and just about every male in town would turn out. The banks and other large businesses would compete to hand out as much liquid refreshment as they could, and I must say, they were not refused. These went on every year until the Chamber got more and more women members. The ladies insisted on being invited, too, and when they saw what was going on they got in a dither and demanded a more proper decorum. Some of this may have come from the wife of the guy who drove his car off a bridge and into the Carlin Park creek after too much barbecue sauce. Anyway, from then on the events just sort of petered out."

## HOW GOVERNMENT GREW UP

Marie Cross had moved to Jupiter in 1945 from Long Island, only to be widowed when her husband died of a heart attack in 1948. She was "at loose ends," she said, until friends urged to get involved by running for town commissioner. Cross filed her candidacy papers, only to learn later that she was running against her own son-in-law. She won, and served as commissioner from 1949 to 1951. "In those days," she recalled, "we held two meetings a month and were paid $5.00."

In 1951, Cross ran for mayor and wound up being the first woman in Florida to hold the position. "I loved being in politics," she said. "I was young and everyone was so nice to me."

She went on to serve three terms, a period when Jupiter saw many "firsts." Its first fire truck, for example. In 1954, during Cross's tenure, the first telephone dial exchange took effect, connecting 120 phones. A new town hall and the Rood-Williams American Legion Post were built. Street signs were acquired and land for a town dump was bought and opened. And Jupiter, which had been bypassed by the Sunshine State Parkway even though it passed nearby, finally wrangled an interchange from the state turnpike board.

Marie Cross' official service ended in 1966 when she lost a re-election bid. It was about that time that Jupiter government took a quantum jump. "The big reason was ad valorem (real estate) taxes," says William S. Wood, who began serving as town attorney in 1967. "Until then Jupiter's income depended on what it could take in from 'fines and forfeitures.' This meant we didn't take in a cent unless we generated it from things like traffic tickets, DUI fines and building permits. The town had never collected a portion of Palm Beach County's real estate taxes because its leaders thought that doing so required majority approval of everyone in town. What they found was that it required only a majority of those *voting* in the election."

Once Jupiter had that real estate money, it more than tripled income and enabled the town to build more roads and expand the police department.

"These new services weren't applauded by everyone," Wood adds. "I remember one Town Council meeting in which a man passionately petitioned us to stop paving the streets and put a fence around the whole town."

The second big change in Jupiter's government came when it commissioned a Philadelphia survey firm (Kindree & Shepherd)

In the years just after the war, Jupiter didn't own a police car. The fire truck (above) was the volunteer fire department's one and only. In the early seventies Jupiter got access to county real estate taxes and local government suddenly got the muscle it needed to serve a growing community. Robert (Bobby) Culpepper (below) presided over much of that era as mayor, then later as a Palm Beach County commissioner. *(Jupiter Courier)*

# WE WUZ ROBBED

In 1971, 16-year-old Anthony Gravett was hiking in J. W. Corbett preserve, aware that the Jupiter-Tequesta Jaycees would be sponsoring a frog jumping contest at Lighthouse Park in a month or so. It must have been Divine Providence, because he came home with a frog he named Jennifer and proceeded with an arduous training and time-trials. When the big race came, and other frogs were being prodded and poked by their owners, Jennifer came out of the starting gate with a 14-foot, 4-inch leap and won the thing by a few furlongs, or however frog races are measured.

The Jaycees had sworn to sponsor the winner in the National Frog Jumping Contest in California, so off Anthony and Jennifer went. In her first heat Jennifer won with such an Olympic bound—humiliating America's finest amphibians— that the judges blew the whistle and huddled with furrowed brows. They ruled that Jennifer was disqualified because she was an illegal alien—an African leopard frog.

Anthony was crestfallen. All he knew was that he caught Jennifer in the Corbett Preserve. Later, back in Jupiter, experts ruled that Jennifer was a Florida leopard frog-as American as Huck Finn. But by then, Jupiter had been denied its moment of glory in the annals of frog racing. *(Ethel Gravett Collection)*

---

to develop a master plan. "Part of that project was our desire to 'square off' the town boundaries," says Wood. "At the time Jupiter was sprawling all over the place and we wanted to draw a straight line south along Marcinski Road. All this made for a lot of annexations. If the town claimed a certain condo or homeowner's association to be within its boundaries and the residents continued to pay taxes, they were deemed to have agreed to annexation. But sometimes they'd file a protest and we'd have to negotiate before they'd consent."

As that process was unfolding, many landowners on the west side of A1A along the beach were getting ready to file claims to be recognized as owners of all beachfront property that lay within their lot lines. "In other words, if you owned 200 feet of land on the west aide of A1A, you'd also own the equivalent 200 feet of beachfront east of it," notes Wood. "Bobby Culpepper was mayor of Jupiter at that time and everyone today can thank him for having the foresight to fight it."

The result is the strand of public beaches and parks that span from Carlin Park to Juno Beach.

## RIDING SHOTGUN WITH THE CONSTABLE

Beverly Jones Mayo vowed she'd never marry a policeman. She grew up in Washington, D.C. amidst a family of seven police officers and had seen her father disabled at age 39 during a car chase. In fact, it was his early retirement that led him to buy six lots on Pennock Point from Mrs. Shirley Floyd and move to Jupiter in 1954.

For Beverly, just out of high school, Jupiter was a cultural wasteland compared to her Georgetown home amidst the nation's finest museums and monuments.

In 1956 her father succumbed to a coronary related to his police injuries.

Six weeks beforehand she had married a policeman.

Well, not exactly. Jupiter didn't even have a "policeman" as such.

In 1955 the governor had appointed Jupiter native Glynn Mayo "constable." He furnished his own car and radio. His territory ranged north-south from the Juno Beach line to Hobe Sound and east-west from the beaches to Port Mayaca on the edge of Lake Okeechobee. His income was dependent on a fee schedule: so much per traffic ticket, per arrest, etc.

Recalls his widow: "Glynn's office was a phone and notepad that he kept in the headboard of our bed. Our home then [still standing] was on Center Street near where Dix Landscaping is now. We backed onto Sims Creek, but you wouldn't use it then for boating or swimming because it was overgrown and full of snakes and scorpions.

"There really wasn't much to do at night, so I'd ride around in the car with Glynn. We didn't have robberies or much crime. His only problems usually came from a bar in what we called 'Colored Town' right where Center Street and Indiantown Road connect. A big banyan tree stood on the corner and under it was a bar people just called 'The Tree.' Sometimes on weekends a rough crowd from Riviera Beach and West Palm would come up there and then you'd have fights and stabbings.

"Watching Glynn walk in there alone was scary, but the fact is that the troublemakers weren't from Jupiter. The local people always supported him. The big problem was that there were no ambulances or hospitals here. If someone were injured badly, Glynn would have to drive them himself all the way to a black hospital in West Palm Beach."

That Mayo wasn't getting rich from the state's strange "fee" system was evident in 1958 when he jumped at an offer to be Jupiter's first official policeman. The pay was $250 a month (again, with car and radio furnished at his own expense). Shortly afterward Beverly began what would be a 35-year career with Community Federal Savings Bank. The Mayo's moved to Pennock Point, this time paying Mrs. Floyd an extravagant $600 for their building lot.

By the early sixties, the "office on the headboard" had given way to a real one. The old Town Hall was expanded, and in the rear of the building were offices for Mayo and a secretary, as well as a cellblock. "He needed the cells only to hold a prisoner before he could run him down to West Palm Beach," says Beverly. "When I'd go over to help Glynn with his paperwork, I'd put our kids in the cell and use it as a playpen. They loved it."

By the late sixties, the police force had outgrown Town Hall and now rented space at Third Street and Old Dixie where Bates Exterminating is today. Chief Glynn Mayo had two policemen and some K-9 dogs. Still, Jupiter remained a small town, a policeman's biggest problem being the growing number of boats now entering the inlet with bales of pot smuggled from the Bahamas.

Dramatic cases? Only a few. Beverly remembers a serial killer named Dennis Whitney, who had rampaged across the U.S. vowing to break James Starkweather's "record" of eleven murders. As fate would have it, Whitney kidnapped an elderly woman and her dog in Miami and killed them in the woods along A1A in Jupiter. Using the volunteer help of Guy Freeman, a veteran animal tracker, Mayo and his posse ran down Whitney at the river's edge and saw that he got sent to prison for life (where he is today).

But dramatic shootouts aren't why a part of Alternate A1A is named *Glynn Mayo Highway* today. "It really was because Glynn worked so hard to get things done in the community," says his wife. "It was the little things, like when we got the first traffic light in Jupiter. Glynn himself went to West Palm Beach and talked the county into giving us one of their old lights. He brought it over to the corner of Indiantown and Loxahatchee Drive and installed it with his own men.

"Glynn knew lots of people all the way to Tallahassee," she adds.

RIGHT: When Glynn Mayo became Jupiter's first police chief he had to supply his own car and radio. But a growing tax base soon brought a fleet of patrol cars. When Mayo retired after some thirty years, the police force had 55 on its payroll. *(Jupiter Courier)*

ABOVE: Glynn and Beverly Mayo at his 25th anniversary dinner. *(Jupiter Courier)*

175

"For example, people in Jupiter were greatly inconvenienced for years because there was no bridge where Indiantown Road now goes over the Intracoastal Waterway. If you wanted to go, say, from the beach to the high school, you'd have to go along A1A and cross on Donald Ross Road or go north across the U.S. 1 bridge over to A1A and double back. It got to be quite a problem when you had storms or medical emergencies.

"The bridge project was well down the state's priority list, and officials here asked Glynn what he could do. He went to Tallahassee with a delegation of local officials, and after a lot of hard work the bridge finally made it to the top of the list."

But "lobbyist" would hardly belong on Mayo's epitaph. Beverly recalls her husband foremost as a Good Samaritan in a *Mayberry* setting. "We couldn't take a family trip on the Turnpike without him stopping to help every stalled car on the way," she says. "I can't count the number of times we'd go out fishing on a Sunday and wind up towing some stranded fisherman back—all with me complaining about my pot roast going to ruin at home. He delivered babies and saw that runaway kids had a place to sleep. When our son Brad was in a car wreck that killed one of his friends, it was Glynn who was there with the Jaws of Life to pry the other kids out.

"When the new Town Hall was opened, they dedicated a plaque to Glynn, and I'm sure that's what he was proudest of."

Glynn Mayo spent just short of thirty years on Jupiter's police force. When he retired in 1986, the staff exceeded fifty. Mayo died in 1991.

## SALHAVEN, OR HOW JUPITER MEDICAL CENTER GOT ITS START

Jupiter's first "big" development went up so fast it reminded folks of Camp Murphy.

It was named Salhaven. Residents called it "Sal's Haven" because its visionary and ardent backer was Sal B. Hoffman, the pint-sized but bulldog-tough boss of the Philadelphia-based Upholsterers Union International. He was not only besmitten by Jupiter, but besotted with the dream of creating a retirement heaven-on-earth for furniture industry workers. And a nice home for himself in the process.

In 1956 the union pension fund acquired an entire 640-acre section (one of the original tracts platted by the federal military reservation in 1855) that now encompasses Jonathan's Landing. In less than two years, Jupiter (pop. 500) was adjoined by a quasi-town (pop. 300) that offered far more public services than the "real" town could dream of. Clusters of trim two-bedroom cottages were arranged 18 to a cul de sac, each well-manicured unit with its own swimming pool (Sal's imposing retreat had its own pool, of course). Surrounding the homes (rent: $35 a month) and overlooking a large man-made lagoon, were an recreation hall, cafeteria, separate water and sewage purification facilities, telephone system, administrative office, a maintenance building and "security" facility containing one jail cell. It even held a prisoner at one point, but no one can remember why.

Next came a health complex that made Jupiter sick with envy: a 34-bed nursing home pavilion, a small clinic, fire truck and an ambulance facility. All Jupiter had was a second-hand fire truck.

Marcia Brown was supervisor of nurses—three RNs and four aides round the clock. "We had two wings and twenty patients in each one," she recalls. "It started out just for the union retirees, but eventually it admitted outsiders.

"The whole operation was first class," says Brown. "The food at the cafeteria was great. They put on plays in the auditorium. The village even had a little upholstery shop where retirees could keep up their skills."

But somewhere in the mid-sixties Sal Hoffman's euphoria evaporated due to the cost of a weighty infrastructure that now supported less than two hundred residents. With membership in the upholsterer's union dwindling, Hoffman had worked out a partial merger with the United Furniture Workers of America; but when the UFW officers looked at the cost of Salhaven on the balance sheet, they blanched.

Lois Shambaugh saw the trouble coming as well. She ran the telephone switchboard and her husband headed up maintenance. "The basic problem," she says, "was that most of these retirees came from big cities like Philadelphia and Chicago. They complained all the time that there was nothing to do in Jupiter."

Salhaven officially went broke in 1971 and a year later remaining residents were induced to move north to the newly built Little Club on the fringe of County Line Road. Later in 1972 the 130 acres making up the village were sold to a group of 23 doctors. A few months later they flipped it to Alcoa Corp., but with the proviso that thirty acres containing the medical facilities be set aside.

While the rest of Salhaven was being bulldozed down as fast as Camp Murphy disappeared, the thirty acres and clinic-nursing home were already metamorphosing into something much bigger. The reason is that by this time a group of Jupiter Island residents had seen Salhaven as a way to bring all kinds of medical services closer to home. So on May 1973, doctors George Ford, Edwin Brown and William Donovan became the incorporators of the nonprofit Palm Beach-Martin County Medical Center. At its core was to be Salhaven Outpatient Clinic and Convalescence Pavilion, leased from Alcoa for $1 a year. In 1976 the first building was completed, and on February 14, 1979 the newly reorganized Jupiter Medical Center opened with 156 single-bed rooms, all with private bath.

## JUPITER GETS A NEWSPAPER

It all started with Mitzi Stieper. A Long Island native who had been an avid vaudevillian, Stieper had come to Jupiter on vacation in 1956 and stayed on to work as a part-time secretary. At the time, the true center of gravity in town was the Post Office and Ralph's Package Store next door. Stieper became fascinated that people seemed to communicate their announcements and things for sale by posting notes on the Post Office wall.

She had a better idea, one that fit nicely with the secretarial service she'd just opened on an extension of Old Dixie north of Center Street (Southern Bell occupies it today). On Oct. 3, 1957, a mimeographed sheet on pink paper debuted. Called *Highlights,* it contained a handful of announcements, a map of the

ABOVE: Union boss Sal Hoffman envisioned Salhaven as a utopia for retired furniture and upholstery tradesmen, complete with an auditorium, recreational building, up-scale eatery and outsized lagoon. Problem was, it took as many people to run it as the number who lived there. "Utopia" lasted until 1972 when a shrinking union could no longer afford it. *(Lois Shambaugh Collection)*

RIGHT: Salhaven had its own police force and utilities system. Its ambulance and fire-rescue fleet far exceeded anything its poor neighbor, Jupiter, could field. *(Lois Shambaugh Collection)*

LOWER RIGHT: Marking the opening of Jupiter Medical Center in 1974, chief of staff (left to right) William E. Leone, Administrator of Kirkwood Outpatient Center; Dr. George L. Ford, Jr., President of Palm Beach-Martin County Medical Center; Margery Harp, RN, Director of Nursing Services, Kirkwood Outpatient Center *(Jupiter Medical Center)*

177

Ives Cary in 1977. The founder of Jupiter's first "real" newspaper, told friends he named it the *Courier* "because I always wanted to be Courier and Ives" after the famous lithographers of early America. For years he drove each issue to Palm Beach for printing and returned with the finished product in the backseat. *(Jupiter Courier)*

Indiantown-to-Center Street "downtown," and ads for businesses therein. *Highlights* was named for the lighthouse to show that its ads covered Jupiter as completely as the beacon.

By 1958 Stieper was cranking out 18-page issues with more than seventy ads. When Pratt & Whitney opened, she saw to it that five hundred extra copies went to the plant site with a special *Welcome!* supplement sponsored by the Jupiter-Tequesta Chamber of Commerce.

In 1962, after illness forced Stieper to sell, *Highlights* bounced from owner to owner. It finally found a long-term champion in Ives Cary, who had been an ad manager of a Florida newspaper until being squeezed out of his job in a merger. In 1964 it became *Courier Highlights,* and by the start of the following year, when Cary let expire the contracts that let advertisers appear on the front page, it began looking more like a real newspaper. But the initial going was rough, and Cary joked to friends at one point that he was a success because in the first two years he parlayed $2,500 in borrowed funds into a debt of $78,000.

In getting out his weekly each Thursday, Cary's personal schedule was unique to say the least. As he described it: "I went to work on Sunday afternoon about two o'clock and I went to bed Thursday morning if I was tired or not. I did that for 16 years. I never made a major decision on Wednesday that I had not already made earlier in the week. I knew that by then I was mentally incompetent."

A good indicator of the Jupiter area's population at the time is that 3,000 copies of *Courier Highlights* were distributed free to residents within a ten-mile radius. Each Wednesday at 6:30 a.m. Cary would arrive with galleys at the *Palm Beach Post-Times* for the weekly printing. Once completed, the 3,000 issues would take up the back and front seats of his Renault Dauphine on the way back.

"The biggest single problem was keeping up with growth," he told a reporter on Jupiter's 25th anniversary in 1983. Between 1964 and 1980 circulation increased from 3,000 to 20,000 free papers.

Cary's biggest worry was rain. "If you're a daily and it rains, you've always got a paper tomorrow," he said. "If it rains on a weekly, you're out for a week."

Soon he hit on a solution that made *Courier Highlights* first in the world. He saw his butcher wrapping meat in plastic containers and decided that's the way his papers would be encased. He admits that at first readers had their troubles trying to figure out how to open them.

In 1972 Cary moved the paper to its present Indiantown Road location and bought a computerized typesetter. "Ads picked up 25 percent in one month because we started to look like a newspaper," he said.

Others noticed, too, and in 1978 Cary cashed in. That year he took an offer from the Scripps-Howard chain, which had already acquired *The Stuart News.* By that time his payroll had increased to 55 and the paper had won some impressive awards from small town publishing associations.

In short order *Courier Highlights* became essentially what it is today—*The Jupiter Courier,* published twice a week, with an all-paid circulation.

## A LITTLE 'JET PROPULSION' FROM PRATT & WHITNEY

Which came first, housing developments or the money to buy the houses?

New development came first in that Jupiter Inlet Colony and Tequesta Country Club had already begun in 1957 when Pratt & Whitney arrived, but it marked a new era of jobs, skilled positions and a large infusion of income for Jupiter's businesses and homebuilders.

But it wasn't exactly an invasion. "Initially, just four or five of us from headquarters in East Hartford [Connecticut] were assigned to investigate Florida because we needed lots of land for a special top-secret project," says Richard Anschutz. "We were working with Lockheed to replace the aging U-2 spy plane. We were convinced we could build a hydrogen-powered engine because it's the most efficient fuel you can use.

"Our dilemma was that you have to store liquid hydrogen at 423 degrees below zero, and a plane flying at Mach 3 generates tremendous heat. Our testing facilities up in East Hartford were in enclosed areas. We had never worked with hydrogen before, and we worried that the size and noise and combustibility of these new engines might cause some kind of disaster. So we began shopping for a big site where we could do the testing outdoors."

The original idea was to recruit and build a skilled technical staff of 1,500 or so without drawing from the 12,000 people at P & W's main plant in East Hartford. Says Anschutz: "When we tested want-ads ads for engineers using several potential locations, Florida drew three or four times more resumes than the others."

As luck would have it, Palm Beach County officials had been courting aerospace titan Howard Hughes by dangling the prospect of 9,000 acres of J.W. Corbett Preserve for an aircraft test site.

When Hughes left them high and dry (he couldn't stand the smell of nearby pesticide sprays) the "reconnaissance team" from P & W showed up. They got the Corbett acreage when P & W agreed to buy the adjacent 13,500-acre Indian Trail Ranch and swap it. As an added incentive, the county agreed to build a road that would afford employees a "beeline" commute to "civilization," i.e. West Palm Beach.

So that's how the Beeline Highway got its name. Ironically, when the original P&W team went house shopping, three of them fell in love with Jupiter Inlet Colony. For years thereafter Pratt & Whitney would carry a Jupiter address, no doubt reflecting the affinities of its top brass.

"By 1959 or so, we already knew there was no way in the world that a few guys from East Hartford were going to train 1,500 people from dozens of different corporate cultures," says Anschutz. The result was a decision to transfer some 1,200 employees from East Hartford. While most of them would wind up in the West Palm Beach orbit, the few hundred who settled in Jupiter-Tequesta had a sudden and profound impact. For nearly thirty years, one might accurately describe P&W as the financial umbilical cord of Jupiter-Tequesta.

"By the mid-sixties, it felt to me that one of every three people in town was from Pratt & Whitney," recalls Anschutz, who served as executive assistant to the president.

"They meant deposits for banks, mortgages for new houses and pledge dollars to build new churches."

At its peak in 1976, the campus on Beeline Highway was a full-fledged P&W division employing 8,000. The effort to develop the hydrogen-powered spy plane had long since been abandoned, but the technology became the basis of the RL10 rocket engine, which has been used in sixty percent of all satellite launchings. By then the sprawling campus would also be developing engines for fighter

Richard Anschutz (left), part of the executive team who "colonized" the Pratt & Whitney plant on Beeline Highway, moved down from the company's Connecticut headquarters in 1956 and never left. Part of being assistant to the president meant escorting visitors like rocket legend Werner Von Braun. *(Richard and Shirley Anschutz Collection)*

jets and the SR71 "Blackbird" spy plane while also serving as the mother corporation's research-development arm.

But as early as 1980 cost cutters at corporate headquarters were beginning to question the need for two separate engineering departments. A gradual wave of consolidation began that today has reduced the facility to testing engines and Sikorsky helicopters. Although Jupiter and Tequesta have certainly felt the withdrawal financially, the housing-banking-retailing infrastructure that Pratt & Whitney spawned remains securely in place.

## CIVIC CLUBS: FROM THE SERVICE TO 'SERVICE'

Returning veterans breathed new life into local civic clubs, and none more so than Roy Rood. In his own words:

*All of us veterans who came back wanted to see our community grow. One organization that we thought would encompass all of us at that time was the American Legion. At first most of the Legionnaires did things like taking care of the cemetery and being part of the volunteer fire department. At the time the fire department was out at Pennock Plantation. Many times we were called out in the middle of the night to fight a fire in the woods. Out of that grew a project to raise $1,100 for a fire truck and its proud display at the post office.*

*The American Legion also got permission to wreck town hall and jail. The plan was to build a smaller town hall and use the remainder of the material to build a Legion hall.*

*Some people yearned to do more in the educational area, which led to formation of the Kiwanis Club of Jupiter. There were five men who had the most to do with it. One of them was Ted Chambers from Hobe Sound. The other four lived in Jupiter. There was Harry Moore, who lived on Center Street and came from Columbus, Ohio. There was Harry Jackson who I've known all my life. Then there was Harry Miller, also from Columbus. Finally there was Harry Phipps from Massachusetts, who lived over at DuBois Park. We called them 'the Four Harry's and they were the ramrods of our Kiwanis Club.*

Rood's affinity for Kiwanis goes back to his childhood.

*When I was a boy and one of eleven children, we didn't have much money, so Mom would take us to West Palm Beach high school to a dental clinic for underprivileged children run by the Kiwanis Club. Back then I thought Kiwanis people were all dentists. When I grew up and finally learned better I always said that when I got in business and joined a civic club it would be Kiwanis. So in 1954 some of us formed the first Kiwanis Club in Jupiter/Tequesta.*

One of its first projects was bringing Little League baseball to Jupiter. It was actually started in Stuart," says Rood. "The league had one team from Jupiter and we had to haul our boys up to Stuart to practice because we didn't have a ball diamond to play on. Then the boys in the Kiwanis came upon the idea that we needed a recreation park in the area for both Hobe Sound and Jupiter."

With some nudging from Kiwanis, the area got its first recreation park, and local Little League teams were playing a year later. Says Rood: "The Kiwanis was involved in managing the

Although he tried his best to blend into everyday life, singer Perry Como was First Citizen of Jupiter from the day in 1956 he moved his family into Jupiter Inlet Colony. Despite a hugely successful weekly TV show and countless network specials all over the globe, Como seemed to find enough time to be around Jupiter to know dozens of people on a first-name basis. Here, in 1967, he's at the Red Lion Pub and Restaurant kicking off the Jupiter-Tequesta Community Fund drive with his own $1,000 donation.
*(Jupiter Courier)*

teams and the concession stands. Pretty soon the job got too big. The main function of the Kiwanis is to begin a project, get it running and then let the community take it over. If the community doesn't take it over, then the project isn't worth its salt."

Still, Roy Rood never let go of his Little League connection. "This was a busy man with his fast-growing landscape business," says Skip Gladwin, "but he would stop everything to haul us kids up to Hobe Sound in his truck. He'd stay and practice with us, then haul us back."

And that wouldn't even begin to cover Rood's civic activities. Adds Gladwin: "He helped many kids become Eagle Scouts, including my two sons and my nephew."

Harry Jackson was another successor to the Carlin-DuBois-Pennock tradition in that he was never too busy to further a worthy cause. Over the years he would become vice president of the state florist's association, secretary of the Palm Beach County Dairy Association, organizer of the Jupiter-Hobe Sound Kiwanis Club, director of a Red Cross fund drive, chairman of the Jupiter Boy Scouts and director of the Loxahatchee Historical Society.

During Jackson's 44 years in Kiwanis, he had 28 years of perfect attendance. He passed away on Jan. 10, 1973 at age 83. The night before his death he had attended a Kiwanis gathering, then left to attend another meeting of the Loxahatchee Historical Society.

In 1971 the Junior Women's Club of Jupiter-Tequesta decided to form the Loxahatchee River Historical Society. What could be a better sendoff than a talk on local history by Bessie DuBois in her home? It had formerly been the DuBois restaurant, and the ceiling beams were made from salvaged timbers when the original Jupiter Beach Bridge was demolished. *(Ethel Gravett Collection)*

## THE CAMP THAT REFUSED TO BUCKLE IN THE WIND

In 1954 the waiting list was so backed up at Girl Scout Camp Margery Daniel on Anchor Point that a regional council met to ponder a new location. Recalls Claudet Benton, one of the leaders: "Someone said 'why don't we get some land from the state park north of Jupiter?' The board said, 'Go to it!' and the dream was born."

Two years later the Council had obtained state permission to use six hundred acres of the park on the topmost extension of the North Fork. In August 1958, after a developer paid $110,000 for the eleven waterfront acres that had housed Camp Margery Daniel, construction began on the much larger Camp Welaka, including a manmade four-acre lake for waterfront activities. Reporting on the dedication ceremonies, the *Palm Beach Post* noted, "A winding road leads to the natural gate of twin pines. You enter. The air is sweet and woody. Close by a mockingbird calls out. Suddenly you understand why so many volunteers have worked so hard to make this possible."

On June 17, 1959, just four days before Camp Welaka was to open, a tornado cut a 150-foot wide swath through the woods of Jonathan Dickinson and straight through the camp's vitals. The lodge was demolished and tent platforms damaged. Trees snapped off and the dike at the west end of the newly created lake was damaged by water turbulence. While the community worked to

The Jaycees and Jupiter-Tequesta Women's Club sponsored Fourth of July parades year after year. From left, Anthony Gravett, Jim Tuning and five-year-old Jeffrey Gravett fife and drum on the back of a float truck.
*(Ethel Gravett Collection)*

ABOVE: Getting access to Camp Welaka meant navigating County Line Road, preferably with a 4-wheel-drive vehicle. Once called "Cemetery Road" by locals, it remained unpaved as late as 1970. *(Claudet Benton Collection)*

RIGHT: Before the camp got a swimming pool, Girl Scouts used the four-acre Lake Akelew. In the eighties, young canoeists would zigzag through the pilings of the old swim dock to test their paddling skills. *(From the book,* Footprints in Time, *by Claudet Benton)*

raise $20,000 for the repairs, the Girl Scouts cleaned up the mess and decided to open with about two-thirds of the facilities that were still intact. On July 5, 1959 the first camp session began.

Postscript: Roy Rood can thank the camp for delivering him a wife.

Patricia says it all started in 1951 when she was teaching school in Louisiana and hoping to land a summer-time job. A friend suggested Camp Margery Daniel in Jupiter. Pat was intrigued because she'd never been to Florida.

She landed the number two staff position at the camp on Anchor Point and enjoyed it. Her one complaint was that the water tasted and smelled bad, so she and the staff would jump at any chance to go into town and get a good glass of water at Jupiter Sundries (where Papa John's is today).

After the latest session of Girl Scouts was checked in, Pat went to Jupiter for the mail and a cool drink. She was sipping her drink and browsing through some greeting cards when in walked Roy Rood.

"I asked what the ladies at the other end of the counter were drinking," he says. "One of the ladies overheard and replied, 'a Key Lime freeze.' So I ordered one and began a conversation with this lady, who turned out to be from Louisiana."

Until then, 34-year-old Roy was so busy building up Rood Landscape that he'd overlooked the matter of marriage. But he was so instantly besmitten and talked to Pat for so long that he walked out without paying for his drink. A few days later he arranged to accompany her to Jupiter Island to pick up materials for the camp's "Christmas in July Party."

TOP: Jupiter mayor Don Faucher (at mike) helps christen the Burt Reynolds Dinner Theater at dedication ceremonies in 1978. Reynolds is seated third from left.

BOTTOM: The star of *Smokey and the Bandit II* gets a tip from director Hal Needham on shooting location at the Reynolds ranch in Jupiter Farms. *(Jupiter Courier)*

They were gone so long that Pat missed dinner at camp and Roy took her home to his mother's for dinner. He popped the question soon thereafter.

## THE ARTS: PUTTING JUPITER–TEQUESTA ON THE MAP

In 1962 it had been five years since Shirley Spitzer had moved to Jupiter from the Cleveland area. She didn't miss winters but she sure missed the theater and other trappings of "culture." One day when she vented her frustrations to choral director Stan Doyle at the Congregational Church on Center Street, she found a kindred spirit.

*Continued on page 186*

# JUPITER CELEBRATES A CENTENNIAL—TWICE!

(All photos: Loxahatchee River Historical Society)

In 1959 Jupiter staged a centennial celebration to commemorate the completion of the lighthouse, which was as good date as any to affix as the town's beginning. Women wore nineteenth century dresses and large sunbonnets.

Beards were prescribed for men and those caught "bare faced" were rounded up by a posse and ordered to serve time in a jail that had been erected in the Piggly-Wiggly parking lot on Route 1 (photo, upper left).

Frank Williamson (right) must have done something especially vexing to the posse to wind up with his head in a noose. "Sheriff" Ralph Crooks (with black hat) asks for his final words.

Even Perry Como couldn't escape the posse. Tracked down at home while taking a nap (beardless, of course), he was hustled off to the jail at the Piggly-Wiggly while still in his shorts. (above right).

All of Jupiter had such fun at the Centennial that when 1966 rolled around, folks decided that the one hundredth anniversary of the relighting of the lighthouse in 1866 deserved another celebration. During the day, Bessie DuBois (far right) Coast Guard officials and others led a ceremony at the foot of the lighthouse to dedicate a plaque marking the occasion.

That evening the stars and moon shone brightly over the lighthouse. On a makeshift stage at the foot of the river on the lighthouse grounds, a pageant was performed depicting the history of Jupiter. Costumed locals portrayed such notables as Maj. Gen. Thomas Jessup, Jonathan Dickinson and George

Meade played, (upper right) by Henry DuBois (with daughter-in-law Agnes). Seminoles, who had set up a camp on the grounds, performed Indian dances and crafts. At the end of it all, the cast stood at attention while Coast Guardsmen marched up in dress uniform. Bessie DuBois was there, of course, and she described "the flags softly waving in the night breeze while the national anthem was played," the flood-lit lighthouse in the background providing "a moving and impressive scene."

By the mid-fifties, Jupiter (pop. 600) had six churches, and all were centers of social life. Above, the girls' choir at Southern Methodist Church. *(Loxahatchee River Historical Society)*

They teamed up to found North County Choral Society, borrowing Salhaven auditorium for the first concert and giving free tickets to all the retirees who lived there. Today the Choral Society is still singing—over 65 voices strong.

In 1964, Dick Anschutz, who had helped spearhead Pratt & Whitney's arrival, yearned for a Jupiter theater group as well. "We ran an ad in the paper to see if anyone felt the same way, and six people showed up for the first meeting at the Beach Club in Jupiter Inlet Colony," he recalls. They formed the Coastal Players, and that June they put on the Kaufman-Hart comedy, *George Washington Slept Here,* with Anschutz and the late Ellie Schmidtke in the leading roles.

Like the choral group, their first stage was the Salhaven auditorium. As Mitzi Stieper would recall for the *Courier* a decade later, "It was so beautifully appointed—all new and first class. There was a magic there. The high curved windows and magnificent long drapes were elegant. And there was no other stage in town except at the Jupiter School, and it wasn't very good."

But Salhaven was too good to be true. By 1972 the financially troubled retiree haven was closing (soon to become Jonathan's Landing and Jupiter Medical Center). The Coastal Players were left without a stage and forced into a nomadic existence, first at the cramped Chamber of Commerce Building on Seabrook Road and then to the Jupiter Civic Center and finally to the American Legion Hall. By then other towns from Boca Raton to Stuart had their own community theater groups and Jupiter was the only town among them that didn't have a facility to offer them.

But they remained strong for many years. A playbill for *The Odd Couple* in 1974 shows over fifty volunteers—from actors to stagehands—taking part in the production.

The year 1977 brought good news for theater lovers all over south Florida, but daunting news if you were part of an amateur troupe like the Coastal Players. Namely, Burt Reynolds and some business partners met with the Town Council and rolled out blueprints of a new Burt Reynolds Dinner Theater (BRDT).

Soon, Jupiter residents could attend a new 378-seat theater with the latest audiovisual technology. The BRDT made its debut in January 1979 with Sally Field performing in *Vanities*. Then came the likes of Farah Fawcett, Julie Harris, Charles Durning, Martin Sheen, Carol Burnett and, of course, Reynolds himself. Jupiter soon got used to a parade of stars performing in the fancy new facility on A1A near the beach.

On the heels of BRDT came the Burt Reynolds Institute for Theater Training for Florida college grads looking to further theatrical careers. The small but well-equipped building on Tequesta Drive afforded locals a chance to see repertory theater at cheap prices.

But Reynolds didn't stop there. His father had been chief of police in Riviera Beach, and when he wanted to retire, Burt helped his parents buy a family spread in Jupiter Farms that became the Burt Reynolds Ranch, complete with tours of his movie memorabilia and oft-used production facilities for filmmaking. Instead of using Hollywood sound stages, Reynolds shot at home when he could, using the ranch and other Jupiter settings for film scenes.

In March 1980, what was probably the biggest accumulation of movie, stage and television luminaries in the area's history gathered at the Burt Reynolds Ranch to film a scene for *Smokey and the Bandit II*. It was the culmination of weeks of film making here and elsewhere in Palm Beach County. On one weekend the Indiantown Road Bridge over the Intracoastal was closed and turned into a movie set for a stunt scene featuring a car toppling off the raised drawbridge.

The big scene at Reynolds' ranch included, in addition to Reynolds, Robert Urich, Lola Falana, Howard Cosell, Robert Fuller, Linda Day George, Mary Ann Mobley, Jayne Kennedy and Anson Williams. *Courier* reporters and other members of the press filled in as extras.

But you had to be there. Moviegoers never saw the scene because it wound up on the cutting room floor.

When Reynolds launched the *B.L. Stryker* television series, Jupiter got used to being a regular stage set, and Mike Daniel is a good example of how it could touch on the lives of local folks. The production company began in Riviera Beach, where Daniel, a professional diver and undersea explorer, owns a marine supply business and dive headquarters named The Sea Chest. Reynolds and his crew became regular Sea Chest customers for marine supplies, and before long Daniel had agreed to be marine coordinator for the series. And because Reynolds' *Stryker* character was a detective who operated from a houseboat, Daniel soon found himself in charge of the houseboat as well. In its second year, when the TV series (and houseboat) moved to Charlie's Crab waterside restaurant in Jupiter, Daniel began decorating sets. Soon he was doing the same when Reynolds used his ranch in Jupiter Farms for scenes from *The Maddening* and *The Man from Left Field*.

Says Daniel of his expanded film career, "It's just typical of Burt. He gave a lot of people opportunities and I was one of them."

Indeed, when The Burt Reynolds and Friends Museum opened in 2003, Mike Daniel had become its president, supervising everything from construction to exhibit design.

## TRAPPER NELSON: THE MYSTIQUE AND THE MYSTERY

War's end meant that boat fuel was no longer a rationed luxury. People had money in their pockets again and *Trapper Nelson's Zoo and Jungle Garden* had more visitors than ever before.

As he approached forty (in 1948) Vince Nelson still had the rippling muscles and a panache polished by hundreds of entertaining wildlife lectures. He cut a cord of wood every day with a specially made two-edge ax that sent chips flying in all directions. During summers his sister Marcie Celmer and her husband Phil would visit from Trenton and lend a hand improving the camp. Phil and his son helped Trapper build a three-car garage and small propane-powered sawmill. Guests were treated to a homemade firing range. And for the first time, Trapper was taking in overnight guests in a newly built cabin.

By 1951 he was also buying more land, but this time to cash in on housing development. He was so convinced that a much-discussed bridge over the river's North Fork would spur development that he bought 215 acres in what today is Riverbend Country Club and Little Club.

By the late fifties *Trapper Nelson's Zoo and Jungle Garden* was flourishing. But Vince Nelson's life was beginning to change forever. His wilderness was closing in on him.

The same population growth that brought more "civilization" also meant more troubles. The people who rented his cabin were

TRAPPER NELSON WITH LIVE ALLIGATOR — BOX 122 — JUPITER, FLA. H7

As 1960 marked a new decade, Vince Nelson still produced postcards posing with his usual jungle prop. But he was 52 and feeling the burdens of poachers, rowdies and rising land taxes. He closed his camp to the public soon afterward. (*Jonathan Dickinson State Park / Celmer Family Collection*)

ABOVE: In what may the last photo of Trapper alive, sometime in 1968, he reclines by a campfire at night. By then he was being treated for prostate problems and was also convinced he had colon cancer. *(Jonathan Dickinson State Park / Celmer Family Collection)*

BELOW: Within days of Trapper Nelson's death, looters invaded his unguarded cabin, trashing everything in a frenzied search for hidden money. Finding none, they hauled off pickup trucks full of plants, trees, firewood and Trapper's personal belongings. Ironically, it galvanized public demand for the state park to acquire and preserve Nelson's 857 acres. *(Jonathan Dickinson State Park / William Lund Collection)*

often roughnecks who got drunk and staggered off to wrestle alligators in their pens at midnight. Teenagers would turn up in gangs to taunt the Legend of the Loxahatchee as a rite of manhood. State regulators nailed him for not paying sales taxes on his visitor income. County authorities frowned on the fact that his animal pens didn't have "sanitary" plumbing. He paid $10,000 to build proper men's and ladies' rooms, but still didn't meet the county code.

In September 1960, Nelson's family got a letter abruptly announcing that he had "closed my camp to the public." He wrote of having "peace of mind" at last, vowing to spend more time at his first love, trapping.

All that locals knew was that Trapper had felled logs across the river to keep boats from reaching his place. Hand-hewn KEEP OUT signs warned as they approached by river or road. If brave souls somehow surmounted those barriers and approached his cabin, they would often be startled when Trapper stepped out from behind a tree, waving them off with a shotgun.

Tranquility at last? The same man who had once homesteaded and hunted with free abandon, was now the owner of over 1,100 acres and three miles of riverfront frontage. His letters now describe himself as "ranch" owner and "businessman" with all the stress that went with wealth. Adding to the worry was that he had become "land poor." As population growth drove up real estate values, his annual taxes exceeded $10,000—far more than he took in from trapping. He worried about liability lawsuits if someone were injured on his property, so he spent more money to fence it. He borrowed $100,000 at 10 percent interest to pay his debts on the bet that he'd sell land in a rising market. But all he got were low-ball offers from crafty developers like John D. MacArthur.

In August 1964, the day the lender was set to foreclose on the $100,000 note (plus considerable interest in arrears) Vince Nelson blinked and sold his 215 acres on the north side of the river. The $328,000 he received in cash seemed like a killing to locals who read about it in the papers. In truth, after paying off his mortgages, back taxes, lawyers and other debts, Trapper was left with perhaps $60,000 on which to live the rest of his life.

Free at last? This time both business and health created inner tensions. Trapper was now well past fifty, and the massive chest was accompanied by a stomach to match. He still trapped and chopped wood, but a lifetime of eating wild game had his stomach churning and his mind gripped with fear that he had colon cancer. Before long an enlarged prostate would result in his doctor prescribing a catheter for urination.

This time the business stress was caused by negotiations with agents for Jonathan Dickinson State Park. The state wanted his 857 remaining acres as the key to preserving the upper Loxahatchee. Trapper was a hard bargainer to the point of driving park officials batty. They were willing to grant him a life estate on a hundred acres surrounding his cabin (the right to live there for the rest of his life), but Trapper also insisted on the right to set traps on all his former lands (which no park full of hikers and bikers could permit).

The negotiations seemed to have hit an impasse in late July 1968 when John DuBois thought he'd better drive out and see why Trapper hadn't come to town for a week to pick up his mail. DuBois was one of only three locals entrusted with a key to Trapper's gate, and as he parked his car and walked down the sandy road to the camp, he was guided by his nose. There under the chickee hut, was the badly decomposed body of Vince Nelson, his shotgun lying at its side.

Many locals insisted that Nelson was done in by someone who knew where he'd stashed the money (that most folks presumed to be buried somewhere out there). But a Martin County coroner's jury found no trace of a scuffle and no evidence that anyone had dug anywhere for money. The verdict was suicide, and it will ignite an argument in Jupiter even today.

One thing for sure: the death of Vince Nelson broke the impasse.

Ironically, the first result was a wave of vandalism. With no one at the camp to step out from behind a tree with a shotgun, the quiet cabins were invaded by vandals, ripping open mattresses, overturning cabinets and smashing jars of preserves in a frenzied search for money. Valuable fruit trees were uprooted and vegetable patches looked like exploded minefields. Pick-up trucks backed up to Trapper's woodpile and loaded up.

Newspapers soon showed photos of the devastation and outraged citizens demanded that the state buy the land and post some security protection on the place. Trapper's relatives in Trenton were willing enough. The land was appraised at $1.3 million and all of it went, as Nelson's will dictated, to Philip Celmer II, his late sister Marcie's son. Even then the looting continued for months because the park system had no immediate budget for providing security.

Today Trapper Nelson's camp, with pains taken to leave it as it was on his death, remains the sightseeing centerpiece for Jonathan Dickinson State Park. It is perhaps ironic that through his untimely death, Vince Nelson has become a symbol of Jupiter's wilderness history, the reason why the upper Loxahatchee was preserved and a catalyst in the river restoration effort that goes on today.

Talk to the rangers and some will insist that his ghost walks the place today.

## THE SEVENTIES: STILL A SMALL TOWN

Some say Trapper Nelson's death symbolized the end of an era and a type of lifestyle that was to surrender forever to the invasion of concrete, cable, cell phones and other symbols of urban frenzy.

Yes, perhaps, for the long-term, but in Jupiter's case, not for several years after Trapper. At a time when places like Fort Lauderdale, Pompano Beach and Deerfield Beach were knitting themselves together with ribbons of cement, Jupiter's small-town ambience continued. It was flanked by 12,000 acres of state park to the north, the groves and livestock lands west of the turnpike, and, to the south, the still-undeveloped tracts owned by John D. MacArthur.

The northern perimeter of "civilization" was County Line Road, but not quite the same one people know today. *Footprints in Time*, Claudet Benton's history of the Girl Scout camp, described it this way in the late fifties: "The term 'road' was used very loosely because only a four-wheel drive vehicle could be sure of getting through. A regular vehicle could only be sure of making it if the sand was a little wet. However, because of the human and natural obstacles from the east, the approach from the west seemed to be the better choice."

That wasn't the case in 1973, however. Florida Power & Light had begun putting power poles down the middle of the road (to serve the new Little Club) and it closed the road just as the camp was about to host a conclave of girl scouts from 35 states and eight foreign countries. As author Benton reported, "Cars and buses couldn't get past the poles without getting stuck in the sand." When the Council's attorney filed a complaint, FP&L stopped long enough to let the meeting take place.

Still a hub for boaters and fishermen was the DuBois dock. *(Loxahatchee River Historical Society)*

Florence Kuschel, who worked many years for the county school district, remembers the day when one of her colleagues said he was headed for Jupiter and asked where the center of town was.

"I remember thinking real hard where that might be," Florence says. "I finally said I guessed it would probably be Ralph's bar on Center Street. It was right around the corner from Town Hall, and that's where people hung out."

In 1952 Al and Florence Kuschel had spent $1,900 for fifty acres along Roebuck Road for a future home site. The road didn't go through all the way to Loxahatchee River Road. It ended at a dump that the Town of Jupiter had bought thinking at the time that no one would ever settle that far out in the woods.

The Kuschel tract lay idle until 1975 when Al retired from the Riviera Beach police department and went to work as chief of security for John D. MacArthur. That's when Al and Florence built their house.

"Those were the happiest days of our lives," says Florence, who kept working for the school district. "When we'd drive to the end of our little dead-end street on a Friday night, we felt we had the whole world to ourselves. Our property stretched to Limestone Creek, and we could ride our horses everywhere. You could ride in the woods past where The Shores is today and go all the way to the turnpike. We had a horse named Coco who lived to be 34. He loved to head out to a big lake where Eagle Landing is today. He'd plunge right in the water and then sit down in it, rider and all."

One day Al saw a car with New York license plates parked in front of the vacant lot next to his. A man in a blue suit was hunched at the wheel, frowning over a map. When Al asked if he could be of help, the man volunteered that he'd just inherited the twelve-acre plot. He thought he'd try to sell it for $7,500. Since it fronted on Limestone Creek, Kuschel said his father might be interested, but didn't think he could pay more than $2,500. The man paused, then said, "Okay, but on one condition." He'd sell it if he didn't have to get out of the car. He said he was scared to death of snakes.

Further north and west just off Loxahatchee River Road, Jupiter River Estates remained sparsely occupied even in the early eighties. Kathleen Forst Putnam, now a nursing educator in Virginia, grew

# RIDING THE RANGE IN JUPITER

In the early seventies, the Sigmund Weizer family owned hundreds of undeveloped acres along Loxahatchee River Road. After son Bill married Patti Brooker in 1971, they lived with their infant son, Troy, in a trailer on the river at the end of 197th Place North. Recalls Lynn Drake: "Whenever I would drive out to see my friend Patti and her baby, the sugar sand was so thick I'd have to park my car and walk twenty minutes to her trailer. "Today it's all the Loxahatchee Point development, but then it was just sand, pine and saw palmetto," says Drake. "Several wild horses roamed about; and although Patti had never ridden a horse, she was able to coax them up to her back door and feed them treats by hand.

"On one of my visits Patti had a surprise for me. She was at the back door as a horse approached, and she suddenly handed me the baby. 'Watch Troy for a few minutes,' she said. 'I'll be right back.' With that, she jumped on the horse bareback and bare feet and away they went. It scared me to death!"

Later, Patti had won over two of the horses to the point where, after teaching her friend Lynn to ride, the two women would saddle up and amble out towards the turnpike. But *tame* would be too strong a word. Says Drake: "Once while riding out near the turnpike, Patti's horse Diablo (right, with Patti) kept trying to bite my feet. My horse proceeded to throw me and the saddle as well. It was a long walk back." *(Lynn Drake Collection)*

up on Jupiter River Drive.

*We used to ride bikes all through the woods, and sometimes the Weizer's cattle would escape from their fences and run wild. Sometimes we'd have cows in the front yard, and then we'd have a cattle roundup on our bikes. There was also an old black man named George White who lived way back in the woods by himself. Mom used to pay him for yard work and for some of the collards he grew*

*When I lived at home, if three cars went by our house in a single day it would be a lot of traffic. As a kid I learned not to be afraid to jump off the small [Island Way] Bridge, but I believe I only jumped off the big bridge once, and that was on a dare. My brother and sister were much braver than me. We used to have a rowboat that we would anchor under the little bridge. We'd take along fishing poles, a stack of comic books and peanut butter and jelly sandwiches, and there we'd spend the afternoon. For a break we'd swim across the river to the other side where a big river barge had been sunk.*

*When I come home for visits, I'm sad that all my old forts in the woods are now backyards of million dollar homes, but I guess that's progress.*

### 'YOU KEEP YOUR DISTANCE, I'LL KEEP MINE'

Sometime around 1957, when northern states were inching toward more integration, south Florida took a lurch in the opposite direction. Ella Preston Rollins, who had been raised with her twelve brothers and sisters in one of Bama's tenant cottages, vaguely recalls a visit from Hank Pennock, who managed the Plantation's nursery. "He said he'd been told that all black families had to be moved out west to the Limestone Creek area," she says.

Who gave such an order? Jupiter had no police. No Ku Klux Klan. No episodes of cross-burning or other violence. Rollins shrugs her shoulders.

It probably stemmed from the fact that the Plantation was being sold off in parcels by the Pennock heirs and it was part of getting the land ready for development. Legal and proper, no doubt, but it was another "push" in the gradual cordoning of African-Americans into a rural ghetto.

For nearly a hundred years until the postwar era, both blacks and whites lived near where they worked. Since no one could commute over long distances, blacks lived in clusters all over a large rural landscape.

At Pennock Plantation, for example, a dozen or so black families lived in a section called "Bama," near where Home Depot is today. Ella Rollins' father worked in the Pennock nursery for forty years, and she remembers how white men would come to Bama on Sunday afternoons to drink "tea" with their black co-workers. They seemed to enjoy the "tea" a lot, singing songs together until they wobbled off into the sunset.

But blacks could get a different reception when, for example, they went to the post office or grocery on Center Street. "There were some rough boys who ran around in gangs," says Rollins. "They'd follow us and shout insults. But I still remember how my daddy put a stop to it. One day he saw them coming down the street and met them head-on. He told them that when he sent his kids to the store, he didn't intend for God *Himself* to bother them.

Iris Hunter was Jupiter High's first black student in 1962. She graduated at the age of 14 after a year of stoically enduring insults by students and teachers alike. *(Lynn Drake Collection)*

Then there were the white folks who worked at Pennock; they'd look after us, too."

This delicate but dependable relationship would begin to erode, however. Unexplainably. An early indicator was the 1945 state census. In 1935 the census for Jupiter had intermingled everyone in the count. The 1945 edition provided one list for whites and another for "colored."

Ironically, the "push" westward in 1957 turned out to be a financial break for some black families. The Pennocks owned some lots around Limestone Creek and Church streets and graciously offered to sell them to Plantation tenants on a "pay me when you can" basis. Ella Rollins had just been married, and Hank Pennock saw to it that her house was slid onto logs and rolled down the road to its new location. In time she and other transplants owned their own homes and gave Limestone Creek a stable foundation that endures today. Yet, from then on it was an unwritten law that no blacks lived east of U.S. 1 from Jupiter to West Palm Beach.

By 1960 it was also "understood" that the Jupiter police cars didn't patrol Limestone. Blacks had a separate volunteer fire department (which soon burned down, leaving no coverage). Ella Rollins remembers Stine's drug store suddenly creating a special side door for "colored." Ida Simmons Harris Connaway recalls no bathrooms available in filling stations. "If you had to go, you went in the bushes," she says. Until then, blacks hadn't thought twice about using whatever beach they wanted. Now they were confined to just one stretch near the inlet.

Yet, as the rest of the South became a civil rights battleground in the sixties, Jupiter never ignited. Why? First, Jupiter was a town

RIGHT: She raised seven children, tended her farm, worked in town and supported her church. But Rebecca Simmons "never thought of herself as anyone special," says her daughter Idella. She was. When this was taken in 1960, her children's last photo of their mother, Mrs. Simmons was still "full of joy and a sense of purpose," says Idella. This, despite the amputation of both legs due to diabetes. She lived four more years.
*(Idella Simmons Harris Connaway Collection)*

FAR RIGHT: Idella at the family's well-tended grave site, Mount Carmel Missionary Baptist Church.
*(Sue S. Snyder)*

of six hundred where blacks were outnumbered three to one. Second, Jupiter had no buses, had no lunch counters big enough to attract a crowd and never rated the attention of a big name civil rights protester. But more than that, Jupiter's black population simply had its roots in a hundred years of small-town ways. As Ida Harris Connaway put it, "If someone says they don't want you on a certain beach, well, you just wouldn't want to go where you're not welcome."

So, blacks made do. As Limestone became a tighter community, churches like Mount Carmel Missionary Baptist and the Church of God took on strength. The grade school, built in 1929, was known as Jupiter Colored School and after 1956 as L.M. Davis School (in honor of the man who had donated the land around it) was as outmoded as the Depression era when it was built. High school kids went off to West Palm Beach, even though Ella Rollins would recall, "We would pass school after school on our bus and wonder why we couldn't go to any of them."

Two bars were social strongholds as well. The most unique was The Tree, a funky open-air tavern set under a massive banyan tree at the northeast corner of the intersection of Indiantown and Center Streets. But a far bigger emporium was the Mexican Bamboo. Most folks called it after its colorful lady owner, Artie ("Jubaby") Sapp, who'd been a vaudevillian in New York. Mexican Bamboo stood on Indiantown Road just east of today's Kentucky Fried Chicken place, and its massive bar was said to run a hundred feet long.

As Artie Sapp got along in years, Mexican Bamboo would open only when she felt up to it. It soon fell to the onslaught of commercialization along Indiantown Road. Brian Marchewka bought the place in 1982 and Brian's Bar quickly became a rollicking country and western emporium with a band booming every night. "People drove up in everything from horses to pickup trucks to Rolls Royces," says Lynn Drake, who worked the bar and package store. "We were open every night until 5 a.m. to accommodate second-shift workers from places like Pratt &

Whitney. We'd spend several hours cleaning up, then open around eleven and do it all over again!"

Blacks used the package store, but the rednecks and their country music made it an entirely different place from Jubaby's.

In 1961 some blacks started pushing in the other direction. With Congress and the courts having dynamited a path for them, five local black educators and civil rights activists at last deemed the signs propitious for Palm Beach County to desegregate its schools. They went to the school district and emerged with a practical plan. Five high schools would integrate that fall by accepting a token group of African-Americans in their senior classes. The icebreakers would expose only one year of their school lives to possible harm and harassment, then they'd resume normal lives. Besides, at the more mature, enlightened senior class level, things might even go smoothly.

Jupiter High was tapped to be the first. Iris Hunter, whose family recently marked a century in Jupiter, learned she'd be one of the black seniors. "At that age, I didn't see it as an awesome experience," she says. "I figured I'd be among my friends."

It was her mentors who got cold feet. A few days before school began, the civil rights leaders were worried. All but one of the group headed for Jupiter High were average students whose grades and chances for higher education might not survive a year long tirade of taunts and turmoil. That left only one girl, Iris Hunter, who had an impressive scholastic record. The black leaders met with Iris and her mother. They lectured her on nonviolence, on turning her cheek to insults. Was she up to the task?

"I was young and naïve," she recalls in a cool, crisp voice.

Iris was just 14.

Her father spent his whole adult life as a gardener on the Chase estate (of Chase Manhattan Bank fame) in Juno Beach. The family owned a "quarter-homestead" (forty acres) on what she now describes as "the south I-95 Interchange onto Indiantown Road."

Thanks to a mother who revered learning, Iris was soon absorbing everything she could at a young age. She hurdled grades

Once freed from peer pressure, the two became friends and remain so today. But the pattern was set for the school year. Iris fought to make good grades, but always with barriers in her way. In typing class, for example, the teacher presented her with a special handicap. Kids laughed as the woman took from a closet shelf an ancient Underwood whose keys seemed to be glued together. Through test after test on typing speed, with the latest Martin Luther King sermon on nonviolence ringing in her ears, Iris managed only D's. After finally appealing to her student counselor, she got a newer model and started to catch up, but it was too late in the year. She wound up with a D.

It would be nice to write that as a result of Iris Hunter's ground-breaking experience, the road was smoothed for other blacks in Jupiter. It was bumpier than that. In 1963, College-educated Ida Harris Connaway remembers how her own daughter quickly rose to the top of her high school class. "Her teacher told her that she ought to drop out because no black student was supposed to be that smart," says Connaway. "I didn't know what else to do but take her out and put her in Roosevelt" [the black high school in West Palm Beach].

But changes did come. In 1963, when Jupiter High went to the state basketball finals for the first time, Willie Mitchell and Robert Williams were its two stars—both from Limestone Creek. By the 1970s, blacks were starring in every team sport at JHS.

And now for the rest of the Iris Hunter story. Upon graduation, she had a scholarship offer from a black college in Alabama, but her mother blocked the way because she was only 15. She enrolled in Palm Beach Junior College, but always the money would run out after a semester or two. Then came marriage and babies. As Iris Hunter Porter she put two sons through Florida State University and Georgia Tech. Now, as Iris Hunter Porter Etheredge, she has helped two stepchildren become a doctor and a radio deejay.

Now it's her turn. As this is written, Iris, at 56, is entering Florida Atlantic University to finish the last semester for a degree in human resources management.

two and three in one year, then four and five in the next. "By the seventh grade I was nine," she says.

Fast forward to the senior year at Jupiter High and Iris' own words.

*I was not allowed on the school bus. Mom had to take me. Federal agents [marshals] in civilian clothes met us at the school gate. On the way in that first day, I saw an elderly woman on a front porch across the street. She was holding up a shotgun and shouting that she'd kill me if I went in.*

*After the first day the routine was the same. I would enter the class only after everyone else was seated and leave only after the others did first. If I went to the bathroom, I was escorted. I was never allowed to walk the school corridors without a teacher assigned to accompany me. They were beside me when I ate lunch in the cafeteria.*

The die was cast on the first day when Iris walked into her senior English class.

*The first day's exercise was a quiz based on Shakespeare's fourteenth sonnet. We had to recite it from memory. I remembered having this great sense of relief because my mother had a set of Shakespeare's works and we both loved to read that particular sonnet. I took the test and felt I had done well.*

*When all the test papers were passed up to the teacher, she looked them over and walked over to me. She showed me the paper, which had a perfect score written on it. Then she turned to the class and said something like: "I'm not used to Niggras in my presence except when they're cleaning my house." She proceeded to tear up the paper in front of the class. She gave me this hard look and said, "If you keep your distance, I'll keep mine."*

*Well, by that time, I was in tears. Nobody said or did anything except the girl in the desk next to me. Her name was Beth Thorne, who later became Mrs. Keith Jones. She took out her box of Kleenex and gave me one.*

Dozens of Jupiter pioneers rest together in a section of the cemetery on County Line Road. *(Sue S. Snyder)*

193

When the Lainharts headed for the weekend at their Loxahatchee River retreat, their children brought lots of friends with them. Posing in 1941 at the Lainhart Dam (rebuilt and still in use today) were, from left, Mickey Chillingworth, Dede Hancock, Charlotte Fowler, Martha Lainhart McKenna, unidentified girl, Dale Simon and another unidentified girl. *(Lainhart Family Collection)*

# CHAPTER 8
# THE LAST BATTLE OF THE LOXAHATCHEE

The Indians who lived for some 5,000 years in the Loxahatchee watershed left little of their history save a few tools, some jewelry pieces and middens of shells and bones.

Yet, in that compressed shellrock were some materials indigenous to Lake Okeechobee as well as stones from as far north as Georgia. These and the fact that carbon dating of artifacts covers thousands of years certainly points toward a society that was well organized and interdependent. And it's quite likely that the Indian's main artery of communication was the "river of grass" that flowed south from the big lake and whose fingers led into the Loxahatchee watershed.

Indeed, the very visible Indian middens that once lined the south side of the Jupiter Inlet were just one example of the civilization that lived and traded within that large watershed. In Jonathan Dickinson State Park, for example, no less than four prehistoric middens and shell scattering sites have been discovered along Kitching Creek. In all, an inventory compiled by the Florida Department of Environmental Protection (DEP) lists 13 prehistoric and/or historic (Seminole) sites in or near the state park that bear further investigation.

That Indians left so little evidence of their lifestyle over some 5,000 years is a monumental statement in itself. They did not try to challenge nature's ways. They blended into it. This was their legacy and their lesson to those who would follow.

## A GENEROUS, FORGIVING RIVER OF PLENTY

The manifest of the Southern Express Company for December 1904 listed all the goods picked up or delivered at each railroad stop from Jacksonville to Miami. The entry for Jupiter showed 2,700 crates of oysters picked up for shipment up north. The nearest any other station came to Jupiter's oyster shipment was 700 crates.

Around 1910, flocks of migrating ducks and geese were so thick they repeatedly flew into the top of the lighthouse, putting the

In the late sixties kids up and down the Loxahatchee estuary would look forward to regular visits from two dolphins they called "Georgie Boy" and "Georgie Girl." They'd spend hours swimming and playing, as one of them demonstrates with (from left) Eddie Mayo, Frank Lund and Mike Mayo. Says Mike's brother Brad Mayo, "They were so tame and playful that we always thought maybe they had been show performers who were turned loose."

One day Georgie Boy was found floating in the water, dead from a shotgun blast. (*Mayo Family Collection*)

In 1976, another dolphin appeared—just as delightful. He'd play with groups of kids and even with Mayor Dorothy Campbell, who would wear her swimsuit under her business clothes in case she spotted him when she drove over a bridge. Sometimes he'd roll over to have his stomach scratched ("it's just like wet velvet," she said). But he liked roughhousing with a gang of kids, too. When kids like Nancy Bracht (left) and her friend Diane Bursey would put their surfboards in the water, the five-and-a-half-foot dolphin would push them through the water.

One day he simply stopped coming back. If any dolphins ply the river today, they are few and far between. (*John Lopinot, Palm Beach Post*)

196

expensive Fresnel lens in such danger that it had to be girded with a metal screen barrier.

---

Growing up around World War I, Carlin White remembers mullet "so thick they would keep us awake at night. Each time the beam of the lighthouse would pass it would startle the mullet into a cascade of splashing." Robert Hepburn would write, "Some mornings the lawns bordering the river would be covered with mullet that had jumped out of the water during the night."

---

In the 1930s migrating ducks still settled so thickly on the river that hunters hardly knew where to begin shooting. Robert Hepburn said he always tried to shoot ducks soon upon their arrival because "if you didn't, they'd soon gorge themselves on fish and spoil their taste."

---

In the late 1930s, Ray Swanson was a teenager wearing his homemade diving helmet and walking on the river bottom just off the DuBois beach. "I remember hearing the hum of a boat engine as it came in the inlet," he says. "As it passed me a few hundred feet away, I could see that it was an old paddle-wheeler, which I'd never seen before. The water was so clear that I could see the paddle-wheel rotating clearly despite the great distance from me underwater."

---

In the early 1960s Lynn Lasseter (Drake) and her childhood chums at Suni Sands would spend hours lying face down on the dock gazing between the planks at the dozens of manatees grazing on the sea grass below. "It was as if you could walk across the top of their backs," she says.

---

In 1972 Palm Beach County processed five million pounds of fish. More than one million pounds of it could be attributed to Jupiter Fisherman's Marina where Pinder's Seafood bought from commercial fishermen.

---

Raymond Baird, who has been guiding fishermen on the river for nearly fifty years, remembers when the riverbed just below Trapper Nelson's camp was six to eight feet deep, with some pools over twenty feet deep. He was there when his friend Dave Brooker caught a 97-pound tarpon in the same spot.

## BULLDOZERS AND BUNGLERS

In less than a hundred years, the inlet and the Loxahatchee have been kneaded like silly putty in the hands of its well-intentioned stewards. In this ecologically brief period the river system has been manipulated and mutilated, drained, dredged, ditched, dammed, developed and depleted.

---

When the original Florida East Coast Railroad Bridge was built over the Loxahatchee in 1896, it narrowed the river's natural width by 1,800 feet. Further bridge work in 1929 choked the river's throat by reducing the width to 581 feet.

---

In the 1930s, the tender of the swing bridge leading to Jupiter Island kept a hundred pound harpoon handy. When a manatee was spotted nibbling sea grass around the bridge pilings, the tender would hoist the heavy harpoon and with all his might send it hurtling down into the manatee's broad back.

"You've got to understand what it was like back in the Depression," says Nathaniel P. Reed, whose father founded the Jupiter Island Club. "The Club provided the only jobs for miles around, and to make them go further, men worked in four shifts of four hours each. That manatee made a meal for several families."

---

In the 1930s the lighthouse and Coast Guard station, providing light and hope for sailors, provided sewage pipes for residents that plunged directly into Jupiter Inlet.

Standards at the lighthouse reservation were hardly unique. From the diary of Wilson Horne, written in the same period:

*A short dead end road (now Eganfuskee) ran past Bowers Store going east. About a hundred yards east, on the south side, there was a huge rubber tree. The Martins lived in a house under the tree with about twenty cats and operated a fish house built on stilts over the edge of the canal. He bought and sold fish. When he cleaned them, the offal fell into the water. There was a jerrybuilt toilet whose receipts also fell into the water. Over the years a big school of two-foot catfish made their home there and immediately, like sharks, ate everything that fell into the water.*

*Anytime I went fishing and had no luck, I would stop by Martins and catch a couple of catfish to take home for supper.*

---

In the 1940s Bridge Road was built to give Hobe Sound an east-west artery. Until then, Kitching Creek ran north toward Cove Road. The new road dammed up water to Kitching Creek and further reduced freshwater flows into the Loxahatchee.

---

In 1947, the Jupiter Inlet District got some tax money again and launched a major dredging project right off DuBois beach. Until then, there was an elongated, hundred-or-so-foot island a few yards from the shoreline. When the project was done (the JID commissioners included one John DuBois), so much sand had been pumped onto the island that it became the peninsula that now comprises most of the waterfront picnic area in DuBois Park.

Skip Gladwin's parents were renting the original DuBois house at the time. To a small boy, it seemed "that the dredging went on and on forever. When it was done the beach in front of the DuBois property was much higher and broader than it had been before."

197

LEFT: In 1947, prior to a major inlet dredging project, a view from the lighthouse south to the DuBois property shows a small island in front. *(Skip Gladwin Collection)*

ABOVE: Looking from the new DuBois beach across the inlet at the area that is now Jupiter Inlet Colony. The extensive dredging extended the DuBois shoreline by several yards and, in the process, incorporated the former island. Today the "island" is the peninsula with beach and picnic tables that juts to the west at DuBois Park. *(Skip Gladwin Collection)*

RIGHT: This weir protruding northeast from the south jetty in the early fifties was supposed to speed the flow of the tidal currents and prevent silting. The reality was that the inlet tended to bend along its historic southward course before dredges made the artificial cut (above) in 1922. So, sand simply piled up along the catchment wall conveniently provided by engineers. *(Loxahatchee River Historical Society)*

In the early fifties the inlet's south jetty was reconfigured so that it stuck out into the channel diagonally toward the northeast. The rationale was that by making the inlet narrower, the current would flow more swiftly and reduce shoaling.

But just the opposite happened. Reason: the artificial cut made in 1922 went through the south end of Jupiter Island. The current's natural inclination was to bend along the inlet's original course, a quarter mile south of its man-made successor. Hence, sand piled up quickly against the new south jetty, documenting another case of man trying to dictate terms to Mother Nature.

In the 1950s various civic and social clubs held weekend fish fries. A sponsor would go to a local fisherman and ask for maybe 150 pounds of fish. "No problem," said the fisherman. He'd grab a mate, motor out to one of the river bridges where snook were stacked up like cordwood, then drop a couple sticks of dynamite over them. Order completed.

Those who have a deepwater dock right on the Southwest Fork of the Loxahatchee may deem the decision to create the C-18 Canal a brilliant stroke. For those whose perspective is the Northwest

Fork, the move by the South Florida Water Management District in 1958 was probably *the* most damaging man-made act in the river's known history.

In order to drain marshlands used by growers and to make sure the budding Pratt & Whitney campus would be free of flooding, the District commissioned the Army Corps of Engineers to dig a straight trench along today's Route I-95 and connect it to several smaller ditches that extended from West Palm Beach to Jupiter Farms. Once the drainage water moved down the wide, straight C-18 ditch and over the dam at Indiantown Road, it dumped directly into what had been a shallow neck of the Loxahatchee that people often waded across in early days. Only now it had become the Southwest Fork, which would drain more than fifty percent of the entire river basin.

Today, says a Loxahatchee River District report, "massive discharges of freshwater from the C-18 canal…occur several times each year. Ongoing research has shown that discharges of over 800 cubic feet per second (cfs) that last four or more days greatly alter the salinity of the estuary (main river) with negative lasting impacts on the native flora and fauna."

Once the bulk of the water from the slough began coursing through the C-18 to the Southwest Fork, the Northwest Fork of the Loxahatchee became like a bathtub with the stopper pulled out. Its flow of fresh water dropped from levels regularly exceeding a hundred cubic feet per second to the point where today, during the

dry months, absolutely nothing from the slough finds its way to the upper river. On days like these, the current slows and silt builds up. Canoers headed from Riverbend Park to Trapper Nelson's must portage often and far.

In the fall of 1965 a company owned by John D. MacArthur announced it would dredge 370,000 cubic yards of Loxahatchee River bottom. The Singer Island land baron owned a tract above (what would become) the Island Way bridges that he wanted to develop as Jupiter River Estates. Martin County commissioners didn't mind having more real estate tax revenue, but a fracas flared up when MacArthur wanted to dredge a couple of shallow creeks so lot buyers could build docks.

Conservationists warned that building bulkheads would ruin the mangroves, drive off wading birds and channelize the pristine upper river into another Fort Lauderdale. Many of the lot owners insisted that dredging would help fishing and boost their property values. MacArthur waded into the fight for public opinion by promising to build bridges across the river from Tequesta so that Pratt & Whitney people could commute faster to work.

Environmentalists, led by the gritty Philip A. (Bill) Lund (himself a builder) took their case to Tallahassee. The same day they appealed to the State Board of Conservation, a huge two-decker dredge named *The Admiral* was moving up the Loxahatchee—still with no county or state permit. As soon as the hearing concluded (the Board promised to "study" the matter) Lund raced back home, jumped in his Boston Whaler and zoomed up to where *The Admiral* was already dredging. But the most he could do was run circles around it and shake his fist at the work crew.

That November, roughly two hundred persons formed a boat-a-cade for a tour of the upper Loxahatchee to call attention to the river's plight. But by then the dredging was a *fait accompli*. MacArthur had shown that one determined man with money could steamroll over a bunch of agitated individuals with no money.

In 1976-77, carloads of oyster beds were dredged from beneath the railroad bridge after *Jupiter Courier* publisher Ives Cary led a relentless crusade. He said the stacks of oysters choked off the tidal currents and kept the river from flushing out to sea. Behind Cary's back, people snickered that it was all because he lived on a canal and couldn't stand looking at the debris that stagnated in back of his picture window. Richard E. Roberts, then the state park's interpretative naturalist, warned that dredging would mean more seawater rushing in as well as out, and that it would damage cypress and other freshwater vegetation. But no matter. Cary had a petition signed by 1,500 citizens and the backing of Jupiter Inlet District. As Roberts wrote a friend that "it's getting lonely sitting out here on a limb by myself," the dredges came and the oysters went.

Extensive research has shown that while mature cypress can withstand salt water intrusion for long periods, new growth like the many cypress knees lining the river here on Kitching Creek will soon succumb, leaving the species without the regeneration needed to continue. *(Sue S. Snyder)*

Today's popular "sand bar" began building up in the seventies. "This was a direct result of beach renourishment projects," insists fishing guide Raymond Baird. That, plus the C-18 canal and dredging of oyster beds by the bridge. "Most of that sand now comes in on the incoming tide, and that's where it collects," he contends.

In August 1972 a group called Concerned Citizens Against Aircraft Noise and Air Pollution demanded that the Palm Beach County commissioners vote to move Palm Beach International Airport into Jonathan Dickinson State Park or somewhere along Beeline Highway "before it becomes an intolerable concrete monster." Spokesman Al Cone said land could be bought "for practically nothing" in the park because fire had destroyed a large part of it (actually more than 4,000 acres) the year before. This, he said, would "stop further degradation of the environment."

The bid failed, but only after a protracted discussion.

In the 1970s scientists first began to register concern over the long-term effects of a rising sea level. In a letter to the Palm Beach County Commission, Dick Roberts wrote: "The latest evidence suggests a rate of about three inches for every hundred years. This does not seem to be very much, but since much of the coastline is of very low elevation and in some areas the surface grade can be as gradual as 0.2 feet per mile, changes in salinities over extensive areas can show up rather quickly."

Soon afterwards, salt water began pouring from household faucets all over Palm Beach County. Tequesta, which got its drinking water from five separate well fields surrounded on three sides by salt water, "is pretty close to the bottom of the bucket," reported Abe Kreitman of the U.S. Geological Survey. "It's not that the county has a lack of fresh water. It's just that in some areas pumping has not matched the mushrooming population."

In 1972, Nelson and Lilly Wilder bought a lot on Merritt Way just west of the Island Way bridges. Their first snapshots of the river's edge show all fresh water vegetation. Within twenty years the same shoreline would consist exclusively of mangroves.

And yet, the Florida Park Service had already realized in the seventies how quickly encroaching salt water was taking its toll upstream in the park. The first to feel its effects were the remaining cypress trees that lined the river within the park boundary. It was a fluke in some respects that there were any cypress left at all. In the 1930s cypress logging was so extensive along the river that one outfit even installed a narrow gauge rail line near Cypress Creek to make hauling easier (the old steam engine is rusting in the woods today). Around 1940, as the loggers were buzzing their way towards the shoreline of Kitching Creek, an exasperated Trapper Nelson called his friend Joseph Verner Reed, founder of the Jupiter Island

Club, with a plea to help him halt the chopping. Later that week, Reed and Nelson paid the logging company foreman a surprise call. With them was Reed's neighbor, heavyweight champ Gene Tunney. After some manly jabbering, some autographed photos and the pressing of greenbacks upon his palm, the foreman agreed to leave the remaining trees along the river standing.

Now it was salt instead of saws that threatened the ancient trees. Even this was disputed for years by many old-timers. They could point to some large, healthy trees downriver where it was saltier. Or as one put it: "Cypress just have tougher hides. When they die naturally, the trunks just stand there and look ugly longer than other trees."

But gradually, study after study began to point to salt as the culprit. In the year 2002, the South Florida Water Management District compiled a scientific literature review of 31 studies on the effects of saltwater intrusion. One of them was a U.S. Geological Survey study in which core samples were collected from 69 baldcypress trees at different parts of the Loxahatchee "to assess if the width of tree rings and their quality had changed over time."

*It was found that although each tree…had endured stress at intermittent levels throughout their life span, the percentage of individuals experiencing stress down gradient of river mile nine [roughly Trapper Nelson's camp] increased substantially. In 1940, the percentage of stressed trees downstream of river mile nine was 30 percent, whereas in 1982 it was 80 percent.*

The District's literature survey concluded that while mature baldcypress trees appeared more able to withstand the effects of saltwater than seedlings, "it is extremely important" to keep salt levels low enough to protect seedlings "because levels that protect only mature adults will not ensure a sustainable population."

Just below Trapper Nelson's camp, several man-made contrivances ganged up to clog and silt the river he had known in his lifetime. Over the years the Florida Turnpike, Bridge Road, Pratt & Whitney Road (S.R. 711), Indiantown Road (S.R. 706) and Beeline Highway (S.R. 710) had all chopped up the natural drainage pattern and brought change to the Loxahatchee.

The onslaught continued. Where Cypress Creek ran into the Loxahatchee a few hundred yards north of the camp, the mouth became choked by vegetation and a lack of water to flush it. Further downstream was Hobe Grove Ditch, a citrus grower's crude attempt to drain

## HISTORICAL HIGHLIGHTS

| | |
|---|---|
| **3000-750 B.C.** | Late Archaic Period. Early Indian encampments built along the river. |
| **750 B.C.-A.D.1750** | Indians live in villages along the river. |
| **1894** | Construction of Florida East Coast Railroad trestle bridge with fill from surrounding wetlands. |
| **1895** | U.S. Army Corps of Engineers dredges and widens Intracoastal Waterway. |
| **1920** | Lainhart and Masten dams privately constructed some ten miles upriver by private fruit growers to help irrigate crops. |
| **1947** | Extensive dredging of Jupiter Inlet. |
| **1958** | Southwest Fork of river is dredged and widened by construction of C-18 Canal, diverting water that once flowed into Northwest Fork. |
| **1965** | John D. MacArthur begins developing Jupiter River Estates by dredging two miles of riverfront west of Island Way bridges. |
| **1970** | Florida acquires Trapper Nelson's 857 acres on river to add to state park system. |
| **1974** | G-92 canal is constructed, allowing some of the flow towards the C-18 Canal to be re-diverted to the Northwest Fork. |
| **1977-78** | Oyster bars are dredged at the railroad bridge to improve flushing of the embayment area. Saltwater intrudes further upriver. |
| **1983** | U.S. Geological Survey team begins series of studies to gather "baseline" scientific data on the Loxahatchee. |
| **1985** | Congress declares the upper Loxahatchee Florida's only federally designated "wild and scenic river." |
| **2001** | Projects get underway to restore hydrology on several creeks and to enhance freshwater flow to Northwest Fork. |
| **2001-2002** | Government/public agencies acquire over 25,000 acres for preservation in Loxahatchee watershed. |
| **2002** | Implementation begins on Comprehensive Everglades Restoration Plan. |

ABOVE: Nathaniel P. Reed of Jupiter Island began a lifetime of conservation leadership as a kid fishing on the Loxahatchee. *(Agnes Brooker Collection)*

RIGHT: Reed as a young Assistant Secretary of the Interior. *(Loxahatchee River Historical Society)*

BELOW: Reed and Bill Lund (left) take part in dedicating the new Loxahatchee River District in 1973. Lund served as its first chairman. *(Gravett Family Collection)*

his field in the wet season. The result was heavy scouring of the canal banks and a sandbar in the river that, among other difficulties, eventually made it a trying task for boats headed upriver to Trapper Nelson's at low tide.

Further upriver from Trapper's camp and south of where the Loxahatchee crosses Indiantown Road, it was safe from saltwater, but not from a century of other intrusions. In the thirties and forties, families like the Reese's, Lainharts, Chillingworths, Potters and Hulls were but honest toilers trying to grow citrus and enjoy their camps on weekends. But in the process of human habitation, the natural hammock that once sheltered thousands of years of Indian settlers was cleared for orange trees and tomato plants. Rough bridges were built over the river in several places so that growers could get to their groves on both sides. Crude dams were built to hold water in the dry season and makeshift canals cut to keep fields from flooding in the summer. In the sixties Dimick Reese also grazed cattle on his land, which left a decaying coral and pits in which cattle were dipped to help control parasites.

All the above left a miniscule imprint compared to what came next. John M. Yount, a developer from Delray Beach, bought a two-mile stretch on the west side of the narrow river south of Indiantown Road. The citrus groves were quickly abandoned as Yount began "improving" his property for development. The river was dredged and the spoil thrown up on the riverbank to control flooding. Fill was trucked in and the land elevated by nearly three feet. More ditches and dikes were built to assure drainage. As his centerpiece, Yount built a large circular canal in the middle of the property so as to offer more "waterfront" lots.

After persuading the Jupiter Town Council to extend the city limits out past his property, Yount was ready to make his killing. In 1968 he sold the land to the developers of Riverbend Park, which became a mobile home community with asphalt roads, sewage and water treatment plants, and concrete slabs for each of the trailers.

Riverbend Park lasted until 1978 when the county bought it for a park (of the same name). By then the landscape had changed to ball fields built atop a meter of fill. The concrete trailer slabs remained along with the abandoned sewage and water facilities. In contrast to the towering cypress and water hickories lining the river's east side (and still occupied by Dimick Reese as a life estate), the park authority inherited what had grown in the fill dirt: Brazilian pepper, Australian pine, Java plum and a tangle of other exotic species. The county also found itself the owner of a quarry pit along the park's southernmost road, which Yount had probably used to mine paver stones. Said a county study in 1995: "The area had apparently become a garbage dump...as a good deal of metallic refuse, including several old automobiles, litter the land here."

And a river ran through it.

## FIGHTING BACK

The Loxahatchee's most redeeming attribute may be that it isn't connected to Lake Okeechobee or any of its canals. If, on top of our existing mistakes, we'd had to suffer the results of the debacles that befell the Kissimmee-Okeechobee-Everglades water chain, the river might have turned into a toxic sludge pond long ago.

Instead, people who lived along and governed the Loxahatchee were beginning to recognize mistakes and fight back during the same timeframe.

In 1950 the newly formed Jupiter Chamber of Commerce lobbied hard for laws barring the use of netting on the river. It said at the time that it had ruined the sport fishing. The commercial fishing lobby proved tougher and the bill lost out. But in time the Chamber prevailed.

By January 1966, Bill Lund had learned a lot from tilting at John D. MacArthur over the dredging at Jupiter River Estates. It was time to mobilize. He helped form the Loxahatchee River Chapter of the Izaak Walton League and became its first president.

A year later he was also president of the Walton League's state chapter and served as advisor to governor Claude R. Kirk Jr. on conservation issues. After Vince Nelson's death in 1968, Lund had the governor's ear when asking the state to acquire Trapper's 857 acres for Jonathan Dickinson State Park.

The Town Council of Jupiter also learned some lessons from MacArthur's upriver dredging and from a developer who had set about on his own to fill in two mangrove islands on the north shore just west of the railroad bridge. Today two short peninsulas jut out from the river in place of the mangrove islands because there were no laws to stop him from building "new" land from river bottom. But Robert Culpepper was mayor at the time and, in his words, "the whole Town Council was alarmed by what this man had done. We saw it as the beginning of the end for the Loxahatchee. If others had been able to follow his example, we'd wind up with a river maybe three hundred feet wide and both sides of it lined with condos built on fill dirt."

The result was a landmark statute in 1967. Says Culpepper: "It states that the natural shoreline of the Loxahatchee shall remain as it was on that date, and the papers filed in the Palm Beach County Courthouse show every foot of shoreline. I'm proud today that we played a small part in saving the river."

Actually, a *huge* part.

Another positive step came in 1973 when voters agreed to create the Loxahatchee River District. For the first time, sewage and wastewater treatment would be in the hands of a single authority for all of the areas bordering the river. The agency would also provide regular monitoring of river conditions and build a scientific database that would help underpin some major restoration decisions in the next century.

Up river, within Jonathan Dickinson State Park (JDSP), other seeds were being planted in the early seventies that would eventually lead to the Loxahatchee becoming Florida's first

waterway to be protected under the federal Wild and Scenic Rivers Act. But how it came about is proof that great movements often begin in a different form.

In 1970 Dick Roberts had no sooner arrived in his new job as park interpretative naturalist for the Florida Park Service—one that now spans over thirty years—when he found himself dealing more with politics than plants. At the time, state highway planners were mapping the course of the new Interstate I-95 linkup through the Jupiter area. The lines on their drawing boards ran smack through the Trapper Nelson property that had just been acquired by Jonathan Dickinson State Park. The I-95 project prompted an ecological impact study by Roberts that led to a decision to reroute the superhighway. In the process, agencies all the way from the Palm Beach County Planning Commission to the U.S. Interior Department began to notice the Loxahatchee and commit themselves to its preservation.

Also thrust on the young biologist in 1970 was a sketchy notion to forge a canoe trail through the river's cypress-canopied upper reaches. Low water was already a problem then, but a bigger one was the objections of some landowners whose property would have been crossed by the waterway. Again, what started as a small project soon gathered so much public support that the state wound up buying some some 600 acres from local growers and garnering another 900 via a MacArthur Foundation donation. The combined tracts ran along the river from south of Indiantown Road to Trapper Nelson's. With the South Florida Water Management District acting as buyer and turning the land over to JDSP for management, the park system now had enough land to protect the cypress swamp and create a world-class canoe trail.

As the preserved land expanded, so did people's horizons. Says Dick Roberts: "Before all this activity, Bill Lund and other environmentalists in the area thought of the Loxahatchee as a 'local' river and they insisted on local control. But they finally realized the need for state and federal involvement if they truly wanted to protect it."

It didn't take long for south Florida legislators to take up the cause. In 1978 they prevailed on Congress to authorize the National Park Service to study the prospect of protecting the upper Loxahatchee under the federal Wild and Scenic Rivers program. Because so little scientific data existed on the Loxahatchee river system, the U.S. Geological Survey was asked to coordinate a three-year, $700,000 study to produce baseline statistics on such topics as agricultural runoff pollution, reduction of fish life, tidal flushing and saltwater intrusion.

By 1985, when Congress officially made the Loxahatchee Florida's first river in the Wild and Scenic Rivers Program, a coalition of local agencies was already putting the finishing touches on a management plan. And that's how today's Loxahatchee River Management Coordinating Council was born.

When the nineties rolled around, people had already gained a greater appreciation of their "wild and scenic" river—and it was soon tested. In 1990 a developer proposed to build on Martin County agricultural land bordering directly on the park for 2.5

miles. The massive project called for 4,700 dwelling units, a million square feet of commercial space and three golf courses. Sustaining thousands of newcomers would mean driving some 2,000 wells into an aquifer, which then supplied about six percent of all the water reaching the Loxahatchee.

All it required for Martin County to swell its tax base overnight was an okay from the Treasure Coast Regional Planning Council and a yes vote from three Martin County commissioners. But by then county residents had seen what happened when John MacArthur ran amok in Jupiter and they rose up en masse. So did the Jonathan Dickinson State Park Interpretative Association (now Friends of JDSP). An ad hoc "town meeting" in Hobe Sound drew a record eight hundred participants. In a straw vote the same night, 97 per cent of the attendees resoundingly opposed the project and dared their commissioners to vote otherwise.

They didn't have to. After three years of maneuvering and probing for chinks in the armor of citizens' groups, the developer quietly withdrew its application. But the episode was a milestone in the evolution of what has become a conservation-first county.

## THE TURNING/TIPPING POINT

Unless you hover over a low tide line for many patient minutes, you won't detect the final feeble ebb and the first tiny splurge of a new tide. A new tide of hope began in the battered history of the Loxahatchee, and it happened soon after the turn of the century. I mean the one we're living in now.

Sometime in 2000 three propitious events occurred to align the stars in proper order. First, a booming economy and a sense of eternal optimism inspired local governments to spend lavishly for some major wetlands acquisitions. Palm Beach County acquired 10,389 more acres of the Loxahatchee Slough. Shortly afterwards, the South Florida Water Management District spent $139 million to buy a former rock quarrying pit and give water managers the ability to store some 10 billion gallons during wet periods instead of dumping it into the river system. Both of these acquisitions

came as various state-county consortia were buying up 4,200 acres of Cypress Creek watershed, roughly 5,000 acres in the Pal-Mar section and the 5,650 Atlantic Ridge Property in Martin County. All would be conserved for serving the Loxahatchee watershed. And some of the newly acquired land is connected, giving wildlife more room to roam.

Second, Congress approved the most ambitious environmental restoration program in history, an $8 billion federal-state program to unscramble the Everglades and re-create a system more in tune with God's original blueprint. At last, real *money* was available to do what people had been talking about for decades.

Third, "average" citizens in Jupiter-Tequesta became more ambitious and aggressive about saving their river. Perhaps it sprang from the growing awareness that the real heart of Jupiter-Tequesta is not Indiantown Road and its shopping centers, but the river and state park. "People are also realizing," says activist Patrick Hayes, "that the term 'Loxahatchee' means not just a ribbon of a river, but the 270-square-mile watershed that it drains."

The best seller, *The Tipping Point*, preaches that dramatic changes in human history are usually triggered when a single symbolic episode galvanizes an otherwise passive public to take notice and take action. The "tipping point" in saving the Loxahatchee may have come after discovering that the upper river was parched for fresh water for much of the year. As the 21st century rolled in, nothing was flowing over the Masten and Lainhart Dams above Trapper Nelson's during the dry seasons. Eric Bailey was cursing because the people who rented his canoes at the Riverbend County Park put-in site were having to portage a good part of the way downstream to Trapper Nelson's. Down at the park concession building, the *Loxahatchee Queen* was forced to cancel trips upriver during low tide.

Back then, Patrick Hayes was just one of the kayakers scratching his head. Today he spends nearly all of his waking hours as a Loxahatchee watchdog and member of the Water Management District's Water Resources Advisory Board.

In 1970, Lilly and Nelson Wilder (above) bought a vacant lot overlooking a channel of the river just east of the Boy Scout camp, there wasn't a mangrove in sight. Today (right) the same view shows nothing but mangroves, the unmistakable markers of a saltwater environment. *(Wilder Family Collection)*

"I got into this innocently enough," he says. I contacted the SFWMD and asked how much of their water flow coming from the Loxahatchee Slough was allocated to the Loxahatchee River.

"I was told it was zero.

"After more questions, I learned that the first mandate in issuing permits is for drinking water, golf courses and other 'consumptive use.' Something like 400 millions a day are drained off for these uses.

"The next priority is surface water management permits, which generally means releasing stormwater down the river and out to sea. This can claim twice that much water— maybe a billion gallons on some days.

"The third and last priority is for 'natural habitat.' Yet," says Hayes, "only one permit in history has ever been issued for that purpose, and it wasn't really what you'd call a permit. It came after someone filed a lawsuit that resulted in a court issuing a consent order. It directs the District to supply the Northwest Fork of the Loxahatchee with 50 cubic feet per second (cfs) in the low season *when possible.*"

In 1995 the Jupiter Inlet District sought to combat the increased surge of salt water upstream. Projects like this one, near the entrance of the state park, sealed off stretches where the river had taken a "shortcut" and broken through its natural course. By restoring the meandering flow, the saltwater barrier would take longer to travel upstream and preserve more cypress trees, leather fern and other hallmarks of the freshwater ecology. *(Jupiter Inlet District)*

When Hayes asked District officials if the agreement had been honored, he was told it hadn't been *possible.*

Fortunately, in 2002 the District was starting to compile its game plan for implementing the $8 billion Comprehensive Everglades Restoration Plan (CERP) and announced a round of hearings to gain public input. Suddenly volunteer groups like Friends of the Loxahatchee, Friends of JDSP, the Jupiter Farms Environmental Council—all with their specialized missions— found a common ground and created the Loxahatchee River Coalition. Members attended CERP meeting after meeting, often wearing big GOT WATER? buttons as attention grabbers. After a year of hearings, the SFWMD pledged to make it happen. Starting in 2006, the river would get no less than 35 cfs during dry spells and more later, when pending studies can pin down the exact amount needed.

The District *can* make it happen because, to its credit, it will have a much larger slough to draw upon, more storage capacity (a la the rock pits) and a better canal system for transporting the freshwater flow to the upper river.

In another forward move, a consortium of local regulatory agencies combined forces to launch an unprecedented number of "fix-up" projects in the river itself. Each year the dozen or so public agencies meet and decide what projects they'd like to tackle under the umbrella of the Loxahatchee River Preservation Initiative. Once approved, the list of projects goes to the state legislature, which (barring a budget crisis) usually matches the local sponsor's cost for each project. Examples of recent work-in-progress include:

• Unclogging Kitching Creek and increasing surface flows;

• Giving Jones Creek new life by removing some 4,000 cubic yards of bottom sediment;

• Creating a deep trap at the end of the C-18 canal to capture sediment before it reaches the main river;

• Restoring the headwaters of Cypress Creek so it will send more freshwater to the North Fork;

• Filling in Hell's Canal, a former citrus grower's ditch that dumped sediment into the main river.

Less glamorous but just as important are several other projects aimed at better monitoring of river conditions. Regular, systematic sampling has taken place only since 1973 when the Loxahatchee River District was created. Today, the LRD maintains 22 long-term monitoring stations.

The state park is pitching in, too. Its impressive five-year plan calls for a $350,000 hydrologic study of Cypress Creek to document scouring caused by heavy rains and the dumping of sedimentation into the Wild and Scenic part of the river. It will also monitor bacteria counts in the newly reopened swimming area and spend $120,000 on testing for heavy metals and pesticides at least twice a year for five years.

Behind much of the new attention to monitoring and testing is the Florida Watershed Restoration Act. It requires that a Total Maximum Daily Load (TMDL) be fixed for each pollutant deemed to be a threat to a given body of water. Should the pollutant exceed the TMDL, the water body will be declared "impaired" and no longer suitable for its intended use (such as swimming, fishing or drinking water).

Guardians of the Loxahatchee have until 2010 to determine TMDL levels for specific possible pollutants in each of five sub-sections. The C-18 Canal, for example, will be assigned a maximum allowable level for dissolved oxygen (DO), coliform bacteria and mercury. The Northwest Fork will get the same for nutrients and dissolved oxygen.

ABOVE: Far above the public walking trail, Kitching Creek is an emaciated version of its former self as it trickles out from Bridge Road. Ongoing restoration work will untangle the overgrowth and increase its flow of freshwater into the Loxahatchee. *(Sue S. Snyder)*

RIGHT: Jerry Metz and David Porter of the Loxahatchee River District's WildPine Ecological Laboratory make one of their regular rounds to collect data from a water quality monitoring station at the entrance of Kitching Creek. It's one of 22 stations maintained on the river by the District to measure salinity, oxygen levels and other water quality data around the clock. *(Sue S. Snyder)*

# HOW TRAPPER NELSON (SORT OF) SAVED THE LOXAHATCHEE

The painstaking ordeal to buy the wild and scenic upper part of the river started with Vince Nelson. On September 10, 1963 he wrote a letter to Alice DeLamar, a Connecticut-Palm Beach widow who had long owned 15 pristine acres adjoining his land. The letter laments that developer John D. MacArthur, owner of 60,000 acres southwest of Trapper's property, is conniving to get the Army Corps of Engineers to create "flood control" canals that would connect his land to the inlet (and boost its value for real estate development).

*Flood control cannot be used for any purpose except water conservation. I'm sure MacArthur is trying to play politics and I am too little to stop him. The park people could stop him if they owned my property, as he would have to come through the middle of my ranch. Why don't you buy my property and donate it to the State Park? I'm sure then that the river could be saved forever. I really cannot hold it much longer, as my county taxes cost me $9 per day. All my mortgage commitments and taxes cost me about $450 per week and my yearly income is less than $500 per year.*

Trapper closed his letter by offering Mrs. DeLamar "one other alternative to saving the river."

*Loan me $200,000 on a 5-year mortgage with 4 percent interest…and I will give you a 5-year option to buy this property and will take [it] off the market. I turned down $1,700 cash per acre a few years ago for this property, so you see I saved the river by buying out numerous owners on borrowed money which I must repay soon or lose it all to the mortgage holders. I have several offers to sell small tracts, but this would be the end of a good river.*

*Will you do something for the river?*

*Trapper*

Mrs. DeLamar probably wasn't as wealthy as Trapper assumed, but his plea struck home. She turned to a good friend, E. Harris Drew, who had been her personal attorney until becoming a justice of the Florida Supreme Court. On September 23, 1963, he replied,

*The last legislature enacted a law levying a tax upon all sporting goods and equipment of that nature for the purpose of acquiring lands and facilities for recreational facilities. I can imagine no better place to invest some of this money than in this area, and Vince's suggestion and your letter may have come at a most opportune time.*

The next day Judge Drew wrote to James Kynes, chief of staff to governor Farris Bryant. He recalled having invited a group of senators and representatives on a tour of the Loxahatchee "many, many years ago" and how they reveled in the "virgin tropical grounds, plants, flowers and trees." Drew talked of "a man by the name of Vince Nelson" who had several hundred acres on the river to sell. He offered to personally organize an inspection trip up the Loxahatchee for a delegation of state notables.

On Feb. 21, 1964, Trapper writes to thank Mrs. DeLamar for her efforts with the state, but now suggests another tack. He reports that the Audubon Society has just bought forty acres adjoining the DeLamar property and surely they'd be interested in buying his land as well.

On April 15, after more letters from Trapper warning that his creditors are getting ready to foreclose, Mrs. DeLamar begins a frantic exchange of letters with Audubon officials. She will even donate her land and pay Audubon $5,000 a year on condition that they also buy Trapper's land. "Time is running out," she warns. "If Trapper Nelson goes bankrupt in the next two months, the wolves will be at the river."

Audubon's interest is genuine. Visits and letters pile up, but both the state and Audubon are still mired in procedural surveys and paperwork as Trapper's creditors set a foreclosure date in August. His back to the wall, Vince Nelson finally accepts a developer's low-ball offer to buy a separate 215-acre plot downriver along today's Riverbed and Turtle Creek country clubs.

Suddenly the pressure is off. Negotiations continue for the upper riverfront land, but Trapper now has cash to live on and can afford to haggle—even to play the state and Audubon off against each other.

But time and illness catch up with him. By January 1970 Trapper is gone and Alice DeLamar vents her frustrations in a letter to a friend. She has long since donated her 15 acres to Audubon. Now she accuses the late Trapper of having been brazenly bullheaded.

*It was so impossible to deal with him or to talk sense to him that everyone gave up hope of getting anything accomplished to save the beautiful wild jungle river while he was still alive. The state park people and Audubon people… all tried to work out some sort of deal in the matter. The Society tried to agree with the trapper to become their official warden at a small compensation, but he was too stupid to agree and of course he would have had to discontinue his trapping activities. Quite a saga…!*

In defense of Vince Nelson, it's unclear as to how much Audubon or the state would have paid him. Or did the Society expect him to donate the land in exchange for a small stipend as "warden"?

All that's left are these facts: Trapper acquired 857 acres of riverfront. He sold little or none of it in small parcels. He never sold to a developer. He died on his land. The site is now preserved. Without Vince Nelson's more than thirty years of occupying and defending the most pristine riverfront in Florida, who else would have been there to save the Loxahatchee?

# THREE KEY QUESTIONS FOR TODAY

## 1. Are we now better off than before?

The best available statistical indicator is the index that the state Department of Environmental Protection has developed to measure relative quality of all surface waters. The Florida Water Quality Index (WQI) is a composite of six parameters: clarity, dissolved oxygen, organic materials, nutrients, bacteria and biological integrity. It ranges from zero (best) to 90 (worst) with anything under 45 deemed to be good quality. From 45 to 60 are fair quality and 60-90 poor.

So how are we doing? Overall, we're around 46—just within in the "fair" range. But it really depends *where* in the watershed one measures. In 2000, the coastal/marine portion rated a sparkling 26. The estuary, or lower, wide part of the river scored an overall 36, but has been declining steadily since the seventies when the first measurements were taken. The Wild and Scenic Northwest Fork rated a "fair" 47, but has been improving somewhat since the seventies. The freshwater tributaries (Kitching Creek, C-18 Canal, etc.) had an unhealthy mean index of 52. However, the long-term pattern of declining water quality seems to have leveled off.

Still, the Water Quality Index offers only a composite of conditions that can change sharply from day to day. Moreover, individual components of the WQI have their own stories to tell. For example, a Loxahatchee River District report shows that nitrogen "has essentially doubled since the 1970s and now exceeds the statewide mean."

Okay, but let's get to the bottom line. Are we better off today? Have we made progress? Richard C. Dent, who heads the Loxahatchee River District, has two ways of looking at the question. "On one hand, analytical works addressing water quality, salinity, hydrology, sedimentation and the biota each indicate declining trends," he says. "On the other hand, consider that we've nearly been able to keep up with the impact of development. After all, we've grown from five hundred people fifty years ago to over 50,000 today. So I'd say that while the trends are going the wrong way, they aren't so terribly out of whack to the point where it can't recover."

Dick Roberts of the Florida Park Service adds this sobering note: "We've now obtained the land and we've set the long-term goals, but it may be another two generations before we see positive changes in the river. The critical issue is to focus on the entire river basin and not just the river. Obtaining the freshwater flows needed for the river's health will be a constant and forever ongoing challenge due to our still rapidly growing population."

## 2. What do we want the river to look like?

Before anyone alters a waterway or its salinity in carrying out the Comprehensive Everglades Restoration Plan (CERP), South Florida Water Management District scientists conduct extensive "what-if" scenarios with computer models.

But we already know we have the ability to change a river's course or tinker with its salt level. The weightier question is: what do we want to accomplish with our money and science?

Example: It's nearly unanimous that we don't want salt water coming up as far as it does now. And we'd like to see more stately cypress trees growing on the riverbanks. But how far back should the salinity line be pushed? Downstream, oysters must grow in a delicate balance of salt and fresh water. Alter that mix and they die. Or take sea grass. It won't grow in water with less than 5 parts per thousand salt. Driving the fresh water barrier downriver just might diminish the area in which sea grass can grow. Manatees wouldn't like that at all.

Ironically, scientists and water managers don't want to make decisions like these. They want the *people* to decide. We'll need to get much wiser than we are now.

## 3. What can you do for the river?

**First,** help find the answers to question number two.

**Second,** you can have a big impact on reducing stormwater runoff. Right now it's one of the most overlooked obligations homeowners have. Says Richard Dent: "Typically, a housing developer gets a permit for a stormwater system and the contractor puts it in according to the plan. Then the home buyers move in and a homeowner's association takes over management. A dozen or

Old World Climbing Fern has gained a stranglehold on several trees alongside lower Kitching Creek in one of Jonathan Dickinson State Park's most popular walking trails. Of the 159 exotic plants found in the park, 37 are now targeted for intensive treatment. The tab for removing Old World Climbing Fern alone is estimated at over $3 million. *(Sue S. Snyder)*

One small step for the river, the re-opening the Jonathan Dickinson State Park swimming area in 2003 was cause for celebration. Leading the ceremonies: Richard E. Roberts, Florida Park Service; Richard C. Dent, Loxahatchee River District; and David R. Struhs, Secretary of the Florida of Department of Protection. The beach had been closed since 1986 due to declining water quality. *(Florida Park Service)*

so years pass by. We go out there for a visit and the stormwater system isn't even close to the original plan. Swales are filled in and ponds are full of yuck from the yards. In the mid-nineties we did some site visits and found a couple hundred homeowners associations that weren't taking care of their stormwater systems."

Bottom line: If you're in a homeowner's association, go to a meeting and raise the issue. You might not be popular, but *somebody's* got to do it.

**Third,** be judicious in using fertilizers and pesticides. Up around Riverbend Park, the streambed still has traces of arsenic from the pesticides in which cattle were dipped to combat tick fever. That was over sixty years ago.

A latter day example is Jupiter Farms. When fertilizers and pesticides (not to mention lots of manure) find their way into the water, bacteria begin "eating" them and consume lots of the river's oxygen in the process.

To test the point, in 1995 and '97 the Loxahatchee River District maintained a test station in two Jupiter Farms canals, another in the C-18 Canal (into which the first two flow) and a third station on the river around Indiantown Bridge. "The results were very clear," says Loxahatchee River District director Dent. "Up in the Farms canals, the dissolved oxygen (DO) was very low. The C-18 station showed high DO. The Indiantown Road station, where some water came from the Farms and the rest from another source, scored midway between the two others. So clearly the problem was coming from the Farms."

The same findings would apply to anyone who uses pesticides and fertilizers where they can run into the river. With the ban on new seawalls and more homes with natural shorelines, the risk of river damage is higher than ever.

**Fourth,** join the war on exotics. Unwanted species colonize just as much from "base camps" in people's backyards as when growing wild. We can all help the cause by concentrating on removal of the top five pest plants on the state's Most Wanted list. They are: Old World climbing fern (*Lygodium microphyllum),* Melaleuca (*Melalauca quinquenervia*), Brazilian Pepper (*Schinus terebinthefolius),* Australian pine (*Casuarina spp.*), and downy rose-myrtle (*Rhodomyrtus tomentosa*).

**Fifth,** do what you can to cut speed, noise and wakes on the river. The docks that line every part of the lower Loxahatchee are a museum of fiberglass behemoths with twin 250 h.p. engines hanging there like so many six-figure assets. To those who truly use them for ocean fishing or hops to the Bahamas, Godspeed. Enjoy them. To those who hang them out back only as trophies of their success, consider *really* enjoying your local river by powering down. A 60 h.p. Whaler gets you to anywhere on the river. You'll save money, make a smaller wake and spew out less fuel.

**Sixth,** join organizations of equally concerned citizens. Examples: Friends of the Loxahatchee, Friends of Jonathan Dickinson State Park, the Jupiter Farms Environmental Council and the Loxahatchee River Coalition. Yes, they have pleasant picnics and the like, but membership means mostly sitting in the hot sun and handing out educational leaflets at some art fair. Or sitting through dreadfully long Town Council meetings while waiting your turn to at the mike for (the maximum allowed) three minutes to speak against a proposed jet-ski concession near your favorite fishing spot. Marge Ketter, who lives near Trapper Nelson's camp, has been sitting through turgid talkathons for over thirty years. "You've got to be prepared to stay late," she says. "That's when the developers like to make their move."

Truly, in this case, the old axiom applies: *Virtue is its own reward.*

Jonathan Dickinson State Park does not own any of its 11,407 acres. It has a lease from the state of Florida that expires on January 23, 2067.

Will the state want to keep it? Knowing the answer would require as much foresight as it would have for the five hundred residents of Jupiter in the 1940s to visualize the Jupiter-Tequesta of today. Perhaps by 2067 Florida's fifty million residents will be so desperate for living space that the legislature will decide that the park can afford to make do with, say, six thousand fewer acres. Perhaps a future planning board will decide that, painful though the fact may be, the park is the only possible site left for the badly needed Southeast Florida International Airport.

The outcome truly depends on who wins the last Battle of the Loxahatchee.

Will it be the river?

I am the Loxahatchee River. I was scenic, wild and free.

My feet were in the wetlands and my mouth is in the sea.

My banks were overshadowed by the emerald canopies

Of cypress that stood stately, thrusting up their knobby knees.

My water's stained to ebony like tea steeped in the sun.

It percolates through fallen leaves and has since time's begun.

The alligators motionless as half submerging logs,

And panthers slipped along my shores through silent morning fogs.

Blue herons and white egrets stalked my shallows for their prey,

While eagles and the ospreys soared above and screamed dismay.


Your quenchless thirst for water drained my slough and your machines

Have dug canals to irrigate your fairways and your greens.

You ration out my water and control my ebb and flow

By diverting what's my birthright just to make your tax rolls grow.

My beaches you've replaced with walls. They've all been concrete curbed,

Where baitfish hid in mangroves and snook prowled undisturbed.

You turned my outlet to an inlet. Now the salty waters flood

With the tides up tributaries to contaminate my blood.

The cypress trunks stand skeletal like tombstones for their dead,

Where vultures perch and watch and wait. They know what lies ahead.


My ecosystem's fragile and it cannot tolerate

Another land development to which you allocate

The water that, by Nature's Law, is mine and mine alone.

Learn lessons from mistakes you've made and scars that I have shown.

The means and opportunity are both within your grip

To protect me from stagnation and the rivulet's final drip.

Open up your floodgates; put an end to all my strife.

Restore my flow so I'll retain some quality of life.

I am the Loxahatchee River. I was scenic, wild and free.

I am the Loxahatchee River and I'm yearning to be me.


Wally McCall / Jupiter: 2003

# RESOURCES & REFERENCES

## Author's note:

Nearly all of the quotes and stories from persons living in 2003 were obtained from personal interviews. Material on others was gleaned in part from the sources listed below, especially, *The Loxahatchee Lament,* that invaluable wellspring of individual recollections on early Jupiter. However, much of the information also came from private files and family letters of those interviewed that would be impractical (and imprudent) to list here. All the same, I wish to give special thanks to:

• Richard E. Roberts, for sharing voluminous personal files ranging from the history of Camp Murphy and Jonathan Dickinson State Park to the ecology of the Loxahatchee;

• Al and Florence Kuschel for the letters of the Tindall family;

• Wilson Horne for his unpublished writings and collection of memorabilia;

• Chuck Milhauser and others who prepared the manual for Lighthouse docents (with valuable facts about its beginnings);

• George Lainhart for his materials on the first settlers along west Indiantown Road and on the founding of Lainhart and Potter;

• Matt Bressler for his written recollections of Jupiter Fisherman's Marina;

• W. Carlin White and the Town of Jupiter Archives for preserving and sharing the unpublished second volume of *Loxahatchee Lament;*

• Ramona Pennock Stark for her detailed records on Pennock Plantation.

## Other helpful sources:

An Archaeological and Historical Assessment of Riverbend Park, Palm Beach County, Florida. February 1995. Study conducted by the Archaeological and Historical Conservancy Inc.

Barnes, Jay. *Florida's Hurricane History.* Chapel Hill, NC: The University of North Carolina Press, 1998.

Bush, Betty. "A Tribute to the Rood Family." *Beacon News,* June 30, 1966, p. 1.

_____ . "Jupiter's Lifesaving Station, 1886." *Beacon News*, June 30, 1966, p. 4.

_____ . "The Story of Jupiter's Little Railroad," *Beacon News,* June 30, 1966. p. 8.

Covington, James W. *The Seminoles of Florida.* Gainesville: University Press of Florida, 1993.

"Cultural Resource Reconnaissance of Hobe Sound National Wildlife Refuge of Martin County, Florida." Report by Cultural Resource Management Inc., Tallahassee, Florida, for the U.S. Fish and Wildlife Service, April, 1980.

Daniel, Mike. "Ponce de Leon and the Discovery of Florida." Unpublished monograph, June 1995.

Dunn, Hampton. *Florida: A Pictorial History.* Norfolk, VA: The Donning Company/Publishers, 1988.

DuBois, Bessie Wilson. "Early County Post Offices," *Beacon News,* June 30, 1966.

_____ . *A History of Juno Beach & Juno, Florida.* Published by the author in 1978. 24 pp.

_____ . *The History of Jupiter Lighthouse.* Published by the author in 1981 as a reprint from *The Journal of the Historical Association of Southern Florida,* Number XX, 1960. 32 pp.

_____ . "Relighting of the Historic Jupiter Light After Civil War," *Beacon News,* June 30, 1966. p. 3.

_____ . "To School by Jungle Waterways. The Schoolboat Maine." *Beacon News,* June 30, 1966.

_____ . *Shipwrecks in the Vicinity of Jupiter Inlet.* Jupiter: 1975. Published by the author. 32 pp.

"The Archeology of Jupiter Inlet and Coastal Palm Beach County." *Florida Anthropologist.* Special Issue: Vol. 55, Nos. 3-4. Published by the Florida Anthropological Society, Inc., September-December 2002.

Hemstock, Kevin. "Tragic Tale of a Doomed Settlement. *Jupiter Courier*. Undated.

Henn, Lt. William. "Caught on a Lee Shore," *The Century Magazine*, June 1893, p. 185.

Hutchinson, Janet. *History of Martin County.* Port Salerno, FL: Florida Classics Library (by agreement with the Martin County Historical Society), 1987.

Ives, Lt. J. C. "Memoir to Accompany a Military Map of the Peninsula of Florida South of Tampa Bay," U.S. War Dept., April 1856. Courtesy of the Historical Society of Palm Beach County.

"Jupiter's Jackson Family." *Beacon News,* June 30, 1966, p. 10. Reprint of a memoir by Elsie Dolby Jackson in 1918.

"Jupiter's Lifesaving Station, 1886." *Beacon News,* June 30, 1966, p. 4.

"Jupiter Schools and Churches Before 1900." *Beacon News,* June 30, 1966, p. 7. Reprint of a memoir by Elsie D. Jackson in 1918.

Keel, James R. *Florida's Trails to History's Treasures.* Fort Lauderdale, FL: Seajay Enterprises Inc., 1981.

*The Loxahatchee Lament.* Vol. I. Jupiter: Cary Publications Inc., 1978. Reprinted by the Town of Jupiter in 1999 for its 75th Anniversary Celebration. (Parts of an unpublished Vol. II are on file in the Town of Jupiter archives and some were cited in this book.)

McGoun, William E. *Southeast Florida Pioneers: The Palm and Treasure Coasts.* Sarasota: Pineapple Press, 1998.

Meredith, David S. III. *Spy Station Jupiter. A History of the U.S. Naval Supplementary Radio Station, Jupiter, Florida.* Privately published (24 pp.) in 1988.

Milanich, Jerald T. *Florida's Indians, from Ancient Times to the Present.* Gainesville: University Press of Florida, 1998.

Mygatt, O.A. "A Winter's Sport in Florida." *Outing Magazine,* November 1889, p. 203.

"Navy Reveals 111 Ships Lost During U-Boat Blitz that Cost 882 Casualties." *Palm Beach Post-Times,* June 4, 1945, p.1. The *Post-Times* (now the *Post*) is an excellent resource for wartime ship sinkings, beginning with the first such episode, reported Nov. 4, 1939, to the final report cited above.

Procyk, Richard J. *Guns Across the Loxahatchee.* Jupiter, FL: Loxahatchee River Historical Society, 1999.

Oppel, Frank and Tony Meisel, editors. *Tales of Old Florida.* Seacaucus, NJ: Castle Div. of Book Sales Inc., 1987.

Rathbone, St. George. "Jupiter Inlet, Florida." *The Outing Magazine*, 1891 (month unknown), p. 53. Article describes the author's fishing trip.

Rinehart, Floyd and Marion. *Victorian Florida: America's Last Frontier.* Atlanta: Peachtree Publishers Limited, 1986.

Thurlow, Sandra Henderson. *Stuart on the St. Lucie: A Pictorial History.* Stuart, FL: Sewall's Point Company, 2001.

Shappee, Nathan D. "The Celestial Railroad to Juno," *Florida Historical Quarterly,* undated reprint, listed as Volume XXXX, Number 4 by the Florida Historical Society.

White, W. Carlin. *History of the Carlin House.* Jupiter: Edited by Lillian M. White. Published by the author in 1988. 78 pp.

_____. *History of the Jupiter Wireless Telegraph Station.* Monograph published by the author in 1992. 48 pp.

# INDEX